Praise for Bel

"In Beloved Chaos, you will learn about the kind of revolutionary love that can change the world . . . which includes yourself. It's a page-turner of a book with a lot of heartache and a lot of beauty, and it will leave its mark on you."

—Brian D. McLaren,
author of *The Great Spiritual Migration*

"As the scaffolding of American evangelicalism collapses, Jamie West Zumwalt offers a hopeful alternative in her newest book. *Beloved Chaos* is a fresh and accessible work of hope, not simply a critique of the shortcomings of religion. Jamie shows us another way of worship: love in action. Jamie's humble, straight-forward reflections invite us back to a simple starting point, one that's accessible in every one of our hearts. As you flip through these pages prepare yourself for a wild and life-changing ride."

—Christopher L. Heuertz,
author of *The Sacred Enneagram: Finding Your Unique Path to Spiritual Growth* and Founding Partner of Gravity, a Center for Contemplative Activism

"Jamie Zumwalt and her crew are extremists for love. The stories she tells will pull you in and shake you up—raw stories of following Jesus in hard ways, and hard places, with hard people. The pain is real, but so is the beauty. Read this book and you will be deeply impacted."

—Craig Greenfield, author of *Subversive Jesus* and Founder of Alongsiders International

"Poverty. Abuse. Pain. Shame. The question becomes not, "Where is God?" but "What is God like, in the middle of these circumstances that form our lives?" Jamie and the Love Gang live out the answers on these pages. Join her and the community at Joe's as they follow The Way of Love. Read. Be convicted. Be healed."

—Jennifer Roemhildt Tunehag, Global Anti-Trafficking
Task Force, World Evangelical Alliance;
Co-founder of European Freedom Network;

"The stories Jamie Zumwalt captures here in this book are not simply stories of individuals. It is the story of how a unique, local community has been drawn together around the Way of Love. With vulnerability and inquiry, Jamie engages in some of the best local theologizing I have ever come across; revealing what Love looks like in the midst of pain, laughter, rejection, joy, loss, violence, care . . . in short: our human experience. And it is indeed, a Beautiful Chaos."

—David Scott Vining,
Community Development Mentor

"Jamie is one of the most courageous women I know. This book is no exception to her boldness. With raw honesty, she reveals the essence of what it means to be belovedly human. The beauty and terror of our humanity seeps through the pages and sparks hope in the hearts of readers that we too might be accepted and find belonging, just as we are. *Beloved Chaos* holds the power to inspire you to create the kind of community we all long for."

—Phileena Heuertz, founding partner, Gravity,
a Center for Contemplative Activism,
author of *Pilgrimage of a Soul* and *Mindful Silence*.

"In 21st Century America, to be on the margins in any way is to be dehumanized by the culture around you. In *Beloved Chaos*, Jamie calls us to hear stories of people as they come to be rehumanized in the beloved, messy, sometimes smelly embrace of community. And if we listen closely, we can hear her telling us there is hope for us, too."
—Hugh Hollowell, Community Pastor at Open Door Mennonite Church, Housing and Hunger Activist

"These stories made me laugh out loud, nearly cry, and feel so many more emotions I simply can't describe adequately. It's an amazing collection! The stories share at least one thing in common: love. And not just ordinary love. The kind of love expressed in strange and unlikely ways to people of diverse backgrounds and unconventional ways of being. I recommend this book to anyone who wants to read about love in action, outrageous love action!"
—Thomas Jay Oord, author of *The Uncontrolling Love of God* and other books

"Jamie Zumwalt has written a love story. A raw, real, unfiltered look at unconditional love in action. Be ready to have your religious sensibilities challenged!"
—Steve Hollingsworth, President/Founder at 4 H. I. M. (His Healing Helping Hands International Ministries)

"In *Beloved Chaos*, Jamie Zumwalt has laid bare her faith in a way that honors God and the people she loves. With weighty vulnerability but without the burden of shame, Jamie describes a world where the last are first and unconditional love and grace abound. If Jesus walked into Joe's Addiction for a coffee, he'd leave a big tip."
—Leia Hollingsworth Johnson, President and Co-founder at Somebody's Mama

"While most American Christians associate "the slums of Calcutta" and poverty in a "third world country" in some "far off location" where Christians might go as missionaries, Zumwalt's true stories narrate the poverty, human brokenness, abuse, and exploitation that take place "over there" is happening right now in American cities. May Zumwalt's stories compel us to act so that actions transform our world that it becomes more on earth, as it is in heaven."

—Marty Michelson Ph. D.,
Founder and Director of The Eupan Global Initiate

BELOVED CHAOS

moving from religion to
Love in a red light district

JAMIE WEST ZUMWALT

Printed in the United States of America

Published by Author Academy Elite
P.O. Box 43, Powell, OH 43035

www.AuthorAcademyElite.com

Paperback ISBN-13: 978-1-64085-480-2
Hardcover ISBN-13: 978-1-64085-481-9

Library of Congress Control Number: 2018960899

Unless otherwise indicated, all Scripture quotations are taken from:

THE HOLY BIBLE, NEW INTERNATIONAL VERSION®, NIV® Copyright © 1973, 1978, 1984, 2011 by Biblica, Inc.® Used by permission. All rights reserved worldwide.

The Message. Copyright © 1993, 1994, 1995, 1996, 2000, 2001, 2002. Used by permission of NavPress Publishing Group.

To the Community of Hope at Joe's Addiction

CONTENTS

SECTION 3: HARD STUFF

SECTION 4: RLOVEUTION

SECTION 5: US THEM WE

FOREWORD

Beloved - "dearly loved, a much loved person."
Chaos - "complete disorder and confusion."

I love the words "beloved" and "chaos" together in the same sentence when it comes to Christian community. For many churches, beloved is common. We talk about being people loved deeply by God, God's beloved, but for most part "chaos" isn't a word that churches would use to describe themselves. In fact, many pride themselves on being efficient, strategic, focused.

Beloved and chaos together?

Yes, that is the way of Jesus.

We have sanitized so much about modern Christianity, tried to do what we could to separate "us" and "them," the believers and non-believers, the ones who need God's love and those of us who know it and feel like it's our job to give it—our way, on our terms.

That is not the way of Jesus.

Jamie Zumwalt's stories will sear your soul in all the right ways. Entering into her story and day-to-day world at Joe's Addiction and seeing up close and personal what beloved chaos looks like in intentional, messy, frustrating, tiring, beautiful messy life together will remind you that there are people in the world willing to do what so many others aren't.

It's easy to think, "Well, I'm glad they are called to do that, but I'm certainly not." (I hear that a lot in our work at The Refuge, a Christian community and mission center in North Denver, too). I fully acknowledge there might be some truth to it. You may not be called to work full-time, scramble to keep the lights on every month, and be taking people to Health and Human Services on a weekly basis. But what I truly believe we are all called to is this: *Being willing to engage in beloved chaos in whatever ways we can.*

- To get our hands dirty.
- To break down the walls between us and them.
- To find our shared humanity instead of seeing how we are "not like those people."
- To weep over the realities of our broken systems and somehow play a part in changing them.
- To remember that Jesus' ways were never sanitized, separated, or sexy. They were simple -so simple that they're brutally hard.

Simple relationship. Cups of black coffee and honest conversations. Presence. Human connection. Hugs. Listening ears. Sharing stories. We underestimate the healing power of all of these things, and Jamie reminds us of them. I hope as you read the stories, you find your heart stirred in ways that deserve listening to. I know mine was.

If you're burned out on organized religion like so many other people I know, I hope this re-kindles a little hope, that Jesus is still showing up through people in ways that often never get recognized or rewarded because they lack "wow" and "strength" and so many other things Christianity has tended to value the most. And if you are wondering what more beloved chaos might look like for you, start with this—listen to someone's story. Hold it tenderly. Share yours, too.

-Kathy Escobar, Co-Pastor, The Refuge,
and author of *Faith Shift: Finding Your Way Forward When Everything You Believe is Coming Apart.*

PREFACE

"All the really good stories, in their juicy truth,
can't be told til everyone is dead."

— John Willis Zumwalt

I once read an author who said, "Don't tell other people's stories. Tell your own story, but their story is not yours to tell." I started to wonder if maybe it is wrong for me to tell these stories. I began to wonder if telling their stories is exploiting them.

As I was mulling over this concern, I went to visit a friend/ mentor of mine. She is pastor of an inner city church in Waterloo, IA (I know, "inner city" in Waterloo, IA? Yes, there is.). She is a few years down the road in front of me, doing a similar kind of work, and so I looked to her for wisdom that comes from experience. I was feeling discouraged, sad about some things happening in our Joe's Addiction community—I was tired.

I started telling her the recent events . . . For each one I told, she jumped in and said, "Oh my! This happened to us," and then she told me of a circumstance that mirrored the same kind of struggle we were experiencing. I had come to visit her looking for encouragement. Where was it? For every pain I shared, she shared one of her own. We commiserated late into the night.

Suddenly, I realized: "such is this kind of work." It just is this way. These are the common experiences of starting a Community of Hope in the midst of the darkness of generational poverty and all of its complexities. I asked my friend, "How do you keep going? How do you keep your faith in the midst of the discouragement?" Without hesitation she said, "You tell the stories. As you tell the stories, you remember why we're doing what we're doing. And you remember what God has done."

I tell these stories also because of ancient wisdom:

"Speak up for the people who have no voice, for the rights of all the down-and-outers. Speak out for justice! Stand up for the poor and destitute!" Proverbs 31:8

All of the people in these pages have a voice of their own, but they have no opportunity to tell their own stories—and their stories need to be told. So I tell them here. Each one of them had a story before I met them, but their story intersected with mine at Joe's Addiction, and so it became *our* story. I hope to honor each one of these precious people who have become my family at Joe's Addiction.

Full Disclosure:

I come from the Jesus tradition, and my language in this book reflects my own history (both negative and positive) with Christianity and the teachings of Jesus. It is my hope that if the reader brings a different faith tradition, or no faith at all, to this reading, you will not be put off or distracted by my perspective, and that through Love, we can together create Beloved Chaos here on earth.

Trigger Warning:

This book may contain triggers. Many of the people in our Joe's Community have suffered abuse of all kinds. I warn you because you might want to be prepared, but I also ask if it is possible for you to press through reading these stories, that you continue. You might receive healing, as many of us at Joe's Addiction have.

SECTION 1
GRAND EXPERIMENT

"To see what is right and not to
do it is want of courage."

— Confucius

CHAPTER 1
NEAR-NAKED GYMNASTICS

"If you do not change direction,
you may end up where you are heading."

— Lao Tzu

My husband, John, who grew up in Taiwan, romanticizes American Christmases. Instead of a beautiful evergreen tree and frosted sugar cookies, his family decorated a palm tree frond and ate steamed, rice cooker cake. From watching "Miracle on 34th Street" and "It's a Wonderful Life," John has conjured the idea that everybody goes Christmas caroling.

So for our first Christmas in Valley Brook, Oklahoma, John proposes this would be a great thing to do. Door to door caroling. What a blessing this will be to the folks in the neighborhood. It will be a way for us to meet people and to announce to the darkness that "Hope" has come.

Armed with "Joy to the World," "We Wish You a Merry Christmas," and a huge dose of idealism and naïveté, we bundle up two of our older kids (10 and 14 at the time) and a few others of our core church planting team, and we head out into the cold, dark streets.

The first house we approach has no porch light, but interior lights are on. We see figures sitting in the living room. We quietly gather around the front step and commence our joyous song. The front door bursts open and a young man in jeans and white tank shirt (known as a "wife beater" in these parts), tattoos on his arms and his neck, charges onto the front porch. Wild eyes flashing, high as a kite and waving his gun, he shouts, "What the fuck?! Get the hell off my porch!"

Apparently, he does not feel "blessed." We mutter some kind of apology and explanation we are just trying to sing some Christmas carols, "Merry Christmas." Stumbling over one another, we rush back to the empty street.

Fear paralyzes me. My children could be shot! What were we thinking? What a stupid idea. Are you kidding me?

I have never seen my husband afraid of anything. Really. He is a brave man. And there he is, marching out in front of us, headed to the next house—to sing some Christmas carols. He looks back at our huddled, trembling, little group of now tentative Christmas joy and says, "What's the matter? Don't we feel like God wanted us to do this? Come on."

We gather together there in the street to regroup. Do we still think God told us to do this? Yes. Is God here with us? Yes. Should we go on? Sigh. Yes. Okay, but . . . together we decide upon three conditions. We will only go to houses that fit these criteria:

1. They must have Christmas decorations, a Santa Claus poster on the door, or lights on a tree in the window. We figure those people would appreciate some Christmas cheer.

2. They must have kids' toys in the yard, a bicycle, scooter, or any sign of children. We think families with kids would be less likely to bring out their guns.

3. If any of us feel we are to sing at a house that does not meet the first two conditions, we all have to be in

agreement. That way if any of us gets shot, there will not be one of us who we can blame.

We all agree. We pray together, asking for courage and protection, and then we set off to belt out "Joy to the World" at the next house bearing Christmas lights.

What an adventure. Our kids receive an education this night. We approach one house surrounded by cars parked in the driveway, on the street, and even in the yard. It looks like a house full of people. As we sing, a woman opens the door. She nods, leaves the door standing open, and then walks back to the couch—where she continues snorting a line of cocaine right there in front of us, as we sing:

Joy to the World, the Savior reigns.
Let earth receive her King.
Let every heart prepare him room.
And heaven and nature sing.
And heaven and nature sing.
And heaven and heaven and nature sing.

I'm sure the quality of our singing is a much better experience for her than it is in reality. Maybe we *are* the angelic choir.

As we stand singing on another porch, the side door of the garage flies open. A young, wide- eyed man in a cloud of billowing pot smoke staggers into the yard shouting, "Is this a bust?! Is this a bust?!" We assure him we are not the police; we are just here to sing some Christmas carols. Eyelids heavy, he listens politely and thanks us.

No more let sin and sorrow grow,
Nor thorns infest the ground.
He comes to make his blessings flow
Far as the curse is found.
Far as the curse is found.
Far as, far as the curse is found.

Do the police usually show up singing Christmas carols?

Our child, Jael, ten years old, possesses the voice of an angel and loves to sing. We position Jael front and center to sing one verse of Silent Night as a solo. Halfway through verse one, a man opens the door with a huge smile on his face. He stands smiling, listening to our beautiful song. One problem . . . His smile is not his most noticeable feature. He is a very large man with a round belly. He was sitting in the privacy and comfort of his own living room when we arrived, and he has forgotten he had unfastened his pants. Down below his belly, at Jael's eye-level, hangs all of his business, there for ten-year-old eyes to behold.

We finish verse one, and without missing a beat, Jael launches into the solo verse.

Silent night, holy night
Shepherds quake at the sight.
Glories stream from heaven above.
Heavenly hosts sing Hallelujah.
Christ the Savior is born.
Christ the Savior is born.

We finish with "We Wish You a Merry Christmas" and hurry back to the "safety" of the street, the man calling his thanks to us, waving and hollering "Merry Christmas" through the screen. The moment his door shuts our children explode in peals of laughter.

At one door, a young father listens to our singing. When we finish he says, "My wife and children are at the store. They've never seen anything like this. I'm sad they missed it. Can you come back in about twenty minutes and do it again?"

What a night. We pray, we tremble, we laugh, and we cry. Precious, elderly people answer their doors with delight. Tears streaming, they say, "We have lived in this neighborhood for 40 years, and no one has ever caroled here. Why are you doing this?" Our simple answer: "We're new in the neighborhood. We've opened the coffee shop over on 59th St. We just want to share the joy of Christmas."

Joe's Addiction

Joe's Addiction is a coffee shop that sits right in the middle of a street lined with strip clubs. You know, the kind where girls perform near-naked gymnastics on stripper poles. The Town of Valley Brook, Oklahoma is its own little city within Oklahoma City. It is only .3 square miles. Not three square miles. Point three square miles. Valley Brook has its own mayor, its own city council, even its own police force for this small tract of land, only .3 square miles.

One reason this little town has maintained its autonomy is because it is zoned for the sex industry. Although state laws supersede, the city's zoning laws allow for every sexual act one's imagination can contrive (some you'd probably never imagine) to be performed for money. Valley Brook clubs boast fully nude dancers, compared to other clubs where the girls dance topless or wear scanty costumes. Some of the clubs employ eighteen year old dancers, attracting those who want to watch younger girls.

Behind the main street of clubs sits a neighborhood of about seven hundred people. The latest census showed the average income in this neighborhood to be $11,000/year. Although some people own and have lived in their houses for forty years, slum landlords own many of the homes and charge cheap rent, but also do not maintain the properties. Functional plumbing is a luxury. Incarceration, drug addiction, mental illness, and homelessness all afflict the neighborhood as well.

How Did We Get Here?

I need to explain why we began this crazy adventure. John and I had been in ministry our whole lives—not only our adult lives. We are second and third generation ministers, and as is true of all missionary and preacher's kids, our parents steeped us in ministry life from the time we could walk and talk. Helping our parents, serving in whatever role they needed, poking our finger in the hole in the dam, wherever there was a gap—this is just normal life for ministry kids.

However, ministry life had not protected me from pain. At fifteen years old, I entered what became a devastatingly abusive relationship with a nineteen-year-old man. I hid the abuse from my parents and my friends, while I suffered in secret physical, emotional, and sexual abuse. When that relationship ended, it was he who broke up with me, so then not only had I been abused, I was also rejected. He hadn't wanted me after all. I dated two other guys through the rest of high school, and both broke up with me as well. So by the end of high school, I had received a message that I was undesirable. No one would want to marry me.

So when I went to college, I grabbed onto the first freshman guy who asked me to some freshman event, fearing no one would ever ask me out again. That relationship turned out to be a carbon copy of the first relationship I had endured when I was fifteen. Date rape resulted in me being pregnant and ashamed. I understood it to be my fault because I should never have let things go as far as they did. I was a preacher's daughter. Sex outside marriage was the worst sin a preacher's daughter could commit in my church culture. With a baby on the way, everyone would know. There would be no hiding from my sin. I saw no hope of redemption, from my church or from God, so I took an overdose of five hundred ibuprofen tablets.

Paramedics and doctors saved my life, and through some serendipitous and personal encounters, I experienced the Love of God, and Love restored hope for my life. I have written about this story and some healing God gave me in my first book, *Simple Obsession, Enjoying the Tender Heart of God*. I met John after my recovery from the overdose, and after I had recommitted my life to follow a call to be a missionary I had received from God as a child.

When we met, it was while pursuing "God's call" on our lives for ministry, and so we entered a relationship with one another as partners in "God's Global Cause." We understood this to mean propagating Christianity around the world. John and I served as missionaries ourselves in Taiwan, and then we founded and led an organization for over twenty years that trained people to travel as missionaries to groups of people in the world who had never heard of Jesus. We shared the dreams, fought the battles, and walked the highs and lows of marriage and this ministry journey together.

When we crashed, we crashed together.

Devastating events collided in a tiny window of time and resulted in a near total loss of faith for both of us. It sounds cliché—and maybe it is, because when it happens to so many, it has become commonplace—but I suppose you could call it our "dark night of the soul."

One:

We were part of a church that started in our living room out of a close-knit group of friends who prayed together for God to bring revival to our city and to our nation. Much weeping over sin and reminding God of God's promises characterized these prayer meetings. Some of these people spent hours a day in prayer. We were a zealous group with a high level of accountability for living holy lives.

Relationships were intimate and committed. We walked with these people for over ten years. Some of them had been family to one another for twenty-five years. It's a long story with many gory and painful details, but the bottom line is the church erupted in conflict. The disagreements had been brewing for years, and bitterness had worked its poison. The church disbanded and everyone went to the four winds. Some of those people have not spoken to one another since. It devastated me.

We had grown up in a denomination that prided itself on a theology that emphasized "holiness." Contrasting with Pentecostals, who believed the evidence of the Holy Spirit in a Christian's life is the gift of speaking in tongues, we believed the Fruit of the Spirit (love, joy, peace, patience, kindness, goodness, faithfulness, gentleness, and self-control) was our evidence. However, we "holiness people" couldn't even be nice to each other.

Two:

The desire of our heart had been to return to Asia to serve as missionaries. We had been training a young man to take John's position as Director of our missionary training program, so we could leave. This young man was talented. His winsome, charismatic personality gathered a host of other young people into our organization.

Perhaps most significant to my ensuing disillusionment was that he was the most disciplined Christian I knew. Our friend woke early every morning to spend time in prayer. He read his Bible every day and the writings of Christian authors from history. He led worship and wrote intimate songs to Jesus and followed a disciplined diet and exercise routine; he expressed his belief that God had called him to be a good steward of his body. He fasted from food regularly, and he led many others into tight accountability regarding these disciplines in their own lives. He was a model leader.

Until . . . he had an extramarital affair. He destroyed his marriage and his family—and he was unrepentant. Turmoil ensued. Many of the young people following him left the organization, and some of them abandoned following Jesus. I was shaken. So many questions. So much confusion. Christianity was not doing what people had taught me all my life it would do.

We had believed a disciplined spiritual life and strong accountability would prevent this kind of moral failure. But instead, we had created a culture of pretending, of little transparency, and no vulnerability. It was acceptable to talk about sins and temptations we had been "delivered" from when we "got saved," but in an ensuing tumult of revelations, we discovered that none of us had the ability to be honest about our current struggles. Shame and fear of disapproval—not only from people, but from God—had caused all of us to hide our real truth.

Three:

Our dear friend and pastor, who served as Mission Director overseeing our missionaries, discovered he had pancreatic cancer. He believed God would heal him. Many in our organization believed God would heal him. Hundreds of people were praying for him. He became sicker and sicker.

We received confrontational emails from people within our own organization claiming there must be "sin in the camp." If we would just repent of our sin, God would heal him. We believed in repentance. We would be happy to repent. Repent from what? . . . He died.

Wait a minute . . . God killed him because of someone else's sin? Is this what God is like? If God is, then God sucks.

Then . . .

I went to India. The director of another missionary organization, a friend of ours, invited me to speak for several events. I was privileged to speak in a church that is serving one of the giant slums in Mumbai. Three hundred very poor people were present that morning, and I felt led to share a message about Jesus being our Good Shepherd. I talked to them about his gentleness and about what it means to be one of his lambs. I told them how a shepherd cares for his sheep, how he provides for his sheep, how the sheep learn to hear his voice, and even how he sometimes disciplines his sheep. Then I invited them to receive the tender, compassionate care of the Shepherd. At the end of the service many came forward to receive prayer.

After the service, Irene, the pastor's wife, asked me if I would like to see where these people lived. I jumped at the chance. She and another Indian woman, a layperson in the church, took me into the slum. My first emotion was fear as we entered the maze of concrete buildings. I was not only afraid of all I might see there, but if I became separated from these two ladies, I might never find my way out of the labyrinth of pathways. The buildings as we entered the slum were simple, square, concrete, box-like rooms with no doors, only openings that led into people's homes.

We took off our shoes and entered a young couple's home. Living with them in a room not much bigger than the size of a full-sized mattress, was the young woman's thirteen-year-old sister and their daughter who had obvious mental and physical disabilities. After we entered, the mother said something to her sister, who then ran out the door and down the lane.

Irene introduced me to them and told me in English he was a rickshaw driver and she a maid. The mother and father would leave early in the morning, and the girls would have nothing to eat all day until mom and dad came home in the evening. Most days they earned enough to provide a simple meal of rice and lentils for the family.

In a few minutes, the little girl returned with three bottles of Sprite, one for each of us visitors. Now, my mama used to give me Sprite when I was sick, so Sprite equals vomit. I could drink it. It's not too terrible, but I also knew this cost so much of their income. I asked Irene if I could give mine to the little girl. She said, "No! They would be so offended. This is their gift to you." So we sat for the duration of our Sprite as Irene told me about this family's new desire to follow Jesus.

When we had finished our Sprite and thanked them for their hospitality, we reentered the lane, only my shoes were no longer by the door. They were now on the feet of a beautiful, naked, little Indian child. When I retrieved them from her, I realized the mud was not only mud, but human and animal feces.

As word went out that a foreign lady was in the slum, I became the Pied Piper. Children gathered from every direction and crowded around me to walk with us. As we continued down the path, a rat the size of a cat darted out and ran right across the top of my right foot. I squealed. But what startled me even more than the rat was the children's response to the rat. They also squealed, but not in fear. Their squeals were of delight, and now I was no longer the center of attention. The rat became the focus. They laughed and shouted as they chased it through the maze. I wondered what they would do with it if they caught it.

In another of these concrete homes, Irene introduced me to a woman with HIV. She told me most of the women in the slum were sex workers. A woman of the slums would need to spend half of what she could make as a maid or nanny—if she could find such a job—on public transportation to and from the rich sector of the city. Sex work is an easy and convenient way to make money, and the market's demand is constant.

This woman in front of me was carrying a baby who was much too small and frail for his age. I asked Irene about him. She told me she was pretty sure the child had AIDS, but the mother refused to allow them to take the baby to a doctor. She would rather not know if her baby was dying.

The farther we walked into the maze, the poorer the houses became. Soon they were no longer made from concrete but from items of trash people had pulled together to form a shelter, pieces of sheet metal, plywood, plastic tarps, and old signboards. The lanes became narrower and the sewage around our feet deeper and wetter.

Shacks teetered upward about three feet above the ground, over piles of everything you would put into your garbage can and everything you would put into your toilet, rotting in 100° temperatures. I cannot describe the stench. My gag reflex lurching, I endeavored to continue smiling at the people who slept a few feet above this foul refuse.

I followed Irene up a rickety ladder made from random trash, into a tiny home where a teenage girl met us. She and her husband lived there with their infant girl, whose body radiated a high fever. The young father was away attempting to earn money pedaling a rickshaw, while the mother had no food to eat to nourish herself, much less her baby.

Good Shepherd?

When we climbed into another dwelling, Irene told me this was a rental house. It was a "second- story apartment" created from trash, and it creaked like it might not hold our weight. About the size of a twin bed, the young woman lived there with her daughter, sleeping together spooning on the floor.

Irene told me the events of this woman's life which had led her to be living in such a condition. As I listened to the tale of hardships, my eyes filled with tears. This young woman knew some English, so I turned to her and apologized. I told her I was sorry so many terrible things had happened to her and that her life was so filled with pain. She interrupted me mid-sentence and said, "No! My life is not terrible. Didn't you tell us this morning in church that Jesus is my Good Shepherd and he is taking care of me?!"

Emotions overcame me and I wept convulsively. How could the "Good News" apply in these conditions? If I had seen their homes before I had spoken that morning, could I have been so confident of Jesus' love and concern for them? I was angry. Beyond angry. I was livid. Because the Gospel message I was taught to believe—the one I had been training people to propagate around the world—bought people a ticket to heaven, where they could go and everything would be good when they died. If all I could offer this woman was a message that said, "Hold on through the hell of this life. Then when you get to heaven, everything will be hunky dory," that just wasn't good enough news.

Then this woman asked me to pray for her. I was the missionary from America, the one with some kind of "power" to bestow upon her, and I had nothing. What could I pray that I could responsibly expect God to do for her? Even if I prayed she would experience God's presence, how do you experience God when you're living in sewage? I couldn't find God.

I came home from India broken. Another blow had pummeled my faith. How could a good God allow so much suffering in the world? How could God be just, when I was born into such comfort, while other people were dying in garbage? Vincent van Gogh had a profound thought: "It always strikes me, and it is very peculiar, that, whenever we see the image of indescribable and unutterable desolation—of loneliness, poverty, and misery, the end and extreme of things—the thought of God comes into one's mind." Perhaps the suffering has nothing to do with God.

The swirling spiral of doubt had begun. We could pretend it wasn't there, but we didn't want to. We were angry. We were sick—and we were tired from many years of working hard for something that we were not sure anymore was even true. I mean Christianity. It was not doing any of the things we understood it promised.

It did not make us holy people—neither in the fruit of kindness toward one another, nor in moral living. The all-powerful God, who we had been raised to worship, did not even protect his own—even one who had served with his whole life and had sacrificed everything to join the cause of missions among the unreached. Who was this God and what was God like, anyway? Did God even exist? Or was this Christianity-thing just the thing our parents had raised us to believe? I had written a book about intimate relationship with God that teaches people how to hear God's voice, and now I didn't know if any of it had been true at all. I will tell you that this spiral of doubt is terrifying. The bottom, the foundation of our life, had crumbled right beneath our feet.

We examined other religions in our grief, pain, and confusion. We saw in Buddhism the cultivation of loving kindness and compassion. I found this attractive, in that perhaps such an emphasis would produce kindness in its followers. I wanted kindness. Taoism held some fascination for us because of our experience in Taiwan. Its emphasis on simplicity and harmony spoke to me. I wanted harmony. Teachings of Hinduism that elevate an awareness of our "oneness," not only as a human species, but with all of creation were compelling, promised connectedness. I wanted connection. We discovered nearly every religion includes something akin to the Christian Golden Rule: do to others what you would have them do to you.

With eyes wide open, we also saw that while a thread of kindness and compassion runs through each of these religions, they (including Christianity) also have contributed to some of the most destructive and repulsive acts in human history.

Religious ideologies, using their "god" as a tribal deity to give justification for the basest human impulses of selfishness and greed, have bolstered oppression, slavery, war, and genocide. No religion is untainted from this kind of history.

To be fair, in our examination of world religions, we had to reexamine what we knew of Jesus. Laid bare, we started over by reading the Gospels—the stories of Jesus in the New Testament. And what we discovered was that not only did he teach compelling ideology: love one another, care for the poor, turn the other cheek, forgive those who hurt you, etc., but he modeled a life of how to do it. Jesus was amazing: how he treated people, his kindness, his mercy, his love, his focus upon the "least of these." Those most rejected by society and most in need of acceptance had his full compassion, while he disassociated from the religious establishment (people like us) which bolstered its power by judgment.

I now saw Jesus' claim when we have seen him, we have seen God. I understood what the Apostle John meant in these words: "The Word became flesh and dwelt among us . . . and through him we beheld the invisible God." God looks like Jesus. Profound. My "holiness" church experience instilled shame and fear in me, embedded in a view of God as a wrathful Judge who sees us as worms worthy of everlasting torture. I decided to start over and learn (by looking at Jesus) what God is like.

Then, we examined the things Jesus taught. In some Bibles, these parts are printed in red letters. Jesus' words, his invitations, his commands—they are subversive to the status quo. He offers a whole new Way of Living. Shane Claiborne, author of The Irresistible Revolution, talks about a similar realization and evolution of his own faith. He writes, "What if Jesus meant the stuff he said?"

Jesus said, "Blessed are the poor, for theirs is the Kingdom of God." Bono, the lead singer of the band, U2, in his activism in the fight against AIDS and extreme poverty in Africa, preaches: "God is in the slums, in the cardboard boxes where the poor play house. God is in the silence of a mother who has infected her child with a virus that will end both their lives.

God is in the cries heard under the rubble of war. God is in the debris of wasted opportunity and lives, and God is with us if we are with them."

I wondered, maybe when we are with the poor, we encounter God.

Jesus told a story which became the basis of Mother Teresa's calling. He said someday he would sit on his throne and separate people, like a shepherd separates sheep and goats from one another. He said he would put the sheep on his right. Here is why:

I was hungry, and you fed me.
I was thirsty, and you gave me a drink.
I was homeless, and you gave me a room.
I was shivering, and you gave me clothes.
I was sick, and you stopped to visit.
I was in prison, and you came to me.

In the story, the sheep then respond to him, "When? What are you talking about? When did we do those things for you?" And he tells them, "Whenever you did one of these things to the least of these, that was me—you did it to me."

After walking by sick and dying people on the streets of Calcutta, India every day, Mother Teresa saw a vision—a personal experience in which she heard Jesus saying this very thing to her. Later, she said she encountered Jesus "in his most distressing disguise." She understood within each human being there is a spark of the Divine, the image and likeness of God. She did not see this story Jesus told as a metaphor, but rather, for her it described reality.

She said, "If our poor die of hunger, it is not because God does not care for them. Rather, it is because neither you nor I are generous enough. It is because we are not instruments of love in the hands of God. We do not recognize Christ when once again He appears to us in the hungry man, in the lonely woman, in the child who is looking for a place to get warm."

Mahatma Gandhi echoed this, "There are people in the world so hungry, that God cannot appear to them except in the form of bread." I saw that God was there in that Mumbai slum, in the sewage and the trash. God was there in the form of Irene and others from her church. God was feeding the poor, healing the sick, teaching the children, and they could feel God's gentle arms around them.

Okay. I was in. I wanted to do this Jesus thing. Divine humans loving divine humans in need. I was ready to follow Jesus, much like a guru, instead of a mascot. I was ready to pack up my children, board a plane, and move to India. But we had responsibilities, and my husband and kids were not eager to move to India. I was angry. I remember praying, "God this isn't fair. You can't just fill my heart with a fire and a passion and then give me no outlet for it." In my spirit I heard, "Take all the compassion you feel and pour it into the slum of Oklahoma City."

I thought of the city dump right next to Valley Brook. We call it Trash Mountain. It is where Oklahoma City deposits the refuse of all the southeast side. The mountain grows each year, and we joke about the possibility that someday it will become Oklahoma's only snow skiing resort. A flame of blue, methane fire breathes like a dragon from its side, and in the summer heat, the smell settles in over the Town of Valley Brook, like a muggy, foul cloud. This man-made mountain stands as a clear metaphor that the poor are the refuse of our society.

Jesus spoke of the garbage dump of his day, a valley called Gehenna, a ravine kings had historically used for child sacrifice. The Jews viewed it as cursed land and designated as the place for the city's trash. Jesus used its continual burning putridness to describe the greatest suffering humans can experience. The English word for this suffering is hell.

Mother Teresa knew Gehenna, "You can find Calcutta anywhere in the world. You only need two eyes to see. Everywhere in the world there are people that are not loved, people that are not wanted nor desired, people that no one will help, people that are pushed away or forgotten. And this is the greatest poverty."

This unique location by the dump seemed perfect for our Grand Experiment. These are the kind of people Jesus hung out with. I grew up in Seattle, WA. Coffee is in my genes. I woke one morning with the thought in my mind, "coffee shop." I took it as inspiration from The Muse (the name I like for God). What better way to get to know people? Folks don't think it's weird to talk to one another in a coffee shop. Maybe regulars would play games. Community activities like open mic nights might inspire connection. We thought if we could create a space where people would feel comfortable to hang out and have natural conversations, maybe relationships would develop.

I could see in my mind the thing we were after. The 1980s television sitcom, *Cheers*, became my mental model. Sam Malone (Ted Danson) an ex-baseball player, owns and runs a cozy bar in Boston that is always filled with quirky customers. People who would never be friends outside this bar become family to one another, as they share life while drinking or working at this place "where everybody knows your name."

I knew we differed from the people in Valley Brook. We were outsiders coming into their neighborhood. Our life experiences are different. Neither John's parents nor mine raised us with a sense of financial abundance, but they met every need. I never lacked for anything. Neither of us struggled with substance abuse or significant mental illness. We had never been to jail. Our nuclear families stayed together to this day. No divorces. We both have bachelor degrees. And we're white. Privilege oozes out of our pores. We didn't know if anyone in this neighborhood would speak to us, much less become our friends, but we wanted to try. We wanted to see if the Love Jesus taught could cross all of those barriers.

I had this picture in my mind when we opened Joe's Addiction in February of 2007, right next door to Valley of the Dolls. I knew nothing about starting a business. Friends who were more capable than I helped with that part. I knew nothing about decorating or creating a cool space. John and some young, talented friends offered their artistic gifts. I knew nothing about making coffee. All I knew was I liked it. A lot. Friends who owned another coffee shop in the city stepped in to train me in the complicated world of espresso, smoothies, and loose-leaf teas.

Most frightening of all, I knew nothing about how to interact with people. I was shy. I was socially awkward. I feared people I didn't know. I often struggled to carry a conversation with people I knew, much less strike up a new one with a total stranger. I remember asking my extroverted husband, "How do you do that?" I had just watched him start and maintain a confident, humorous, not awkward chat with the proprietor of a garage sale. By the end of our shopping and exchange of a few dollars, John knew the man's name, where he'd had grown up, what kind of soda he liked to drink, and that his mother was suffering from cancer and dying in hospice care! "How do you do that?" I asked him. He said, "You just ask questions. People love to talk about themselves. Ask a question. They start talking, and then you don't have to do any of the work."

That's what I saw Sam Malone do. I thought I might be able to do that. So I started there. Taking an order for a regular cup of joe, I'd ask, "How you doin' today?" and wait for a response. This would be a Grand Experiment indeed.

Making your way in the world today
takes everything you've got.
Taking a break from all your worries, sure would help a lot.

Wouldn't you like to get away?

Sometimes you want to go
Where everybody knows your name,
and they're always glad you came.
You wanna be where you can see,
our troubles are all the same.
You wanna be where everybody knows
Your name.

— Portnoy and Judy Hart Angelo

CHAPTER 2
INTO THE RABBIT HOLE

"Perhaps there is no more dangerous place for
a Christian to be than in safety and comfort,
detached from the suffering of others."

— Shane Claiborne

I drag into Joe's at 7:00 a.m., turn on the "OPEN" sign and make a pot of Brazilian Santos. A young friend of ours had roasted coffee earlier in the week, and the smoky aroma had been intoxicating as the beans rolled over and over in the roasting drum. I plan to make the most of this slow, groggy Saturday morning by sitting on the comfy couch and savoring the crazy goodness of Brazilian Santos. The morning passes with only a few customers, and then Bill comes in.

Bill is an older man. He has long, gray, stringy hair and a long raggedy beard. He is wiry, and he walks with a significant limp. Bill is carrying a large, thermal coffee cup. He sits down at the table near me and begins to talk. Right away I can tell Bill has some mental challenges. He rattles on about things I don't quite understand, repeating phrases over and over. He says something about his sister and his mother, his house, and a long walk.

Raising my eyes from my book, I catch Bill's eyes. Tacked onto the end of a slurred and run-on sentence, Bill holds up his mug and asks, "Hey, can I have a cup of coffee?" He is not asking if he can *buy* a cup of coffee. He is asking if he can *have* one.

I remember the words of Jesus, "Give to those who ask of you," and by this point, it usually isn't hard for me follow through. But this morning, I hesitate—it's Brazilian Santos. My friend roasted only one pound. It would be gone soon. And it's Bill. He wouldn't know the difference between it and Folger's, and that thermos cup is so big.

My hesitation lasts only a second as these thoughts speed through my mind, followed by conviction. Of course, he can have a cup of coffee. How could I say no? "Give to those who ask of you." So I say with a smile, "Sure, go ahead."

Then, as I watch Bill push himself up from the chair and limp his way over to the coffee pot, I remember a similar encounter Jesus once had.

The people were all tipsy. They were enjoying the celebration. Weddings don't happen every day. Jesus' mother was distressed. The wine for the party had run out. The family would be embarrassed. Their reputation was at stake. She asked Jesus, would he do a miracle for them?

Then, not only did Jesus turn the water into wine—it was the best wine ever. Naturally. But most, being under the influence, wouldn't even realize this. They wouldn't even appreciate the quality of his delightful elixir. The best wine ever would be wasted on the clueless . . . but Jesus didn't consider it a waste.

Bill sits down, and I lay aside my book. I want to pay attention to the picture The Muse has just brought to my mind. I ask questions. Through that broken and slurred speech, I learn that thirty years ago Bill was in an accident. He was hanging out with some guys, and his friend ran out of cigarettes. He tells me he didn't even smoke cigarettes himself, but he jumped on his motorcycle to ride to the corner store and buy cigarettes for his friend.

Zooming down the road toward the store, Bill looked down for just a second—precisely the second a car backed out of a driveway. When he looked up, it was too late. He slammed into the side of the car at full speed. He never even put on his brakes. The driver of the car had been drinking.

Bill tells me about his injuries—his broken bones, his shredded skin, and his crushed skull which doctors repaired with metal plates. He spent three months in a coma. I learn that Bill receives a disability check, and until recently he has been living with his mother. She died and left her house to him. Now his sister pays his bills for him, but there is never any money left over—not even for bus fare. But Bill can run.

Learning all these things about Bill takes a long time because Bill does not talk in straight lines. His story comes out in bits and pieces, with parts being told again and again, while he leaves others of my questions unanswered. However, repeated over and again, between unrelated sections, he keeps saying, "But I can run."

I later find out this is true. Bill has run marathons. I can hardly picture that scene, his scrawny body limping its way across the finish line. A real life Forrest Gump.

Bill tells me he comes every day to the clubs. In fact, this morning he is hanging out at Joe's Addiction waiting for the clubs to open. He has nothing else to do. He can't work, can't read. He has nobody to do things with him. I wonder about the value of even having survived the crash so many years ago. Thirty years of life lived in that condition. "But I can run."

Somewhere in the story of Bill's life, he asks me for another cup of coffee, and I smile. Of course, he can have another.

When Bill sits down again, it's like his mind gets stuck in a loop. He talks about Valley of the Dolls, the club next door. He says, "I don't have no money to buy beer from them, so I bring my coffee from home. But they won't let me take it in."

I keep asking Bill questions about his life, trying to learn more about him and express interest in him, but he won't answer my questions anymore. He's stuck. He keeps holding up his mug and coming back to the phrase, "They won't even let me take my coffee cup in there."

I feel sad. The semi-lucid moment has passed. It is clear I won't learn anything more about Bill today. We can't even converse anymore. He keeps repeating the same thing over and over again. All I know to do is sympathize with his frustration and apologize to him for the treatment he so often receives.

Bill asks me what time it is. It is after eleven, and I know the clubs will be open now. Bill rises to leave. He holds up his mug, thanks me again for the coffee, and then heads out the door. I watch him limp down the sidewalk past the front window, but after he passes out of site, there he is again—limping back toward the door. He must have forgotten something, or maybe the club isn't open yet.

Bill opens the front door and pokes his head in. He grins, holds up his giant, thermal mug, and says, "Thank you. They won't even let me take my coffee cup in there. Thank you." He closes the door and limps back down the sidewalk.

Suddenly I get it. Bill hadn't been stuck in a loop. He had been trying to tell me something. For the whole last part of our conversation he had been comparing me to the way they treated him next door, and he had been trying to thank me.

Jesus had healed ten lepers—an amazing miracle, a sacrifice of his own reputation (as lepers were regarded as unclean), a beautiful act of kindness toward the rejects of society. And yet, only one returned to thank him. Only one. The most rejected of all. The one who was a Samaritan—hated and cursed by the Jews.

It was not a waste. Bill *did* appreciate my coffee gift. Not because it was Brazilian Santos. But because he was accustomed to a miserable life of rejection, and my coffee was kindness.

Leon Dufour, a world-renowned Jesuit theologian and Scripture scholar, a year before he died at ninety-nine, confided to a Jesuit priest who was caring for him, "I have written so many books on God, but after all that, what do I really know? I think, in the end, God is the person you're talking to, the one

right in front of you." I had spent Saturday morning at Joe's
Addiction with "the least of these"—with Jesus.

This being human is a guest house.
Every morning a new arrival.

A joy, a depression, a meanness,
some momentary awareness comes
as an unexpected visitor.

Welcome and entertain them all!
Even if they are a crowd of sorrows,
who violently sweep your house
empty of its furniture,
still, treat each guest honorably.
He may be clearing you out
for some new delight.

The dark thought, the shame, the malice.
meet them at the door laughing and invite them in.

Be grateful for whatever comes,
because each has been sent
as a guide from beyond.

— Jalaluddin Rumi

A wiry man in tight jeans and a black leather jacket rides
his motorcycle up to the front door. He comes in and orders
black coffee. "Nothin' fancy," he says, "Just black. And no lid."
He asks, "What took you so long to get this place open?" It had
taken us a few months to design the space because we didn't
have all the money up front. Little by little, we had painted the
walls, added espresso machine and bar, then tables and chairs.
He says, "I been waitin' ta get some coffee for months now."
He smiles—not a full smile—but a slight smirk, accompanied
by a twinkle in his eye.

I invite him to sit at a table with me near the counter and we learn a bit about one another. His name is Clint. He lives in the neighborhood and is happy for coffee. We have a nice friendly conversation. When he's finishes his coffee, he stands and turns to go. It is then I see the large patch near the bottom on the back of his jacket: "Fuck you. I have enough friends." Clint comes every day for coffee. Sometimes two, sometimes three times a day. And every time he comes, we learn a little more about each other.

During the daylight hours, the neighborhood is relatively safe, and our daughter, Jessi, works at Joe's Addiction. She is fourteen. One afternoon, during a lull in business, she sits on the couch crocheting beanies for her friends. A tall, stylish man with broad shoulders and a full head of salt and pepper hair walks in for coffee. Noticing Jessi's crochet, he flamboyantly announces, "I love to crochet!" He drives home to find his yarn and crochet hook.

He and Jessi spend countless hours crocheting hats and scarves, or playing cards. Robert brings a couple of friends, and soon nearly every afternoon a lively round of cards is being played. We also discover that Robert is the town gossip. He has lived in Valley Brook his whole life and knows everything about everybody. We learn many things about people in the neighborhood from Robert.

One afternoon Robert tells Jessi about his family, about some of his struggles. He talks with her about the contempt he has received from people who disapprove of him. He tells her about his sadness, of a father who was cold and distant and a mother whose religious zeal rejected him. We wonder at his openness with our daughter, and we are glad he feels safe to share some of his pain.

Clint comes in for his afternoon coffee. I lay my cards down and head to the counter. Robert looks up from the cards and says mischievously, "Well, hi, Muffin."

Clint stops in his tracks and says, "Really?"

The air is tense for a moment. Clint moves to the counter to pay for the cup of coffee I have already filled, and I ask, "Do you know Robert?"

He says, "Oh yeah. We go back a ways."

He pays for his coffee. Then I ask, "Do you wanna play cards?"

"I don't play cards," he says. He walks over to the table and sits down in the empty seat between Robert and where I had been sitting. I return to the game, and for the duration of Clint's cup of coffee, he sits watching while Robert whoops me at a game of Skipbo.

When Clint stands and heads for the door, Robert says, "See ya next time, Muffin." And sure enough, the next afternoon, Clint drinks his coffee and chats with me, while we play another round of cards.

Patty comes every morning after dropping her kids off at school. She orders a cup of coffee and then hangs out for an hour. One morning she says, "This is my meeting, you know." I am not sure what she means. She looks nervous but starts to talk, so I sit back to listen to her story.

Patty and her husband had been notorious meth dealers. Not only did they sell the drug, but they cooked it in their house. One night, the police crashed through their door. Patty and her husband were two of more than a hundred people arrested in a city-wide sting operation that night that included arrests of Irish Mob leaders.

Tears spill over as she tells me the most agonizing piece of her humiliation. The police arrived in hazmat suits, as they consider meth a dangerous chemical, and pulled them to their front yard where firemen hosed them off in front of her three children and her husband's father. The shame is raw in Patty's lowered eyes and burning face, as she remembers her father-in-law watching from his nextdoor porch.

She tells me the story of her struggle for freedom from her addiction and the lengthy and difficult process of earning the right to recover custody of her children. She is now a few years into her sober life. Her children are healthy and growing. She still goes to Narcotics Anonymous meetings, but she tells me her daily visits to Joe's Addiction help her set her day straight—to remember what she is doing and why. After coffee and a conversation at Joe's, she feels ready to face the day.

Some mornings when Patty and I are drinking coffee and chatting, Clint joins us. I learn that Patty's husband and Clint also go "way back." I wonder, does everyone in this town know each other? They seem to. I am the one who has come late to the party, but I'm catching up and they seem to welcome me into the cast of characters who have already done lots of life together.

Chocolat

The powerful movie *Chocolat* tells the story of a mysterious woman, Vianne (played by Juliette Binoche) and her daughter who arrive in a tranquil, little French town. The town is steeped in strict, religious tradition. Vianne opens a chocolate shop across the square from the church, just as the season of Lent begins. Expectations of religious fasting and sacrifice clash with the tempting offer of delicious chocolate and kindness extended by the chocolaterie.

In this, I saw what I hoped for at Joe's Addiction. Vianne and her chocolate represent Love as she uncannily anticipates what each customer might desire. Her kindness attracts into her shop a community of people who, much like the *Cheers* crowd, are varied and unique in their social quirks, their backgrounds, and their emotional wounds. The townspeople consider some of them the "dregs" of their social hierarchy. Together they move away from religious rigidity and instead experience the Love of One Another in a community where everyone is a misfit and everyone belongs. Vianne even becomes one of "them" by the end of the story.

People of the Valley Brook neighborhood know religion. Like much of America, especially in the Bible-belt, they have been surrounded by it their whole life. They know what religion requires of them, and they have failed. They have felt judgment from family and church as they quit trying years ago. They know how church people view them, and, even if it isn't true of you or of your church, they have their guard up expecting rejection.

We did our best to come into Valley Brook without judgment. We carefully chose the design elements at Joe's Addiction to include nothing religious. No Bible quotes. No Christian clichés. We don't serve the coffee with a "God bless you," and we most certainly do not play Christian music. We wanted to make a space where *everyone* feels comfortable, where *everyone* is welcome. We defined the decor as a quirky blend of a Moroccan cafe and grandma's living room. (What that means is we purchased the furniture at thrift stores.) Jesus said all the law and the prophets, all of our religious rules and traditions, are summed up in Love. We wondered, if we offer Love—if we practice Love—what would happen?

Mr. and Mrs. Pig Pen

During our first winter, a young couple starts coming to Joe's Addiction every day. My husband calls them "Mr. and Mrs. Pig Pen." (Not to their face, of course.) It isn't very nice, but it is an accurate picture. As with Pig Pen of the *Peanuts* cartoons, this couple carries with them a cloud, not only of dust and dirt, but a cloud of a most overwhelming smell.

They come into Joe's with a laptop computer. We have free WI-FI, so they plug in, sit down (on the comfortable, *fabric,* odor-capturing couch) and play games and watch movies all day. I mean *all* day—until closing time.

When I say "overwhelming smell," I am not exaggerating. If it has a color, I imagine it as a green fog. I can see it spreading, as other customers raise their heads from their books, and with crinkled noses and questioning eyes look around the room. Conversations halt, necks swivel, and brows furrow.

What to do? Joe's is a business. I have paying customers. Consider the options: I could open the door to let in the fresh air. Too cold. Oklahoma winter is outside. I could tell them to use our WI-FI, they need to purchase something. What if they can't? Didn't we open this place to make relationships with people like them? Should I set a time limit for how long you can sit on the couch or be on the WI-FI? Hadn't we been hoping God would bring needy people to us?

I settle on my first course of action: incense. Every time I see them coming, I light a stick of jasmine in the shop. I'm sure they think this is just part of the ambiance of this cool coffee shop. I buy a large bottle of Febreze and spray the couch every night.

I talk with them, get to know them. They are boyfriend and girlfriend, living together in the neighborhood. They are excited about this coffee shop, happy for a place to hang out. Her name is Louann. His is Claude. He is much older than she. Or is he? She seems awfully young. She tells me she is twenty-one. Hmmm.

But the smell . . . what to do? I think by now I can be considered a friend. Friends give gifts, right? I go to the mall and buy lovely bath products: vanilla bean shower gel, a loofah and smell-good body spray. I wrap it all in a beautiful gift bag with a pretty card saying I am thinking of her and I love her. She hugs me and thanks me for the gift. I figure a hint and the ability to do a little "spa day" might send the message.

But no. The next day she comes back to Joe's—smelling like vanilla stink. She has not bathed. She has merely put the vanilla on top.

I ask more questions, get to know them a little more. They tell me they are grateful for a place to be during the day because the gas company turned off their gas. I ask why and discover Louann receives a disability check. She has since she was a child. She has been in and out of mental institutions for most of her life. Her mother is her "Payee," as she only has the mental/emotional capacity of about five years old and cannot manage her own money. Mom is supposed to pay her bills out of the check, but for the last couple of months, bills have not been paid.

They ask if I can help them with their laundry. They have no washer or dryer, and the clothes are piling up. Well, that is easy. I can do that. They bring me garbage sacks of clothes to wash. Oh, the stench. I can't understand why the clothes smell so bad. They come into Joe's wearing clothes I have just washed and yet now smell of what? What is that? Urine? Body odor? Sweat? How could the clothes become saturated so quickly.

We do church right in the coffee shop every Sunday morning. It's not like any church I ever went to growing up. Perhaps it feels more like an Alcoholics Anonymous meeting with karaoke than a church service. We sing songs about Love and community, and every week we look at the stories and teachings of Jesus. We discuss them and then commit together to practice them throughout the week.

Louann and Claude start coming to our church service. Louann loves to dance (well, more like jump). Soon she asks (every Sunday) if we will sing her favorite song, "You Never Give Up," by Matt Redman:

Oh no, You never let go
Through the calm and through the storm.
Oh no, You never let go
In every high and every low.
Oh no, You never let go.
God, You never let go of me.

One day, Claude shows up at church in his cowboy hat, stiff jeans, and a clean button-down, western shirt. He looks spiffy, and he knows it. He whispers, "I washed this shirt myself in our kitchen sink. I took a shower even though the water is cold. I wanted to dress up for church." Progress.

Claude asks if we can help them clean up their house. He explains they aren't very good at keeping things tidy; they have a lot of stuff that we can just throw out, and it has become overwhelming for them. Our not yet son-in-law, Scott, and our son, Josiah, help them clean up.

Now, you probably know you have to pay a fee for the trash truck to come to your house every week and pick up your garbage. For most of us, this is just a given, but this young couple has not paid their trash bill in many months. Instead, they have designated the one bedroom as the trash room. They have stuffed into this room everything you would throw in a garbage can. The door to the room no longer closes, and the heaps spill into the living room. The garbage piles chest high. My two boys put on gloves, hold their breath, and begin scooping into bags. They take two truckloads to the dump.

They find soiled undergarments stuffed here and there, behind the couch and hidden in cabinets. I know this is graphic and gross, and maybe you would rather not know. But this is life when you're mentally five years old and have no money for feminine hygiene products. Wendell Berry said, "You have to be able to imagine lives that are not yours," and I'm trying to help you do just that.

There are holes in the floors and in the walls that let in not only the outside temperature but also the neighborhood cats. Piles of cat poo sit on the floor, on the couch (where the couple sleeps) and—on stacks of clean laundry I have just washed days before.

And the cockroaches. Oh, the cockroaches.

The picture is becoming more clear. We clean up the place, and we talk to them about how to keep it clean. But what about the trash bill?

"Why is your mom not paying your bills?"

"Well, she feels she deserves the money for herself, because she has been taking care of my daughter for the last five years."

"You have a daughter?" Sigh.

"Okay, but there is other money for your daughter's needs. That check is supposed to take care of *your* needs."

Louann then asks me, "Will *you* become my Social Security Payee?"

I catch my breath. It hits me like a ton of bricks. Wait a minute, now. That is an awfully big responsibility. I'm already a very busy person. I'm doing well if I remember to pay my *own* trash bill on time each month. I may be getting in over my head here. Out loud I say, "Let me think about it, and I'll get back to you."

All the while, the stink has not improved. I know we have lost customers at Joe's Addiction. Some come in and see "Mr. and Mrs. Pig Pen" sitting on the couch, and they turn right around and leave. The incense is just not powerful enough to do the job. And that poor couch—it will never be the same.

The day comes when John says, "You're going to have to talk to her about her smell."

I throw back, "*You* talk to her about her smell." He reminds me I am the one who has built the strongest relationship with them. They know I love them. She would most likely be able to hear it coming from me. I know he is right, but . . . ugh.

I ask The Muse to help me, to let me know when the appropriate time is, to help me say things gently, to prepare their hearts to receive and to not feel hurt.

One day Louann and Claude come to me at Joe's. They are bouncing with excitement. They say, "We love it here. We want to volunteer. You know we have plenty of free time. We want you to train us to work as baristas!" Then they stand there, eyes twinkling, awaiting my response.

Here it is. I take them into the kitchen and tell them I need to talk with them about something. I explain that the Health Department will not allow me to let them work at Joe's because they are not clean. As gently as I can, I talk about her smell and about her need to bathe. I do the best I can; really, I do. But as I feared, tears fill her eyes, angry hurt clenches her face, and she runs out of the kitchen. I follow, but she keeps running, right out the front door. Standing at the door, I call to her, but she does not look back.

I tell Claude I am so sorry. I can't chase after her because I have to keep watch of the store. I feel horrible. He motions for me to follow him back into the kitchen.

"Jamie," he says, "You have to know her story." Everyone has a story.

Louann's story is this: when she was five years old, her parents divorced. Like so many children, her parents shared her back and forth. But unlike most children, every time she went to stay at dad's house he raped her, sometimes himself, sometimes with objects, household tools —once with a curling iron—and most often in the bathtub. Claude says, "There's no getting her anywhere near the tub."

Suddenly the puzzle pieces fit. It makes sense why she is "stuck" at five years old. It makes sense why I have taken her to the doctor several times for bladder infections. It makes sense why she has told me she and Claude are "a couple," but there is not much sex happening between them.

A picture comes to my mind. With my gift bags and washing of laundry, giving free coffee and an occasional muffin, even cleaning their house, I have been trying to stick a band-aid on a hemorrhaging wound.

I know God is asking me, "Are you all in?" We have seen this little coffee shop-church thing as sort of a "hobby on the side." But, the Kingdom of God is not a "hobby on the side" or a weekend activity. It's not a "drive-by mission-trip." The Jesus Way is a Way of Life. It is *who* we are. The Kingdom of God is a community. It is a family—a family especially for the least of these.

The question is, "Will I become Louann's family? Will I become a mom to her?" "As one whom his mother comforts, So I will comfort you," Isaiah 66:13.

Yes, The Muse sometimes does this for us by the Spirit. But sometimes a mom needs arms, she needs a voice, she needs to pay the bills.

I know the question is in front of me. Will I go all in on this thing we set out to do? The whole thing seems daunting. The people in this neighborhood are so different from me and so needy. I have no hope of ever understanding them and helping. That just seems like too large of a task. I decide to take the plunge.

"Start by doing what's necessary;
then do what's possible;
and suddenly you are doing the impossible."

— Francis of Assisi

CHAPTER 3
COMMUNITY IS A BETTER WAY

"Ministry is the least important thing.
You cannot not minister if you are in communion."

— Henri Nouwen

Ace has been hanging around the Joe's Addiction community for more than a year. He lives outside, so he takes advantage of the air conditioning in the summer and the heat in the winter. He drinks free coffee and borrows the phone, and sometimes he causes trouble. Ace is angry all the time.

Once, when I ask Ace to leave because he is yelling and threatening violence, he blurts out, "I did time in prison." His soul overflows with bitterness that comes from being at the butt end of injustice.

Ace tells me that when he was nineteen years old, he was living with his girlfriend. She was fifteen. "Her mother was fine with it," he says, "She was living right there in the same house with us. She knew we were sleeping together and didn't care—until . . ." He and his girlfriend's mom had a conflict. They fought, said awful things. The next thing he knew, the police were arresting him. She had made the call. Charged with statutory rape, he did a prison sentence of three years.

Betrayal is a painful wound. Added to the scars of a less than desirable childhood, Ace shoved the bitterness deep down inside. His years in prison only taught him violence as a way to survive. Ace joined a gang that became his family, his community, and his protection. When he left prison, the bonds of the gang provided him with an instant family on the outside as well.

Ace is thirty years old now, a telltale teardrop tattoo on his cheek, and still part of that family when he comes to Joe's Addiction. I don't know Ace well. He doesn't talk much. Mostly, Ace stays with his group of homies, hanging out in the coffee shop, and occasionally bursting out strings of expletives and threats of violence that cause us to ask him to take a walk and come back to Joe's another day.

Someone overhears Ace say something about Jesus in a conversation. The person interjects, "Oh Ace, you don't really care about Jesus. You're just here for the free food." Ace grunts, "Sure I do. I think Jesus is pretty cool." The community member suggests, "Well, then maybe you ought to come on Sundays. That is when we talk about what Jesus taught, and we learn how to follow The Way he taught us to live." Ace mumbles some quiet profanity under his breath and goes outside to smoke.

Around this same time, a nineteen-year-old girl in our community who has Hepatitis C announces the news that she is receiving a liver transplant. We rejoice together. New Life. But then . . . it does not take. Her new liver gives her a few extra months, close to a year, but she is going to die.

I go to the hospital to see her that morning. Her family gathers around her bloated, yellow body. She lies face down in a bed that rotates every half hour as the doctors try to evenly distribute the fluids which have collected in all her cells. Her coughed up blood has splattered the floor under the bed. She is unrecognizable and unconscious. I pray with the family, try my best to comfort her mother and her brothers, and then ask them to call me if they need anything. No one can predict how long it will be, maybe hours, maybe days, but it is just a matter of time.

That afternoon, as I am serving coffee at Joe's, the phone rings. She is gone. Can I come to the hospital right away? They need me. There are just a few people in the coffee shop, so I announce that Caroline has died, and I am going to the hospital.

As I move toward the door, one of our men who is homeless asks, "Can I go with you? I wanna make my apologies to the family." Then, another man asks if he can go. He desires to become a pastor and says, "I want to watch how you minister to the family, so I might know how to do it myself." I had driven our old Suburban and knew I had room. I think, "Well, okay. This is community. Maybe it will be a blessing for a small crowd to show up with our love."

Then here comes Ace. He rushes to me with, "Can I go?" I am surprised. I don't think Ace even knew this girl. I don't think he knows the family at all. Why would he want to go?

I say, "Of course, I have room. But why do you want to go? Did you know Caroline?"

"No," he blurts, "But I just need to go. I need to go."

I shrug and tell him to jump in the car.

Ace rides shotgun and talks the whole way to the hospital. His words, full of emotion, pour like a waterfall he has been damming for years. He tells me about his fiancé, the love of his life. He was engaged to her a few years ago. "Oh, I been with other girls along the way, but she was the only woman I ever truly loved."

Zooming down a country highway in their pickup truck, they had driven right over a snake that was stretched across the road. They stopped to take a look. She bent over, reaching out to pick it up, when its head raised and fangs launched. They drove three hours to the nearest hospital, but it was too far. By the time they arrived, the venom had coursed its way through her blood. Tears pour down his face, as he tells me of holding her in his arms, as she breathed her last in the Emergency Room.

He says, "I've never talked to nobody about this. I don't know why, but I have to go to the hospital. I know it's not her there in that bed, but I have to say, 'Goodbye.'"

I wish I had film footage of the next couple of hours. I cannot adequately describe the complexity—no, the chaos, and the beauty.

The family, as you might imagine, is wracked with grief. The mother is in tears. Grandmother, trying to hold it together, is barking instructions. One of the young brothers punches a wall and screams his anger, pacing and hollering until security escorts him outside to take a break. Another brother asks me, "Why? Why would God take my sister? She was the purest, kindest person I knew—a much better person than me. Why did he take her and not me?"

The man who is homeless suffers from paranoid schizophrenia. The moment we step out of the elevator into the intensity of these emotions, he wanders down the hall, talking out loud to himself, poking his head into occupied rooms. Uh oh. Need to keep an eye on him.

Pastor-Wanna-Be says, "I guess we assure them that God's will is always the best. Even when we don't understand it, right?"

I nearly shout, "No!" at him. That is the last thing I would want to hear in my grief—this is God's will, that God did this to my daughter, because God knows best. No. That cannot be what God is like. But now is not the time for theological debate. I tell him not to feel like he needs to say much or give any answers at all. Just a shoulder to those who are crying. I tell him we will talk about "God's will" later.

The family has no money. Hospital personnel is asking, "Where do we send the body?" We all know if they release her body to a funeral home, there will be a bill they cannot pay. What to do? Do I have any advice? Surely the state has a plan for this. Yes. A stack of papers with spaces to fill and lines to sign, and then the county will pay to have her cremated.

Another round of wailing and punching ensues as little brother hears. "They're gonna burn my sister?! I want her buried!

How will I visit her?" We assure him her ashes will come home to him where they can decide together how best to honor her.

In the thick of this bedlam, I suddenly remember our schizophrenic friend. I scan the small waiting room. Where is he? What is he up to? Oh no. There he is, leaning against a wall, standing still, Pastor-Wanna-Be's hand on his shoulder transmuting peace. He smiles at me and nods. I nod back. He'll make a good pastor.

Then there is Ace. He has been standing near me the whole time. He has said nothing. He isn't in the way, but he isn't involved. He is just there. When my eye catches his, he asks, "Can I see her?"

The mother looks startled. "Why?"

"I just need to say, 'Goodbye.'"

She nods. Everyone stands and moves toward the door. Okay, we're *all* going.

They have disconnected the machines. No more beeping. No more dripping. Her body lies still, under a clean white sheet—but it isn't her. The room is so quiet, as one at a time, brothers and mother go to her side, touch her hand and say, "Goodbye." The only noise is the quiet muttering of our friend who is homeless who stands in the corner, wringing his hands.

Suddenly, Ace breaks the stillness with a mad dash grab for the trash can and vomits.

As a pastor, these moments in that hospital are some of the most difficult and most profoundly precious. Maybe other pastors have, but I never took a course in "How to Comfort Grieving Families" or "Answers to Give When Life Just Sucks." Mostly, we pastors just beg The Muse to guide us, to inspire us, to be present in our hugs, to be sensed in our out loud prayers, and then we weep with those who weep. It is hard. I don't like pain. In fact, I've spent most of my life trying to avoid it. And yet, it is these moments of entering into another's pain that have been the sweetest, most intimate moments of community for me. "Blessed are those who mourn, for they will be comforted."

When all decisions have been made, papers signed, instructions left with hospital personnel, goodbyes said, and nothing is left to do, the family asks if they can ride back to Joe's Addiction with me. I whisper a thank you to The Muse that I drove the Suburban. I have just enough seats.

Ten people crowd in one elevator to leave. We are eight, and two are strangers who already occupy the elevator when we step in. They don't seem to know one another and are standing in different parts of the space. I have to describe these people, so you can imagine the scene.

Pastor-Wanna-Be is an eccentric, older man. He is wearing a sweater vest, a buttoned-up shirt and a gothic cross on a chain around his neck. His salt and pepper hair comes down to his shoulders, and he neatly waxes his curled handlebar mustache.

The woman who is a stranger to us appears to be middle class and middle-aged. She is wearing a "mom sweater," and her eyes widen as our crew enters the elevator.

Our schizophrenic friend is wearing six layers of clothing and a knitted winter hat the whole time we've been at the hospital, even though it is now 300° in this elevator.

One son is long overdue for a shower. His hair is unkempt, and he is in need of clean clothes. He smells ripe.

Ace is skittish. He has trouble standing still. His eyes (one bordered by that tear drop tattoo) dart back and forth.

The mother's hair has not been washed in days. Caring for her daughter has consumed her this last week. She is talking on her cell phone as we enter the elevator.

The man in the corner, who we don't know, is thin. His hair is graying. He owns the corner, putting his hands on the rails to both his sides, making his personal space clear.

The youngest brother is cute. His cherubic, round face and eyes have swollen from crying. His shoulders sag, and he is quiet.

The mother's boyfriend is tall, his beard is scruffy. He, too, needs rest and a shower.

Then there is me. I am wearing a loud, multi-colored patchwork skirt, a patterned scarf and peace earrings. Pastor-Wanna-Be has already informed me once I don't look very professional.

As the door closes, the younger son says, "I hate this elevator. I hate all elevators. I don't like this feeling." Our schizophrenic friend looks at the ceiling and shouts, "Where's the escape hatch?! If we get stuck, how we gonna get out of here? Can we climb out the top?" The mother is talking on her cell phone, telling someone the details of her daughter's death and explaining we are in an elevator. Maybe that's why the person can't hear her. The mother's boyfriend begins explaining what he knows about elevators, and there shouldn't be any danger. Ace says, "I'm gonna need a smoke before we drive home. It won't take me long. Jamie, can you wait for me to smoke?" Pastor-Wanna-Be starts giving instructions to everyone about not smoking in my car and then explaining to the middle-aged stranger that we have not just come from a party, but rather the death of our young friend. The youngest brother is still wiping tears from his eyes. All of this is happening at once, and . . . I burst out laughing. Pastor-Wanna-Be sends me a scolding scowl. I can't help it. How did I get here?

The mother informs me she doesn't want to go home. She would like to spend the evening at Joe's Addiction with people. So after a group smoke, we all pile into my Suburban. The drive back to Joe's is no less chaotic, as all these characters are now confined in a *very* tight space. And of course, we hit rush hour traffic. Why wouldn't we?

Pastor-Wanna-Be rides shotgun, so he can ask me practical questions about which Bible verses he should know for this kind of situation. Our friend who is homeless, sitting in the back, is talking incessantly—loudly now. One boy is sobbing, his head on older brother's shoulder. The mother is still on her cell phone. She's making call after call, telling and retelling the details of the last moments of her daughter's life to everyone who needs to know.

Ace, who is sitting next to her, points out a truck he likes and calls it a Ford. Pastor-Wanna-Be corrects him, saying it is a GMC. Ace informs Pastor-Wanna-Be that GMCs and Fords have the same engine, so he wasn't wrong. Ace says what he really wants though is a 1970s Volkswagen bug, because,

"They get 40 miles to the gallon!" Pastor-Wanna-Be starts to say something, then looks at me and says, "Never mind."

From the back seat, our friend who is homeless yells he wants a Karmann Ghia. "Anybody ever seen one of those? They're the coolest. I'm gonna get me one of those someday." Pastor-Wanna-Be sputters. Someone yells, "It's hot in here!" I tell them I have the heater off. It must be the body heat. Someone else yells, "It's Mom! It's all that hot air! Mom stop talking so much!"

Then, amid all the noise, my ear tunes in to a voice over my left shoulder. It is Ace. He is murmuring to himself. "Joe's Addiction is a good place. Good people there. Really good people there." I hear him, and a tear runs down my face. Ace says, "It's mostly peaceful there. Except sometimes. I should be Joe's Addiction Security."

Pastor-Wanna-Be looks at me and bursts out laughing. "See!" I say. "What a beautiful chaos we are!"

This is the day Ace comes *into* community. And maybe it is the day I realize that community is the point. With great wisdom from his many years of experience loving gang members, Fr. Gregory Boyle says, "You stand with the least likely to succeed until success is succeeded by something more valuable: kinship. You stand with the belligerent, the surly, and the badly behaved until bad behavior is recognized for the language it is: the vocabulary of the deeply wounded and of those whose burdens are more than they can bear." We are seeing that he is right.

The next Sunday, Ace is in church, listening to the teachings of Jesus. He begins little by little to let us know more about his life. I learn a lot about gang culture from Ace. I also learn more of the story of his childhood. He listens when I talk to him about his anger and encourage him to obey his boss so he won't lose his job. And then he tells me he has HIV. I begin to make sure Ace eats better, and that he is in a program that can provide his retroviral medication.

Utopia Stuff

As we reexamined the life and teachings of Jesus, we saw that he talked about the Kingdom of God all the time. He described it as being something that exists in the present and something that will also exist in the future. He invited people to enter it.

In the Gospel of Luke's telling of Jesus' life, he stood up in the synagogue and read an Old Testament prophecy from the Book of Isaiah:

> "The Spirit of the Lord is on me, because he has anointed me to proclaim good news to the poor. He has sent me to proclaim freedom for the prisoners and recovery of sight for the blind, to set the oppressed free, to proclaim the year of God's favor."

We have something in our American culture that helps us understand what Jesus was doing. Each time we hold elections for the presidency, we watch the candidates campaign. They appear on television and speak in debates. They hold town hall meetings, run advertisements. What they are saying is, "If you elect me, this is what I will do." (Give us better healthcare. Pull us out of this war. Whatever it is they hope to do if we elect that candidate as our president.)

In a real sense, this is what Jesus was doing at the beginning of his ministry. He stood up in the town hall meeting and he declared, "This is what I am here to do." Then for the next three years, Jesus walked around healing sick people, touching diseased and outcast people, feeding hungry people, holding little children.

And he taught about a different Way to live, a *better* Way, a Way that he summed up as loving God and loving one another as much as we love ourselves. Then he invited people to enter, or to join, what he called his "kingdom"—a kingdom that is characterized by Love. Love instead of hatred. Love instead of power. Love instead of riches. Love instead of selfishness.

When I was a little girl, I memorized this prayer:

"Our father, who art in heaven, hallowed be thy name. Thy kingdom come, thy will be done, on earth as it is in heaven."

But I think the way we really prayed it in our hearts went more along these lines:

"Our father, who art in heaven, hallowed be thy name. Would you hurry up and send Jesus back down here to take us up to heaven where your kingdom is and where your will is being done? Because, honestly, things are kinda goin' to hell in a hand basket down here."

Of course, had I prayed it like that out loud as a little girl, I would have been in big trouble. But that was how we believed, and how we lived. We huddled in a little "Christian huddle," waiting for the day when Jesus would take us up to heaven where everything would be hunky dory.

But that is not how Jesus taught us to pray, nor how he taught us to live our lives. He taught us to pray that his will would be done, his kingdom would come *on earth* as it is in heaven.

The point was not to take us up to heaven. The point was to bring heaven to earth. As Brian McLaren has said, "The Gospel is a transformational plan, not an evacuation plan."

We read in the Book of Acts that, in the early days of people following the Way Jesus taught that:

"All believers were together, and they had all things in common. They sold their possessions and goods and shared what they had with anyone who was in need . . . There were no needy among them." (Acts 2:44, 4:34)

Can you imagine? There was a community (what Jesus called a kingdom) in which there were *no* needy. Everyone had what they needed. Acts 2:47 tells us they were being "added to daily those who were being saved." Now who wouldn't want to get into a community like that? What a dream society. I think this is what John Lennon was dreaming when he wrote:

Imagine there's no heaven
It's easy if you try
No hell below us
Above us only sky
Imagine all the people living for today

Imagine there's no countries
It isn't hard to do
Nothing to kill or die for
And no religion too
Imagine all the people living life in peace

Imagine no possessions
I wonder if you can
No need for greed or hunger
A brotherhood of man
Imagine all the people sharing all the world

You may say I'm a dreamer
But I'm not the only one
I hope someday you'll join us
And the world will be as one

This is what Martin Luther King, Jr. was talking about when he gave his famous "I Have a Dream" speech. He was dreaming God's Dream—the dream of a world in which powerful people do not oppress vulnerable people. A world in which each person has enough. A world in which the children and the elderly are cared for. A world where Love for our neighbor is the guiding principle. Where Love reigns.

He said, "I refuse to accept the idea that the 'isness' of man's present nature makes him morally incapable of reaching up for the eternal 'oughtness' that forever confronts him."

Kingdoms are no longer a cultural reality in our day and age, so we need a new term. Martin Luther King, Jr. called it the Beloved Community. Community is what we are trying to create at Joe's Addiction. Dorothy Day, the Legendary Catholic Social Activist, said, "We have all known the long loneliness, and we have learned that the only solution is love and that love comes with community."

We began speaking of this utopia as the Community of Love, or the Community of Hope. It is the people who have committed to living the Way of Love that Jesus taught, and who dream of his Way bringing peace to a troubled world. We cannot change the whole planet, but we can live it in a small corner of Oklahoma City and hope our tiny stone, thrown into the massive pond, will join with the ripples of other stones, until they impact the whole pond.

Ace's Gang Life

Not long after the hospital experience, Ace comes into Joe's Addiction with a swollen, black and blue eye, and scrapes across his nose and his cheekbone. I ask him what happened. He says "some dude" showed up at the homeless camp and just attacked him, beat him up "for no reason."

I know there is more to the story. There always is. I also know Ace is still in the gang. We talk about it. He explains why you just can't leave the gang. He tells me you have to fight not only to defend yourself, but to protect yourself from future attack. "If the homies think you're weak, they might even kill you." I talk with him about the Way of Peace that Jesus taught, but in his culture, Jesus' Way seems impossible to him. I give him some ibuprofen, free coffee, and a couch to sit on. Sigh. I'm always sighing, it seems.

The next day, I am again serving coffee to Ace. He has just turned to the butcher block/ condiment table and poured creamer and sugar, when the front door opens. In walks a young man I have never seen before. Ace turns and through gritted teeth whispers, "That's him. That's the guy who beat me up! What do I do? What should I do?"

I pick up the phone just in case I might need to call the police for help and walk over and stand next to Ace. I lay my hand on his shoulder and whisper, "Why don't you do what Jesus taught us to do? Turn the other cheek. Forgive him. The violence has to stop somewhere."

Ace stands there contemplating revenge, every muscle tense and ready to spring into action, head bowed, slowly stirring the cream and sugar into his coffee. His anger is tangible under my hand. I wait, as his breath moves in and out in quiet snorts.

Finally, Ace takes in a deep breath, exhales loudly, slumps his shoulders, turns and walks over to the young man and sits down at the table with him. "How's it goin'?" Ace asks.

This is the day Ace decides to follow Jesus. There is no weeping at an altar. There is no sinner's prayer. Like Matthew, the disciple of Jesus who left his tax collecting table, Ace enters The Narrow Way that leads to Life. He knows the Broad Way all too well and has experienced its destruction every day. For a gang member, following the Way of Jesus is dangerous; it can mean losing one's life. But isn't that what Jesus said, "Whoever would lose his life for my sake will find it."

Most of us "good church folks" have imagined what it might be like to be martyred for Jesus. We have contemplated our decision if faced with the threat to deny him or be shot, and it is not out of the realm of possibility. As I write this, 600 Christians have this week been beheaded in Iraq simply because they claimed to follow Jesus.

Yet I wonder if martyrdom more often takes the form of losing friends and family, even Christian friends and family, when we decide to live the peaceful teachings of Jesus—to love our enemies instead of fight them, to not protect and defend ourselves, to speak kindness to a culture steeped in the violence of torture and war, to advocate for care for the poor, to welcome the aliens, to include the "sinner" in our family circle.

Ace risks the loss of his "family" and the potential loss of his life. I think of Jesus' words that "whoever loses father, mother, sisters, brothers, for my sake and the gospel's, will receive in this lifetime and the next a hundredfold fathers, mothers, sisters, and brothers."

A Coupon

This story has one more piece. A couple of days later, Ace becomes really sick. He forgot to fill out paperwork and the program did not renew his HIV medication. He didn't ask me for help, and maybe he didn't think it was a big deal, but late at night, out at the campsite, he knows it is bad. His fever is high and he can't breathe. The young man who beat him up takes him to the Emergency Room—and he sits with Ace through the night, while the doctors diagnose him with pneumonia.

Ace comes into Joe's Addiction the next morning looking terrible. He walks up to the counter, hands me a piece of paper, and then gingerly lies down on the couch. I hurry over to find out what is going on. He tells me his new friend took him, and they diagnosed him with pneumonia, but because he has no insurance, the hospital did not admit him. They gave him a prescription and sent him on his way. That is the paper he shoved in my hand.

I ask him, "Why did you come here? Why didn't you go straight to the pharmacy and get this medicine?" He shouts, "I can't afford it! The damn medicine is $140.00!" I tell him that can't be right. It is just an antibiotic. I am sure it can't be *that* expensive. "Maybe it's on Walmart's $4 list. I'll call and ask." I call the pharmacist, and sure enough, she says it is $140.00. Because of his HIV, he needs a high-powered antibiotic. I sit down next to Ace and tell him what she said.

He spouts, "That's what I told you! I can't afford it."

I ask him about his medication program. Is there a way the program can get it for him?

He says, "Maybe. Good luck trying to get a hold of my case worker."

By now, it is about 4:30 in the afternoon. I know it is unlikely anyone will answer the phone this late. I also know there will be paperwork involved. No way I can make this happen before 5:00.

Martin Luther King, Jr., whose life was all about justice for the poor and the marginalized said, "When I am commanded to love, I am commanded to restore community, to resist injustice, and to meet the needs of my brothers."

I text a friend of mine for advice. She is a physician's assistant, and she suggests I go to the pharmacy and ask them to just fill one pill of the prescription. Then the next day maybe I can track down a way to acquire the rest of it.

It is worth a shot, so I go. I ask the pharmacist if it is possible to purchase just one of these pills. I explain that we don't have enough money to buy the whole prescription, but we want to start it and hope to come back the next day to buy the rest. She seems surprised, but says, "Yeah, we can do that. It'll be about a forty-minute wait though. There's a long line in front of you." I tell her Okay and then pick up my phone.

I can't wait for the pill because I have plans to teach a class that evening in a nearby city and need to leave soon. I call Pastor-Wanna-Be and tell him the situation. I ask if he can come and pick up this prescription and take it to Ace at the coffee shop. He is glad to do it. (Because of course, this is what it means to be a pastor.)

During the break in my class, I see the text message that has come from him. *"Call me as soon as you can."*

When he answers the phone he says, "You're never gonna believe this."

He tells me he went to the pharmacy to pick up the pill, and as he was waiting in line, the thought came to him, "You have not, because you ask not . . . It can't hurt to ask." When his turn came to move to the counter, he explained to the pharmacist, "Ma'am there is a reason we are only buying one pill of this prescription. We are just a small church in a very poor part of town. This medicine is for a guy in our community who is homeless. He is very sick. He is HIV positive and now has pneumonia. If he doesn't take this medicine, he could die. Is there any way we can purchase this any cheaper?"

The pharmacist said, "Hold on a sec. Let me check something." She came back a few minutes later and asked, "Could you pay $11.53 for the whole prescription?"

Pastor-Wanna-Be asked, "*Can* we do that?"

She said, "I have a coupon."

WHAT?

The next Sunday, Ace stands in church. He thanks the community and tells how God has provided his medication for him. As Pastor-Wanna-Be stands and fills in the details of the story, someone shouts out. "It must have been a Jesus Coupon!"

Beloved Chaos

The cast of characters at Joe's Addiction is precisely that. A bunch of characters. We are a motley crew from varied social and economic classes, multiple kinds of upbringing and religious and political perspectives. Add in the messiness of brokenness and addiction, and you have chaos, but right in the midst of the daily chaos, we encounter beauty. Beauty in belonging. Beauty in kindness. Beauty in transformation. Beauty in the Love we experience together. Perhaps it is best to call the Kingdom of God a *Beloved Chaos*.

"Love in action is a harsh and dreadful thing compared with love in dreams. You are not hoping for a utopia to suddenly appear in the sweet by-and-by. You are not waiting for Jesus to come whip everybody into shape once and for all. No, you are learning that Jesus is risen and that he's coming again. He's coming for supper tonight, and he's not alone. Jesus is bringing with him Ms. Lewis and Ray, Quinton and Greg, Gary and Ant, Marie and Steven. He's standing at your door with someone whose name you don't yet know. They are sitting now at your dinner table—a peculiar family, for sure—ready to pass the butter and tell you a story about what happened today."

— Fyodor Dostoyevsky

CHAPTER 4
BELONGING

"Hope" is the thing with feathers
That perches in the soul
And sings the tune without the words
And never stops - at all

And sweetest - in the gale - is heard
And sore must be the storm
That could abash the little bird
That kept so many warm

I've heard it in the chillest land
And on the strangest sea
Yet - never - in extremity
It asked a crumb - of me."

— Emily Dickinson

Regularly, people in our Joe's Addiction community must go and spend some time in jail. Most often it is because they cannot pay the fines and court costs associated with their crimes. A judge will allow them to "sit out" their fines, off-setting a dollar amount per day toward what they owe. Chuck committed his crime in another county, so when the marshals come looking for him, they take him to a jail about two hours away.

A few weeks later, Chuck shows up at Joe's exhausted and teary. He has made his way back to Oklahoma City only to find that while he was away, his tent flooded. All of his possessions are ruined by mold. He slumps down into a chair across from me and starts to talk. "I know I'll be all right. My stuff isn't that important," he says, "I'm just glad to get back here." He details the saga of his return.

The county jail released him in the middle of the night. (This is common. The day's clock ends at midnight, so they dump people out on the street.) He found a spot to sleep on the ground until daylight. Then he started walking. He went to two different churches, asking if they could help him buy a bus ticket back to Oklahoma City. Both told him it wasn't in their budgets to do that kind of thing.

Chuck walked north along the shoulder of the freeway. He saw a sign that read, "Oklahoma City 95 miles," and he thought, "Well, I'll get there when I get there." When night fell, he pulled out a flashlight. He was grateful the marshals had taken him with his full backpack. His heart raced, and he tried not to think about the snakes that might be in the grass. He wanted to walk on the asphalt, but the trucks flew by with such speed, he feared that even if one didn't hit him, the gust of wind might blow him over.

He followed an exit to a truck stop, hoping he might catch a ride. A large truck painted with "Jesus Is Lord" on the side idled in the parking lot. He thought, "Surely this guy will help," but the trucker said, "I'm not going to OKC. I have to be in Ada in an hour to drop this load." He offered Chuck some money to buy dinner, and Chuck told him, "I don't need your money. I just need to get home."

Chuck pauses his tale. His eyes fill with tears, and he says, "I'm sorry. That's all I wanted. I just needed to come home."

After he composes himself, he starts telling me again. "The guy went ahead and bought me dinner. He even prayed for me.

He was a real nice guy." Chuck started out on foot again. As he neared the on ramp for the freeway, a truck pulled up next to him. The man who had bought his dinner called from the open window. "Chuck, Chuck. If you're willing to ride with me to Ada and drop off this load, I'll take you to OKC after!"

Chuck tells me what he told the driver of that truck as they rode the long way "home." "If you're ever in OKC, you've got to come to this coffee shop. Even better, if you're there on a Sunday, you need to come to church. When you walk in the doors and you hear the music playing, you can just feel the love. You know this is where you belong."

Joe's Addiction has become a place where people who have lost their family have found a new one. Some have lost family due to death. Others, their families have rejected them because of crimes they have committed. Emotional pain of grief and rejection crimp and stymie our ability to live free and whole. We end up being less than fully human. Unconditional Love restores. It makes us whole again.

Lucille and Timothy

The Valley Brook City Clerk calls me and asks if we might be able to help a family in need in the neighborhood. I am thrilled that someone in city hall sees us as a help, and, of course, say yes! We welcome Lucille, her five-year-old son, and her mother-in-law into our community at Joe's. The daddy has recently died from cancer. The two women cared for him at home during those last days of his life, and they are reeling from the grief.

The woman at city hall tells me they have nothing, no food, no heat, and she is right about "nothing." Little Timothy's face is caked with dirt and his tears have worn trenches through the mud. I wonder when was the last time he has taken a bath. The women in our community take turns caring for Timothy, some even taking him home for "babysitting" spells, just so they can clean him up. This proves to be more difficult than we expected. Baths terrify him, and he flails and shrieks through the whole experience.

One day I ask Timothy if he is hungry, and he nods. I make him a peanut butter and jelly sandwich. When I bring it to him, he asks, "What is it?" I tell him, but he looks at me with a blank stare. I sit down at the table with him.

"Haven't you ever had peanut butter and jelly before?" He shakes his head. "Well, I think you're gonna like it,"

He picks up a half and puts it in his mouth. His teeth move up and down, up and down. Then he takes it out of his mouth and asks, "How do I eat it?" The child does not know or even have the instinct to bite down and and tear off a piece with his teeth.

I fight back the tears as I ask him, "What do you usually eat?" He grins and says, "Mac-n-cheese and Dr. Pepper."

"How 'bout for breakfast? What do you eat for breakfast?" He says, "Mac-n-cheese and Dr. Pepper."

I later find out he is not pulling my leg. That is all this child has ever eaten. I don't know if it is because he doesn't like other things, and mom just doesn't want the fight, or if she doesn't know how to make anything else for him. As we spend time with her, it becomes clear she has learning disabilities and emotional wounding that have stunted her ability to take care of herself, much less a little boy.

But Lucille loves her son, and she and her mother-in-law spend time at Joe's every day. The community comes together and provides clothing for Timothy (when we met him, he didn't own a single pair of underpants). We help Lucille enroll him in school and buy him some uniforms. One lady in the community provides financial counseling and accountability, so Lucille can pay her bills and afford groceries.

About a month into our relationship with Lucille, the woman who has been helping her budget comes to me. She is bouncing up and down. "Jamie, Velma is not Lucille's mother-in-law. She's . . . well, I'm not sure what to call her."

I ask, "Is she Lucille's mom then? Because Timothy calls her "Grandma."

"No," she tells me, "She's Timothy's daddy's wife." What? She says, "You better sit down. It's a long story."

Timothy's daddy was married to the older woman who Timothy called "Grandma." He had brought Lucille into the house as his mistress. Of course, his wife was angry, but she could do nothing about it. Timothy's daddy was the one paying the bills. He was kind enough to not kick her out to the street, so he told his wife she could continue living there if she wanted to. She had nowhere else to go. No way to provide for herself. So she stayed.

Over the years, the two women developed a tolerable relationship. Lucille had a child, and they all decided to have him consider Velma his grandma. She was old enough for that position. The three adults made life work together, and I am sure little Timothy never understood the oddity of his family situation. He loved his daddy, his mama, and his grandma, and they made it work. The two women even developed some affection for one another, particularly when the man they both loved was dying.

However, the power differential shifted when Timothy's daddy died. Velma was the legal wife. Her name was on the papers. So upon his death, she began receiving a monthly veteran's check as his beneficiary. After all those years of humiliation, Velma now took her place at the top, and she wielded her power with minimal mercy. She loved Timothy. He truly was a grandson to her. But Lucille? For the sake of Timothy, she threw a bone Lucille's way from time to time.

How do you navigate the complexities of this situation? Pointing out "sin," calling out "immorality" is not helpful. It is what it is. Fr. Boyle in speaking of how to help people develop resilience has said that in the community of unconditional love, we are "to model not the 'one false move' God but the 'no matter whatness' of God." God has entrusted fragile people to our care. Love is the only Way. We care for all three of them.

We love Lucille. We provide material things she needs to do life. We share our knowledge of life skills and encourage her to go to Community College.

We love Velma. It is not difficult to empathize with her bitterness. We appeal to her love for Timothy and encourage her to be kind. As Lucille grows in independence, Velma's health begins to fail. The best option for her is a nursing home. The monthly check she receives is just enough to make this possible.

And we love little Timothy, the most vulnerable of them all. He becomes a shining light in our community. He excels in school, and we all celebrated together. We howl in laughter as he sings, "All about that bass, 'bout that bass, 'bout that bass." And we cry together when Lucille finally tells us the trauma that caused his fear of the bathtub.

Our relationship with this family brings to the forefront words from the little book in the New Testament written by Jesus' brother, James. "Religion that God our Father accepts as pure and faultless is this: to look after orphans and widows in their distress." From this time on, widows and orphans take priority over every other need in our community, and we become their new family.

Eye Surgery

Cliff lives outside. He is a Vietnam veteran and suffers from PTSD and paranoid schizophrenia. He also is nearly blind when he comes to Joe's Addiction. Cataracts cloud his vision so all he can see are vague, foggy images. Consequently, Cliff has no social value for personal space. He always stands too close, and when I take a step backward, he follows and leans in, putting his face only inches from mine. Suffice it to say, I have ingested Cliff's spit on more than one occasion.

Cliff is resourceful and, without a doubt, the most adept at living outside of all my friends. He keeps his campsite clean, carrying trash out daily. He creates a fire pit with a comfortable seating area, stools and chairs made from old crates and oil cans. He knows how to endure the weather each Oklahoma season throws at him, utilizing padding and coverings, blankets and tarps in winter and motorized fans in the summer heat.

I have often thought Cliff would win a million dollars if he could audition for *Survivor*.

Cliff receives disability benefits including medical care, so when I see him struggling with his vision, I help make the calls and ask the questions to sign him up to receive cataract surgery. I take him to the pre-surgery appointments and make sure he understands what to expect, where to meet me to pick him up the morning of surgery, and that he is not to eat or drink anything after midnight the night before. This shouldn't be too difficult, right? He would be sleeping then, anyway.

At the appointed time the next morning, Cliff is standing on the corner right where I told him to be. He climbs in my car, and immediately I smell the alcohol. Oh, no. I say, "Cliff, you've been drinking." I remind him he wasn't supposed to eat or drink anything after midnight. He says, "It's okay," and pulls out a bottle of cologne and starts spraying himself. "I'll just spray a little of this on me. They won't even know."

They can't do the surgery that morning. Alcohol thins the blood, and they will not take the risk. We reschedule the surgery, a whole month away.

I receive a call from Cliff on the Joe's Addiction phone. He says, "Can you come and get me?" I ask him where he is. He doesn't know. He tells me he walked to the mall (about a mile and a half from Joe's). He knew the road well, so he had no problem. But when he came out of the mall, he must have exited a different door. He followed the road, but it didn't lead to Joe's. He can't tell me where he is because he can't see any landmarks. After a lengthy and frustrating attempt to locate him, he finally puts someone else on the phone. He is at a gas station four miles away.

The day of his surgery comes, and this time we arrange for a man in our community to stay with him all night to make sure he doesn't eat or drink. He arrives at surgery sober and ready. In the pre-op procedure, he introduces me to his nurse. He says, "She puts hope in your mind and gives you a vision for the future, and it's a life of good things." When the nurse asks, "Do you have a family?" he responds pointing at me, "This is my family. It's been a long journey to get into this chair."

Cliff is right. He is my family. My children see him as a grandfather kind of figure. He loves them, and they love him back. His love language is gift giving. He finds special things and passes them on to us, things he knows we would like. A necklace. A toy. A book. His alcoholism and schizophrenia make relationships complicated and impossible to maintain, but we receive his gifts as the pronouncements of Love that they are.

After the surgery, when he is in recovery, the nurse asks him to read the letters on the wall. There is a long silence. She tells him he can read whenever he is ready. "Now, I gotta wait a minute and know for sure what I feel like it is in my heart before I say." A couple minutes pass, then Cliff rattles off the letters perfectly. Hope has 20/20 vision.

The poet Shelley writes, "To love and bear, to hope till hope creates from its own wreck the thing it contemplates."

Hope Is a Good Thing

Early on, in the first year, one of our regulars said, "You'll never know what you opening this coffee shop did for our neighborhood." I was surprised and not sure what he meant, so I asked. He said, "Well, cool coffee shops are on the north side of town. This is the south side. You know. Nobody opens a coffee shop here. When we saw a coffee shop was opening right here in Valley Brook, we thought, 'Wow. We've moved up in the world.'"

We cannot fix the problems of generational poverty and the loss of dignity that comes with it overnight, and even as we share what we have with one another, the problems still continue.

But we had no idea that simply creating this space would elevate the sense of dignity for a whole neighborhood of people who had always felt they were "less than."

Before the idea for a coffee shop had even come to mind, we drove the neighborhood, praying and exploring possibilities.

We could feel a heavy weight, like a blanket or a low pressure system; the pressure was almost palpable. It took some time to make friends before we identified it as *despair*. Never enough. Always a struggle. Can't get on top. It will always be this way. We realized what we desired to create was a Community of Hope.

Andy, the protagonist in the movie Shawshank Redemption, says to a fellow inmate in prison, "Remember Red, hope is a good thing, maybe the best of things, and no good thing ever dies." Hope is the anticipation of good. It's rare. Maybe priceless. We all need it to survive. To keep going. We want to be purveyors of hope, pointing the direction to the possibilities of goodness. To the anticipation—maybe even the expectation—that things could be better.

SECTION 2
RUBBER MEETS ROAD

"Love is a prisoner who stays up night after night with a sharpened toothbrush, working away at a crack in the wall until, finally, he breaks through. A way opens, not over the wall but through it. It helps, of course, to have someone working from the other side—someone who will meet you in the middle. But wherever the encounter takes place, this opening in the wall of suspicion and fear finally makes a relationship possible. This opening, you learn, is called trust."

— Jonathan Wilson-Hartgrove

CHAPTER 5
THE WAY

"Life itself is a haphazard,
untidy, messy affair."

— Dorothy Day

Marilyn and her husband, Roy, move to Valley Brook a few years after we start Joe's Addiction. They don't have a coffee pot, so the morning after they move in, she comes looking for coffee—not at Joe's—at the convenience store next door to us. As she rounds the corner of the building, a man in our community greets her on the sidewalk. She mumbles, "I'm going to the store to get coffee." He says, "Well this is a coffee shop, right here." Later she tells us she had seen the name Joe's Addiction and thought it was a "head shop" (a store that sells marijuana paraphernalia).

She never buys a coffee pot for her house and instead drinks coffee at Joe's every morning. She brings a book with her and reads. After a while, she gets to know some of the folks, and someone invites her to church. She shows up. Later, she tells me when she went home after, her husband asked her how it was. She told him, "That was no church. I don't know what that was. But that was *not* church."

One Wednesday morning, Marilyn comes to buy her coffee, but Joe's is closed. She calls Foster, our manager, on his cell phone. "Why's the coffee shop closed?" she asks. He explains to her that we currently don't have a volunteer to serve Wednesday mornings. "That's not right," she barks, "I need my coffee!" Foster asks, "Well, Marilyn, would you like to serve Wednesday morning's shift?" Marilyn becomes a barista.

Marilyn is strong and capable and she likes to keep busy. She goes to work. When the person running our Free Store needs a break, she steps in. When we need a cook for Thanksgiving Dinner, Marilyn volunteers. She notices the flower beds in the backyard and asks if she might plant cucumbers and tomatoes. (This is the beginning of our Community Garden.) When people donate toys for Christmas, Marilyn organizes a Christmas Store for the neighborhood.

Drill Sergeant might be a fitting picture of Marilyn, and her vocabulary fits the role just fine. She doesn't ask. Marilyn tells people what she needs done, and they jump right up to help. She expects no one to work harder than she does, she'll do it right there alongside, but she's not going to do it by herself when there's a "room full of guys sitting on their asses doin' nothin'." This is Marilyn's view on life. She motivates participation from the most unlikely places.

It might not be too extreme to say men in our community are afraid of Marilyn. Big strong men who have been in prison will not cross her. Once a tenant living in her rented room tries to sneak out without paying rent. Seeing all his stuff loaded in his car, she lets all the air out of his tires, removes his license plate, and then she tells him, "You try an' leave, and I'll cut your balls right off."

Two years into Marilyn being a part of our community, she verbally assaults a disrespectful teenage boy and bans him from ever coming back to Joe's Addiction. As gently as I know how, I explain to Marilyn why her response is just a little over the top, when she says, "Jamie, can we go to lunch? I think I'm ready to tell you my story."

As a young girl, Marilyn and her sister lived with her grandmother because her daddy was in the federal penitentiary and her mama was emotionally unstable. She shows me scars on her arms where her mother burned her when she was only eighteen months old. On her fifth birthday, her mother used a metal key from a can of Spam to cut off the balls of her little feet— the padded portion of her soles, between her toes and the arches of her feet—she just filleted them to the bone. When I ask, "Why?" Marilyn only shrugs, "I was running in the house."

Living with her grandma brought good memories of a nice time in her life. She remembers going to church with grandma and loving it. Church meant playing "dress-up." She wore a white bonnet, white gloves and patent leather shoes. On Sundays, she was "queen for a day."

When she was four and her sister just a bit older, daddy showed up at grandma's house. He was out of prison, and he had come to take the girls to eat. They went to a diner not far down the street and sat together in a booth by the big, front window. In the middle of their meal, daddy stood up and told the girls not to go anywhere, he would be right back. They watched their daddy walk outside, cross the street and go into the pawn shop. A few moments later, he came out the door with a shotgun and gunned a man down, right there in the street—as his little girls watched from their diner booth, picture window. He then walked back into the restaurant and sat down at the table as though nothing unusual had happened. Police swarmed the place and took daddy away again.

Not long after that experience, the girls were playing in grandma's yard when their mama came and snatched them. She took them on a long ride to another state where nobody would know them. For the next few years, to say life was hell would be an understatement. In fits of rage, her mother beat them, but even worse, all of her mother's male friends were allowed to have their way with the girls.

Marilyn remembers the day her mother received a certain phone call. She remembers it because her mom was afraid. After the call, mom packed their things. On the way to the airport, she handed a piece of paper to both girls and told them to memorize everything on this paper. She said, "This is who you really are." As Marilyn read the paper, she discovered her real name, who her relatives were and where she was from. They were going to live with their daddy.

Marilyn remembers walking down the long airport ramp, tightly gripping the hand of her older sister. She remembers the crowd of people waiting to greet the passengers and her sister saying, "That's our daddy"—the scary-looking man with a long, shaggy beard and piercing blue eyes. Turning to her sister, Marilyn said, "Pick another one."

Daddy had married a woman who had children of her own, and the next years were what Marilyn describes as a "Cinderella story from hell." The stepmother resented these daughters from another woman, and she did everything she could to let them know they were worthless. Marilyn wished she could go back to live with her mother. She says, "The mental and emotional abuse were worse than anything we experienced with our mom." By the age of twelve, Marilyn believed she was mentally disabled, she couldn't learn, and she would never amount to anything.

Her older sister ran away, and Marilyn found herself before a judge where she stood up for herself for the first time. "I will NOT continue to live with this woman. You take me out of this home." The court placed Marilyn in a foster home where the father of the home molested her. After four months, she called her case worker from the school office telephone. She said, "You come and pick me up, and you put me in another family, or I will run away and no one will ever see me again." The case worker met her at the door of the school.

The next season of Marilyn's life was maybe the best. She was placed with a Pentecostal family. She remembers the mother of the home sitting down with her and going through her things—her one, small box of personal belongings. The woman asked her, "Is this all you have?" Marilyn nodded, and the lady said, "We have to get you some stuff."

The woman asked her, "Do you know about our religion?" Marilyn remembered church with her grandma, so she said, "Yes." "Well," the lady went on, "our religion does not allow women to wear makeup or jewelry, and we always wear a dress. Now, with you not bein' our own daughter, we will not require all the same things of you. We do ask that you not wear makeup or jewelry, but it's okay with us if you want to wear pants. We would like it though if your pants are not all jeans, if you wear slacks sometimes. Are you okay with this?" Marilyn was thrilled. This meant she would have seven pairs of pants. Three jeans and four slacks.

This family not only loved and took care of Marilyn, but the woman of the home taught her everything Marilyn is now contributing to our Joe's Addiction community. She learned how to clean, how to cook, how to garden, how to can vegetables. Life was good for a time.

Then the day came when her case worker informed her she would have to leave this home. The Pentecostal woman had become sick. They assured Marilyn as soon as the woman recovered, she could come back. That never happened. Marilyn was placed in a girls' "reform school."

After a short, and unpleasant "one-night-stand," Marilyn found herself teenaged and pregnant. Shortly after, she fell in love with a young man, and they got married. She quickly became a young mama of three. Two boys and a little girl. The marriage was a nightmare. Her husband drank a lot, and when he did, he beat her. Feeling stronger than when she was a girl, Marilyn always called the police. The police took pictures. Her husband spent time in jail. But to the dismay of her older sister who now worked as a topless dancer, Marilyn always took him back. Her sister pleaded with her, scolded and berated her for her "stupidity," but Marilyn always let him come back home.

One morning, about 5 a.m., Marilyn awoke to fists pounding her face. This was the last time. Not only the last time he would beat her, but the last time *anyone* would ever hurt her again.

She reached for the gun she had hidden under the pillow and she shot her husband. The bullet landed in his groin, barely missing a testicle.

As he lay, blood pooling on the floor, Marilyn packed, randomly grabbing things of hers and the children's. Eyes wide, she tells me, "I was done. That was all I was going to do. I was leaving."

But then her husband began to beg. He cried, "Please, don't hurt me. Please, don't hurt me."

Tears brimming in her eyes, Marilyn asks me, "How many times? How many times had I said those same words? How many times had I begged him not to hurt me?"

Marilyn picked up the gun and shot. Again and again and again—until the bullets were gone, just the repeated clicking, clicking, clicking of the trigger. She dropped the gun, picked up her baby girl and her bag, and walked out the door with her little boys following close beside.

Two weeks later, at her sister's home, where life had just begun to develop a routine, the police showed up. They arrested her and told her that her husband had not died. The District Attorney charged Marilyn with First-Degree Attempted Murder. Her actions had been premeditated.

Calls to the police, trips to emergency rooms, photos of bruises, arrest records—her attorney presented all of these things in court, and Marilyn was acquitted. The jury ruled the shooting "justifiable."

You might think this was her opportunity to get her life in order, but Marilyn tells me, "I think I had a nervous breakdown. Maybe a mental breakdown." She dove into all sorts of crazy living. Crime. Drugs. Wild behavior. She fell in with a crowd of friends who did these things, and before long, she had joined them in robbing a Savings and Loan.

She fled the state with her friends and with her three little ones in tow. They hid out for a short time, while she did a lot of thinking. She realized the police would catch her—and when they did, they would take her babies away from her. She loved her children, and she did not want to see them grow up the way she had. What had she done?

She walked into a police station and turned herself in. Marilyn spent three years, four months and twenty-eight days in prison. The whole time she was there she was thinking of her children. She wrote to them, and she wished for a visit from them. No one ever brought them to see her. She worked hard in prison and was released early on parole.

Before she left prison, no one told her anything about what she could and couldn't do regarding her children, so she went straight from prison to the home where her children had been living for the past three years. Her now seven-year-old son was playing in the yard. He looked up and cried, "Mama! Mama!" then said, "Stay right there! Don't move. Don't go anywhere," and he took off running. He returned holding the hand of a precious, now four-year-old little girl. Leading her to Marilyn, he pointed and said, "That is our Mama."

Marilyn received custody of her children, and she began to live her life. She worked two jobs, helped her children with their homework. She kept a home. She loved her kids.

A few months after her release, a large group of friends gathered for a cookout. Time to enjoy the weather and have fun. The women were preparing the meal, and the men took the many children for a boat ride. Forty-five minutes later, as the boat docked, Marilyn's son came running, shouting. Her precious daughter had fallen overboard. With the crowd of kids and all the activity, no one had even seen her fall. She was gone.

Tears are streaming down Marilyn's cheeks and mine as she tells me her story. Our Thai food sits, forgotten and cold. She says, "I haven't cried in as long as I can remember. Look at what you've done to me!" I laugh, but I don't know how one recovers. How does a person even go on? Marilyn is a survivor—perhaps the strongest woman I have ever met.

She had two other children to raise—boys she loved, boys she wanted to have a good life—and she raised her boys by herself. Marilyn worked hard, kept her boys in school, made them do their chores. She fed them well and disciplined them consistently. She was determined her boys would grow up to be decent young men, and that they would one day have families of their own —grand babies for her to enjoy. She did it.

After the boys had grown, Marilyn took a chance on love with her now husband, and this time it has been good. They determined from the outset as long as they are happy 85% of the time, they will stay together. They have been together for sixteen years now, and their relationship is fun to watch. They work together well and have fun together. They respect one another and their differences. Somehow, she was blessed with a good man this time around.

Before Marilyn told me her story, I often appealed to her to have mercy for others in the Joe's Community. The day she told me her story I began to appeal to others to have mercy for her. Each of us has wounds and emotional baggage contributing to who we are today. Judgment is easy when we don't know the whys of people's lives. We must give room for trust to grow, for healing to take place, and it takes time. We don't overlook one another's flaws, or continue to allow people to mistreat each other. We aim to follow the Way of Love. But it means as we expect people to change, we do so with mercy, patience, and understanding.

Marilyn is tough. She is an enforcer of the rules, and everybody complies. One day, I am sitting on the coffee table in Joe's, talking with someone sitting nearby. She walks over, slaps me on the shoulder and says, "Coffee tables are for glasses. Not for asses." I think, "Are you kidding me? This is *my* coffee table, I can sit on it if I want," but my body obeys immediately.

Marilyn still loves to dress up for church. She often wears a pretty dress and matching jewelry on Sundays, a throwback to those "queen for a day" little girl church experiences with her grandma. She sits at a table near the door, and she loves to sing. On a Sunday, not too long after she told me her story, I look around the room and see Marilyn still seated at her table, one hand raised and tears streaming down her cheeks. The words of the song we are singing say,

"Like an apple on a tree,
hiding out behind the leaves,
I was difficult to reach,
but you picked me.
Like a shell upon the shore,
just another pretty piece,
I was difficult to see,
but you picked me."
— *Allison Sudol (A Fine Frenzy)*

We serve communion. Although we always open the table to anyone who wants to come, communion has become a rite of passage for some. A public statement. When we give the invitation and people come forward to receive the bread and grape juice, a few make for the door. They seize the opportunity to take a smoke break.

But this Sunday, when the line finishes, Marilyn comes to me. She smiles and says, "I took communion today. Did you see?" I know she means she is "in." She has decided to give her whole self to this thing we call the Community of Hope. She has determined to follow the Way of Jesus. Because I know Marilyn makes no decision lightly, and because I know her strength, I know she will be one of his most determined followers ever.

Following Jesus

Growing up in our brand of Evangelicalism, I understood the process of training to be a good Christian as something we church people called "discipleship." An older person called a discipler/mentor (usually older in age, but most importantly older in length of time being a Christian) met with a younger person once a week to help them "grow." Growing included things like reading the Bible together and sometimes discussing an instructional teaching book. The mentor would ask pertinent questions about what the student had read and help to apply it to the student's life experience.

"Accountability" was a strong focus of these discipleship meetings, so often "sin issues" were discussed. The mentor would ask pointed questions, and the student would confess sinful actions or sinful thoughts they had committed in the last week. The mentor offered counsel and suggestions for how to avoid sin in the future. These meetings often included a strong emphasis on avoiding sexual immorality as sexual purity was most important to staying "holy." The idea was if you knew your mentor would ask you next week if you had committed such-and-such sin, then you would be less likely to do so during the week.

These meetings included the high value of understanding and knowing the Bible. We memorized passages of Scripture. We analyzed outside sources, commentaries, that would help us understand what the writers of the New Testament meant when they used large words like "propitiation" and "justification." One of my goals as a young person was to "wield the Scriptures like a sword." It is revealing that I wanted to learn to use it as a weapon. I did, and I used it frequently in judgment against other people. I could cut them to the quick. I trained well as a Jedi of the Bible.

All those years, I had understood that what I was doing was "following Jesus," but when I nearly quit my faith entirely, and I went back to looking at the Jesus life, I discovered something very different from what I had experienced.

First, I saw what Fr. Richard Rohr points out: "Jesus's common phrase, 'Go in peace, your faith has made you whole!' He said this to people who had made no dogmatic affirmations, did not think he was 'God,' did not pass any moral checklist, and often did not belong to the 'correct' group! They were simply people who trustfully affirmed, with open hearts, the grace of their own hungry experience—in that moment—and that God could care about it!" Disillusionment had made me hungry.

Jesus offered an invitation. An invitation to live a New Way. The Jesus Way. THE Way. He taught of this Way, inviting the rich to share with the poor. He invited wounded people to forgive their offenders. He encouraged oppressors to be kind and merciful. He told stories of a "kingdom," in which every person is cared for. He summed up the entirety of his Way as simply Loving God and Loving Others. In fact, the earliest self-descriptive title we know of his followers was not "Christian," but rather, "Followers of The Way" (Acts 9:2; 11:26).

Then Jesus *showed* his friends how to do it. In everyday situations, as he encountered people, he demonstrated this Way. He modeled how to treat women, how to touch lepers, how to hold children. When his disciples wanted to call down fire on people, he said, "Come on now guys, that's not how we do things in this Way." When they pushed little children aside, he said, "Unless you become like these little ones, you can't experience the Kingdom of God." When religious people confronted him about obeying the rules, Jesus said, "Whoever is without sin can cast the first stone." Then he released and forgave the accused.

The people who decided they wanted to follow Jesus were called his disciples. A disciple is a person who follows a teacher. In India, Hindu people follow various gurus. Gurus are teachers of the faith, enlightened ones, who understand truth and expound upon realities of life the common person may not see. This is the kind of teacher Jesus was. We could say he was a guru, a teacher of The Way.

Jesus didn't meet once a week with his disciples. Rather, as they experienced daily life together, he led them. They became Apprentices of the Way. At the beginning of Joe's Addiction, I decided I wanted to follow, to learn, and to practice the Way of Love, and that included doing life together with the poor.

Every Sunday in church, we look at another story, another section of the Gospels, especially the parts that have often been printed in red letters. What did Jesus say? What did he teach? And then we try to practice it through the week. We remind one another of his teaching, and those of us who have been practicing longer (albeit imperfectly) model for others how to walk this Way— in everyday situations—reminding one another to "put down the sword," because "those who live by the sword die by the sword," that forgiving is better than revenge, that caring for the "least" in our community is the greatest thing we can do.

Forklift

On a Sunday morning in church, we read the story in the Book of Matthew, where some religious leaders confronted Jesus about his disciples not obeying all the religious laws. They noticed the disciples didn't wash their hands before they ate, and they wanted to know why. Jesus had just performed a miracle which fed 5000 hungry people, and they wanted to confront Jesus about hand washing? Jesus responded to them by calling them hypocrites and telling them they were missing the point.

The Southern Baptist Convention had recently released a statement that, as a denomination, they were denouncing the movie, "The Blindside," because it contains profanity. (I guess this book will probably be banned also.) They had wanted to make it known they did not approve of such language. I show a trailer of the movie to the people sitting in Joe's Addiction.

The movie is based on the true story of Michael Oher, who became a professional football player in the NFL. It tells the struggles of an impoverished and tremendously large, African American young man who has drifted in and out of school and develops relationship with a wealthy, white woman (played by Sandra Bullock), a Christian woman, who compassionately welcomes him into her home. Her family becomes his family, and so their family love of football becomes his family culture. His new mama sees his immense strength and protective instincts as football skills, and advocates for his education and football opportunities. It is an inspiring story, and my motive in showing the trailer is to point out that often religious people pick at the "gnat" in their bowl of soup, and miss the delicious meal laid out before them. (My paraphrase of Jesus' words.)

After the service, Marilyn, our tough, enforcer of the rules—the woman who had built a wall of concrete around her soul—comes to me and says, "Jamie, I think me and Roy's supposed to take Forklift into our home." Forklift has committed violent and heinous crimes as a youth and has spent much of his life in prison. He is a member of a violent gang and even has knifed other prisoners. I ask her, "Marilyn, are you sure?" She says, "Jamie, he's never had a real mama. He's been in prison his whole life. He just needs a chance. Everybody needs a chance."

"I'm not sure what the theme of my homily today ought to be. Do I want to speak of the miracle of Our Lord's divine transformation? Not really, no. I don't want to talk about His divinity. I'd rather talk about His humanity. I mean, you know, how He lived His life, here on Earth. His *kindness*, His *tolerance* . . . Listen, here's what I think. I think that we can't go around measuring our goodness by what we don't do. By what we deny ourselves, what we resist, and who we exclude. I think we've got to measure goodness by what we *embrace*, what we create, and who we include."

— Father Père Henri from *Chocolat*

CHAPTER 6
ROSE-COLORED GLASSES

"It is certainly true that you can't judge a book
by its cover, nor can you judge a book by its first
chapter—even if that chapter is twenty years long."

— Fr. Gregory Boyle

We have a time called "Prouds and Sorries" in our church service at Joe's every week. It is an opportunity for anyone to share something they are proud of from the last week. Perhaps a success they have had in walking the Way of Jesus. Maybe an achievement. A good decision they made. Or they can share something for which they feel sorry. A failure. A confession. An apology.

This is my favorite part of our service. The people in our community do a lot of life together. Much of it happens right in the coffee shop. Some of our people come in as we open the doors in the early morning and stay until we close at night. There are many opportunities for us to get on one another's nerves. There is also a lot of opportunity to practice the things Jesus taught about being kind to one another.

The Valley Brook neighborhood is small. Everyone knows everyone else's business. The rumor mill spins quickly and effectively. We call it "The Joe's Vine." I would say our most common sin as a community is gossip. When somebody does something they shouldn't have done, by Sunday, everybody has already heard some version of the story. But brutal honesty is also a strong value in the Joe's Addiction community. Maybe it is part of AA and NA culture, but folks have no problem just laying their shortcomings and failures out there for all to see.

Opening a church service for anyone to speak is a risk. Speakers can be long-winded. One might give TMI (too much information)—if you know what I mean. Another might take the opportunity to preach. In our community, the risk is greater. The number of people attending church on any given Sunday depends on who is sober enough to make it to church, so you never know what level of "under the influence" might affect a proud or sorry that is shared. With the amount of mental illness represented in the room, well, let's just say Prouds and Sorries can be an adventure for the person up front facilitating the time.

Common prouds are people telling of having walked away, rather than punching someone, or celebrating days or months of sobriety. Once a lady announced she had quit using meth (that morning, since she'd used the night before.) People excitedly give reports of jobs attained or family relationships restored. Sometimes a person will declare a proud for another person— some way they saw another serving the community. Prouds are always followed by congratulations and applause from the whole room.

Sorries are often apologies for having used drugs again and commitments to start over. Someone will say, "You all saw me yell and cuss at So-and-So the other day." Then they make their public apology to the person they yelled at and to all who witnessed the altercation. Sometimes the apologies are for damage done to the whole community—stealing from the store, causing trouble, stirring up gossip or violence. Many times the confessions are personal failures and expressions of wanting to follow the Way of Jesus better. After someone makes an apology, the whole room erupts in, "We forgive you!," and we pronounce grace for a new start.

One Sunday, Oscar confesses that he "picked up a prostitute." He tells how he got drunk with her, then drove his car. A policeman pulled him over. He did not have a driver's license, and the girl had marijuana in the car. He was arrested. It is a *long* story. Then Oscar goes on to say, "That's my old man. God knew it would all happen before it happened. That's the sovereignty of God. I keep asking God why he's taking so long to change me." Sigh.

Old Man Tom lives in his car. One Sunday he shares that he had been at McDonald's and "some homeless guy" came in selling hats. "I only had twenty dollars, but somethin' told me to buy a hat. I don't even need a hat. See?" he says, pointing to the dingy, white cap on his head. "Well, I bought a hat. Now, I only got $9 for the rest of the month, but I think I did what God wanted me to do." The crowd applauds. "Good for you! You won't go hungry. Just let us know if you need something to eat."

Another day after church, Big Bob pulls me to the side. He fidgets, shifting his weight from side to side. He seems on the verge of tears. I ask him, "What's up, man?" He starts by telling me he had planned to stand up in church and go off on everybody. He was mad. Some people in the room had done him wrong, and he was just tired of being "shitted on." He had prepared a speech. He intended to point at the "Conduct Code" on the wall and ask, "How many of you really live what that sign says?" He was going to "call out everybody's dirt."

As soon as I had called for Prouds and Sorries, Jim stood up. He wanted to tell everyone he was sorry he'd been judging others in the room. He said, "I have a problem with judging, and I want to stop. I ain't better than any of the rest of you sittin' here. I got no right to judge."

Before the crowd had finished saying, "We forgive you," another man had stood and turned to Big Bob. He told Bob in front of everyone he had been angry at him for things others had told him about Bob. He said, "That's gossip, and I never should have listened. I'm sorry, Bob." Bob mumbled, "I forgive you," with the rest of the room.

Taken off guard, Big Bob missed his chance, and another man stood. This guy had stolen another man's girlfriend. She was in the wrong herself as the whole community was aware she was sleeping with three different guys at the same time. Conflict had erupted. People had taken sides. Violence had threatened. The story had been ongoing for some time, and though I had spoken privately with each party multiple times, appealing to goodness, the man who stood had not been in church for a few months. In fact, he hadn't been around the coffee shop much for quite some time. I was glad to see him.

The room was silent. Everybody knew. The man stood with bowed head and said, "I have caused a lot of harm to this whole community." He told the story of his illicit affair and the intentional spite he had inflicted upon other men in the community and apologized for the pain he had brought, for the confusion and the strife. He told of the destruction his choices had brought in his own life and asked for forgiveness. Then he asked if he could come back. The room erupted in cries, "We forgive you. We forgive you. We love you! You were always welcome! Please come back!"

As Big Bob reviews the prouds and sorries of the day, tears overflow and drop to his cheeks. He says, "I was going to call out their dirt, but there was nothing more to say. All the dirt was on the carpet. It's like everybody here just airs their dirty laundry all the time. I ain't never seen nothin' like it!"

Another Sunday, a tall, very big and very drunk, Native American, ex-con, gang member stands. He almost never comes to church, and the room is stunned into silence. He starts speaking:

"I'm a son of a bitch. I've killed people. I have cirrhosis of the liver from drinkin.' I'm drunk now. You don't know me. I'm a son of a bitch. I'm Indian Brotherhood. Got the patch right here. In prison I cut sex offenders. I still hate sex offenders. In prison I killed 'em. But I'll tell you something. I love that man. And I love that man right there. I love that woman (pointing to me). I love Marilyn and others of y'all. Here at this place I learned to love sex offenders. This place helped me. Now, I don't believe in God. I don't want that Jesus stuff. But I'll tell ya. People love in this place. Y'all have loved me. And I love y'all."

People are quietly encouraging him and thanking him. It is a bit awkward. One of the men gently takes him outside to get some air.

After he leaves, Old Man Tom says, "He might not believe in God, but I'll tell ya God believes in him! You all remember who I was a few months ago. I didn't want nothin' to do with God and look at me now!" The room erupts in cheers, applause, laughter, and tears.

It's true. I've never seen anything like it either. Following the Way of Jesus is not an easy thing to do. The things Jesus taught go against the way we've done things in our past. They go against our natural instincts. Turn the other cheek? Are you kidding me? Fighting back is what makes sense. Forgive those who hurt you? Why? They don't deserve forgiveness. They're not even sorry for what they've done. Love your enemies? How is that even possible?

Transformation, as Dallas Willard speaks of it, is a difficult thing: "Spiritual formation cannot, in the nature of the case, be a 'private' thing, because it is a matter of whole-life transformation. You need to seek out others in your community who are pursuing the renovation of the heart." Thinking differently, seeing the world a new way, valuing people over rules, valuing people over things, becoming a loving person—how does one make the change? It's a slow and painful process. It takes time and practice. And it's messy.

Old Man Tom

Old Man Tom is what we call him. He is a mean, old cuss, and he likes his reputation. He doesn't talk to anybody, and he doesn't want anybody to talk to him. He just wants a latte, and he wants it how he wants it. He shuffles and limps his way over to *his* table, opens a paperback western and sits for hours. Tom's scruffy, yellowish white hair pokes out from under his trucker's cap. A white beard and long mustache mostly camouflage the fact he has no teeth. Sometimes he takes off his cap and lays his head on the table to "rest his eyes," because last night's sleep wasn't so good. Often he comes up from these naps, hair standing wildly on end, so I teasingly call him Einstein.

Tom drives a 1984 white Lincoln Continental that we eventually figure out is his home. The back seat holds all his worldly possessions, and the passenger floorboard functions as his trash can. Tom doesn't like it when I ask questions, so I mostly just try to make his drink the way he likes it and serve him as kindly and politely as I can.

Occasionally Tom looks up from his book and grunts some cuss words at one of the young people who is being loud or unruly. Once, he yells at the girl who is volunteering as a barista. Later, in tears, she swears she made his drink exactly the same way I do, but he had hollered her incompetency to the whole store. I try to talk with him about it, but he tells me the girl is "an imbecile." We pretty much leave Tom to himself . . . until I have a bit of a run in with him.

A young man called Rabbit also hangs out at Joe's Addiction. Rabbit's mental and emotional problems and a seizure disorder make his life extra difficult. He is loud and abrasive and basically has no social skills. He often demands attention and that he receive it now. We have been loving this young man for more than five years, so I know his story.

His life was hard. His mother did not know what to do with him, so he grew up in the foster care system, ran away from foster homes multiple times, got in trouble with the law, and spent years in juvenile detention centers for violent crimes. He had few relationships—rejected by nearly everyone he had known—and he angrily wondered why a God who says he is our good Father would allow him to experience so much pain.

What Old Man Tom, who is new to Joe's, does *not* know is the Rabbit he is encountering is light years better than the Rabbit we first met. Rabbit now is attending counseling. He is on medications that help him have fewer seizures and help him focus his mind. He has been paying his court costs and fines and is just a few months from being finished with probation. Rabbit is looking forward to some hopes and dreams for his life.

Rabbit is rattling away, telling me in detail about some video he has just seen on *YouTube*, and Tom rudely interrupts to tell me he wants a brownie. He says to Rabbit, "Go away. Nobody cares about what you're saying."

I am startled. I turn to Tom and say, "You are being disrespectful. Rabbit is talking to me, and I will get you a brownie when he's finished." To which Tom in a huff replies, "Well, if you don't want my business, I'll just go somewhere else."

Rabbit quickly says, "It's okay. It's not that important," and goes to sit down at a table.

I put my hand on Tom's shoulder, hoping my gentle touch will settle him down. It seems to. He sits, and we talk. I ask him where that came from, and he begins to tell me his frustrations with Rabbit, with how disrespectful *he* is. Not only Rabbit, but others who come to Joe's and just take, take, take, and then are ungrateful. He says, "It's not right. I just can't stand it. I don't like 'im, and the next time that boy mouths off, I'm gonna pop 'im one. And I will. I'll do it. I been to prison. I know how to do that life. I don't mind goin' back.' At boy needs to be put in his place, and I know how to do it."

I point to the "Conduct Code" we have posted on the wall. Only two rules: "Love your neighbor as yourself" and "Do to others what you would have them do to you." I remind Tom these are the teachings of Jesus, and this is what we ask of people who hang out at Joe's Addiction. Tom responds, "I'll do to him however he does to me, all right. If he disrespects me, I'm gonna disrespect him." I laugh and tell him, "No Tom. It's the other way around. We do to others what we wish or hope they would do to us. We love them." He says, "Are you kidding me? You can't teach an old dog new tricks! I'm not gonna love that piece of shit."

I explain to him we will not tolerate violence of any kind. Joe's needs to feel safe for everyone, and that includes boys with no manners. I tell him if he ever threatens again, I will not allow him to hang out at Joe's Addiction. He pushes back his chair, picks up his book, and walks out the door without a word.

We don't see Tom for a week or so. I know I have hurt his pride. A whole room of people saw him take a verbal lickin' from a woman. I am sad, but I know I did the right thing. Deciding where boundaries should lie is a difficult task, but one thing is always clear. Our job is to protect the weaker, the more vulnerable. In this case, that is Rabbit.

To my surprise, a few mornings later, Old Man Tom shuffles through the door. He walks up to the counter, orders a vanilla latte, takes it to *his* table, pulls out his book and begins to read.

Months go by, and Tom becomes a fixture in our community. Sometimes he engages in conversation. Occasionally he offers advice. Most of the time, he is surly, and most likely, unless it is me making his drink, the barista can't make it right. But we grow to love grumpy Old Man Tom.

Winter comes, and he still lives in his car. We give him an electric blanket that plugs into his cigarette lighter. He sputters and cusses. He doesn't say, "Thank you," but he takes it.

One afternoon, a lady in our community comes to me and whispers, "There's a mess in the bathroom." I go to check, and sure enough, there is poop all over the floor. I clean it up and then start trying to figure out whose it was.

There aren't many people in the coffee shop this afternoon, and it doesn't take much to observe that Tom isn't quite himself. I ask him if he is okay, and he says he is a bit under the weather. He puts his head down on the table to rest for a while.

The same night two members of our community—the woman who reported the mess in the bathroom and her boyfriend—find Tom's car parked at Walmart. They have brought him some medicine. When he opens the window, the stench gives him away. It is all over himself and the seat. He is so ashamed. My wonderful friends take him to a motel and pay for a room. In the cold of the dark parking lot, they clean Tom's car, while he takes the first hot shower he has had in months.

The next Sunday, Tom is in church. He doesn't sing. He doesn't even look up from his paperback western, but he is there. At *his* table. On Sunday morning. Drinking a latte. And every Sunday after.

A few weeks later, Tom pulls me aside and says, "Something happened to me. I gotta tell ya." I sit down at his table, and he begins.

"I had a dream the other night. We were all here, at Joe's, and you were walkin' around serving people chicken and cleaning up their messes. I was thinkin', 'Why does she do that? These people are totally ungrateful. They don't deserve her help.' Then I realized we were both wearing glasses. My glasses made me see everything in black and white, but you was wearin' 'rose-colored glasses.' That was it. I woke up from the dream, an' I was thinkin' God *gave* you those glasses. They help you see the good in people. It's a gift from God, but *I* don't have that gift!"

Tom tells me that the morning after the dream he came to Joe's as usual and there was Rabbit—and as usual, Rabbit was getting on his nerves. He sat and watched for a while, fuming, thinking somebody needs to teach that boy a lesson. Tom says, "If I'd have acted like him when I was young, my daddy woulda whooped me." Then something just snapped inside him. He jumped up, headed toward Rabbit to punch him out. But on the short walk of about 15 feet, something came over Tom. It was like a rush of peace. He felt it pour from his head to his feet, and by the time he reached Rabbit his fists had relaxed.

He says, "I sat down with the boy and gave him a piece of my mind." I could just imagine Tom with his wild, Einstein-hair waving, giving Rabbit a "talkin-to." He told a little story illustrating disrespect and asked if Rabbit thought that kind of behavior was acceptable, to which Rabbit said, "No, man. That's not cool." Tom said, "That is how you're acting, and it needs to stop." Rabbit responded to him, "I get it. I do."

As Tom is sharing this experience with me, tears well up in his eyes and his voice cracks. He says, "I think just maybe God can give me those rose-colored glasses." I laugh, "You see! An old dog *can* learn new tricks."

Months go by. Tom is sitting at a table on the front sidewalk, smoking a cigarette when I notice him motioning for me to come over. I go out and ask, "Can I get you something?" He says, "If you got a minute, I'd like to talk to you about somethin'." I take the seat opposite of him and wait. He takes a few more drags on his cigarette, puts it out, then he starts:

"Preacher, I think I'm gettin' a conscience, and I don' like it. I am used to seein' everything black and white. Right or wrong. Last night, I gave Jack (another man in our community) a talking to. Told him he is not worth the powder it'd take to blow him up. He's usin' people. Takin' advantage. I just won't have it. I told him, and I didn't feel bad about it at all, but today it started buggin' me, in the back of my mind."

He is talking faster now, like he knows he has to finish what he set out to say. "I don' like it. I don' wanna change, but I don' wanna to make the Old Man mad at me. (He points up.) I don' wanna piss 'im off. I think I got a foot in the door with 'im. I prayed and asked 'im to forgive all my sins. I pray to 'im every night. I think 'e knows I don' talk to nobody in the mornings, and 'e's okay with 'at. I think 'e's goin' ta let me inta heaven. But I don' wanna get him pissed off. Ya think 'e's gonna let me in?"

"Yes, Tom. He's gonna let you into heaven."

In response to my quick and what he seems to feel too-easy a pronouncement, Tom goes on. He tells me that twenty years ago, he walked into his bedroom and saw his wife having sex with another man. Tom kicked the man in the head. The guy fell over the back side of the bed onto the floor. Tom jumped over the bed and landed hard—on the man's chest and head. The man died. When the judge asked him, "Did you kill this man," Tom said, "Yes sir. I did. I didn' mean to kill 'im. I was just gonna to beat 'im within a inch of his life, then piss on him and walk out of the room." Tom did five years in prison for involuntary manslaughter.

Tom lowers his head and pauses. He sighs a deep sigh. Then he looks me in the eye and says, "I am sleepin' with a married woman. I *am* the man I killed. You think God will let me inta heaven?

I suddenly realize I have the greatest privilege in the world. Each of us has direct access to God. We can hear from God; we can talk to God. But when one is drowning in the dark waters of shame, it is impossible to lift one's head enough to see, enough to hear, enough to *feel* the Love right there available to us all. Tom needs a priest. He needs a go-between. I want to tell him he doesn't, but he does. He needs to hear that God accepts him, God has forgiven him, God loves him—no matter what.

Over and again, we see Jesus telling sick and hurting people, "Your sins are forgiven." The Pharisees hated him for it. They were the only ones who could guarantee forgiveness, and much like the indulgences of medieval Catholicism, forgiveness could only be bought at the price of a sacrificial goat or two turtle doves (which the temple market offered for sale). Power corrupts; absolute power corrupts absolutely, the axiom says. I'm afraid the religious systems of our day continue to operate from the same foundation.

But the Jesus Way turns power on its head. No longer does the religious hierarchy wield the scepter of forgiveness. He demolished the system. Jesus' words from the cross, "Father forgive them for they know not what they do," echo through the ages, his final cry putting an end to the question of who is worthy and who is not. "It is finished." Judgment has been made, and Love rules the day.

As followers of the Jesus Way, he is our example. We imitate him. Wait a minute. Am I saying *we* can forgive sin? Yes.

Before you decry me as a heretic, listen to the words of Jesus: "If you forgive anyone's sins, they are forgiven." (John 20:23) We are channels of Divine Love, and we not only have the ability to do so, but as we follow the Jesus Way, he has commissioned us to pronounce forgiveness to the sinner. To dispense it freely. "Freely you have received, freely you must give." (Jesus' words in Matthew 10:8) What an amazing privilege—setting the captive free.

I tell Tom these things. God's forgiveness is for everyone. Nothing is required. Then I ask him a question, "What if God wants to create a better version of Tom? A better version of the world even?"

Tom leans back in his chair. "What? This is the best version there is. It's pretty great, don't ya think?" He laughs.

He says, "I don' want your gift of seein' the good in people."

"Why not?" I ask. He says, "Because what if it comes back on me? What if I think they're good, but then the bad surprises me and comes at me?" I tell him the bad certainly came at Jesus. They killed him. He says, "Yes, ma'am. That's what I mean!"

The next Sunday, during Prouds and Sorries, Tom stands to his feet. He takes off his hat and holds it in his hands. The room is silent. Looking at the floor, he says, "You all know me. I ain't a nice person, but somethin' is happenin' to me. Somehow I got a conscience, and now I gotta make some apologies. I ain't apologized in as long as I can 'member. Always considered it a sign a weakness." He looks around the room, then calls out two young ladies' names. The baristas he made cry. He says, "I been mean ta you young ladies, and I'm sorry. You don' deserve that, and I'm gonna try an' be a nicer person." He looks again around the room. "I mean 'at for everyone. That's all. I'm just gonna try an' be nicer to ya all." He sits down.

There is stunned silence for just a moment. Everyone looks at each other, then back at Tom. One of the girls says, "I forgive you, Tom." Then the other speaks up, "I do too, Tom. I forgive you." Then the whole room erupts with, "We forgive you," "We love you," and "We're glad you're here."

CHAPTER 7
JESUS BULLSHIT

"To love with understanding
And without understanding.
To love blindly, and to folly.
To see only what is lovable.
To think only of these things.
To see the best in everyone around,
Their virtues rather than their faults.
To see Christ in them!"

— Dorothy Day

Foster is an eloquent speaker, a master of grammar, and he always carefully articulates what he desires to communicate. He holds a degree in political science and has strong opinions about government and public policy. He is a passionate debater.

However, this is not the man we met when Foster first came to Joe's Addiction.

If Foster, our Pastor-Wanna-Be, told you his own story, he would say for fifty years of his life he considered himself a "nihilist." He would explain, "If I was working at a counter, and a customer came complaining of my service and asked if they could speak to my 'superior,' my response would be, "You can speak to my 'supervisor,' but there is no one on this earth superior to me." He would also describe himself as having many material possessions. He was able to buy things, and so he did. He controlled his own life.

At fifty years old, Foster was married with a fifteen-year-old daughter when the darkness he had entertained in his life overtook him. Foster was a writer of horror stories, and for most of his adult life he wore no other color than black. He prided himself on creating the most evil, fictional characters a twisted mind could imagine. He posted his written pieces in chat rooms for feedback and for the sense of community he found with other fans of horror.

There, online, he met a fifteen-year-old girl who admired his work and his personality. Their relationship snowballed quickly and before long, Foster had committed inappropriate acts with her via webcam. He never met her in person, but in one fell swoop, multiple lives were destroyed—hers, his wife's, his daughter's, his parents', his own. Catastrophic devastation.

When his crime was discovered, he lost everything—his home, his material possessions, his family, even his pets. He did not go to prison but was instead given a suspended sentence to be monitored closely by a probation officer. When his coworkers found out, he lost his job. Friends disappeared. Upon seeing his "sex offender" label, landlords would not rent to him. He sold his possessions to pay attorney and court fees and ended up living in his car, but the most devastating loss was relationship with his teenage daughter.

Foster contemplated suicide, but his father had raised him to believe suicide is the "coward's way out." Realizing he could never redeem himself, Foster fled the country. He sold his remaining possessions and bought a ticket to Paris. A lover of culture and history, Foster had always wanted to see the world. He dropped his backpack in a hotel and headed out to view the sights.

Upon entering the Notre Dame Cathedral, the overwhelming presence and grandeur of God struck Foster. He had not been in church since he was a young child and had never prayed as an adult, but he knelt in a private alcove and poured out his remorse. He asked God to somehow heal and repair the damage he had done—to his victim, to his family, to his friends, most of all to his own daughter.

After taking in the city, Foster returned to his hotel room to find someone had robbed him, his bag pilfered. They took everything he owned. Destitute and alone in a foreign country, he felt God was saying to him, "You cannot run away from what you did. You must go back and face it." He called his father and found kindness on the other end of the phone. His dad paid for a plane ticket to return him to Oklahoma.

The day after Foster' return, his probation officer showed up at his parents' house looking for him. She said, "I have found a place for you to live."

Two hours after being dropped off at the half-way-house-trailer-park down the street, Foster walks through the door of Joe's Addiction. I remember that night clearly, because Foster is a memorable character. Dressed in a black trench coat and puffy, Russian-looking fur hat, his gaunt face is made more grim by the salt and pepper goatee on his chin.

He looks around the room as people greet him, and a smile spreads across his face. When he removes his coat, the black continues—from head to toe. I notice a dangly earring hanging from one earlobe and a long, silver necklace resting on his chest. He finds a table near an outlet and plugs in his laptop computer. He orders a "Bottomless Joe" (never ending refills of coffee) and spends the whole evening typing something.

He comes back on Saturday and spends the whole day the same way, sitting in the same chair, at the same table, typing.

Sunday morning, Foster comes to Joe's again. Only this time when he walks in he is confused. People are standing facing the stage. A band is playing, and everyone is singing. He realizes it is a church service. He looks around, and some are not standing. Some play games on their computers. Some engage in quiet conversations. He isn't sure what to do, but he doesn't want to leave. He also doesn't feel it would be respectful to sit down, so he stands near the door until the music ends.

Then, finding a table, he plugs in his computer once again. Soon the sermon begins. Foster tells us later he has never heard God spoken of in that way. The awareness of Love surprises him.

Foster keeps coming back. Every day. Little by little we get to know him. Another night, a crowd packs the room. A Christmas performance is happening on the stage, when Foster rushes through the door. Not even bothering to take off his hat or coat, he drops to his knees on the floor beside me. His face is red from the cold walk, but his eyes are flashing with excitement and intense emotion. He says, "I have to tell you something!"

The half-way house requires the men to attend a weekly Bible study, and most of them put in their time sitting quietly until they are "released" from the obligatory hour. Foster had been sitting in this Bible study, not listening to the speaking man, but contemplating the devastation of his life, mulling over the loss, the pain, the irreparable damage he had done—and he was angry.

He had been awaiting a hearing, in which a judge would decide whether he could move from this trailer park to live with his sister. He could not wait to leave that place. Not only was it cold, but many of the other men used drugs, had poor hygiene, and were even violent. It was not a pleasant place.

He was scheduled for a hearing that day, but for some unknown reason the judge pushed the hearing back six more weeks. In frustration he thought, "God, why did you allow my hearing to be moved?" Immediately he had an awareness that *God* had moved it. His next thought was, "What? Why?" Then in the quiet of the next few moments, he looked around the room at the men. He describes them to me as "zombies."

Many of these men do not know what to do after they are released from prison. They don't know how to find a job, how to fill out applications, how to dress for interviews, follow up with phone calls, etc. This contributes to the depression they already experience, and some of them go back to their "old life."

In those few moments, Foster had actually *seen* these men. Kneeling there on the floor next to me at Joe's, he gushes, "I am a teacher! . . . I know how to do all these things! I can teach them how to do life! I have skills!" He says, "I know this sounds strange, but I think God has been in this whole mess I have made of my life. God now has me in a place where I can help other people! Had I never screwed things up so badly, I would never have even considered helping!" Eyes bright with tears and face glowing, Foster says, "God has given me a purpose!"

I am reminded of the story of Zacchaeus, the tax collector, a man who had made himself wealthy by cheating his friends and neighbors. Jesus invited himself over to the man's house for dinner. The crowd muttered, "He's gone to a *sinner's* home." The Bible doesn't tell us what Jesus talked about at the meal. It doesn't say he preached a sermon or gave an invitation for people to "pray a prayer." We can only imagine Jesus was who we see Jesus always being, the kind and gracious guest. Perhaps he told some of the stories he was known to tell. They broke bread and enjoyed one another's company.

Then, unsolicited, Zacchaeus stood up and said to Jesus, "Look, Lord! Here and now I give half of my possessions to the poor, and if I have cheated anybody out of anything, I will pay back four times the amount." Jesus said, "Today salvation has come to this house. The Son of Man came to seek and to save the lost."

Foster didn't pray a prayer. He didn't ask Jesus into his heart. He didn't ascribe to a list of doctrines. In fact, on a Sunday after he had shared some of his story with me, Foster pulls me aside. He tells me he wants me to understand he doesn't really want to call himself a "Christian." I laugh and tell him, "That's okay. I'm not too sure I want to be called one either!" He says, "I have lived fifty years of my life entirely for myself. That's a long time. I know how to do that. I am starting to live a different way now, not for myself, but for others. It's new to me. It's a way I want to go. I think I'm going a new way. But I don't want to start calling myself something until I'm really sure I am actually able to go this new direction."

Foster is one of many of us at Joe's Addiction who used to walk his own selfish way but turned around and began to walk the Jesus Way, the way of loving God and loving his neighbors. The hows of this path are not defined from the outset of the walk. It is a daily, step-by-step journey of walking in kinship with God and with those around us.

A few months later, during the "smoke break" in the middle of our church service, Foster comes to me concerned. He says, "I know you have noticed I don't express myself like some of the others do in worship. I don't clap or raise my hands or even move around much. But I want you to know I am worshipping in my heart. Physical expression just isn't who I am." I assure him it's okay. Everyone at Joe's is free to participate as much or as little as they feel comfortable, and no one is considered less or more—for any reason.

The very next week, I am standing on the stage, playing the keyboard, helping to lead the music, when I look out into the group. Foster is down on his knees, arms extended, hands up to the sky, eyes closed, tears pouring down his face. I think, "Wow, something's happening for him."

Later Foster tells me. For a few days, he had been feeling another round of despair, the weight of the consequences of his crime, the pain he had caused others, the devastation. From time to time it nagged at him, but these few days it would not let go. He was sad. He was depressed. As we began to sing our songs, Foster' bowed his head. He didn't even want to participate. But then he saw something. There in front of him stood a door. He could see light coming in through the cracks around the door, and somehow he was aware Jesus was on the other side.

He heard a voice saying to him, "Please open the door. Let me in. I will take that ten-ton weight you are carrying on your back, if you will just let me." The vision was so real to Foster he extended his hand to open the door. Suddenly the burden on his back fell away. He said he physically felt it fall off. Then Jesus himself came and put his arms around Foster. Foster could feel him. Over and over, he heard Jesus say, "It's going to be all right. I am here. Everything will be all right," as tears poured down Foster' face.

Not everyone experiences God in the way Foster did that Sunday. One might find God in a song. Another in a flower. Another in the mountains of Colorado. My husband always finds God in the ocean. Whatever our story is, we each carry with us the weight of the pains we have inflicted upon others and the wounds others have given to us. However we encounter The Muse it is always through Love, to heal, to restore—and Love makes us able to love in response.

The path of healing and transformation is not a smooth one. Rather, the road most often bumps and winds, with twists, turns and even terrors along the way that make us frightened to keep going forward. And there is no requirement to continue along the Way. No one is holding our feet to the fire, so to speak. Instead, there is a constant invitation to take another step. To make another change. To allow a little more healing. To receive a little more Love. And to make another commitment.

Forklift

In the story of Jesus' life, near the end, we find Jesus in the Garden of Gethsemane with his disciples. He has spent three years teaching them, walking with them, modeling for them how to live the Way of Love, and now he will be arrested, tried, and crucified. As the Roman soldiers arrive, painfully and dramatically, Jesus' dear friend Judas betrays him with a kiss, and the soldiers step in to take Jesus away. Peter pulls out his sword and slices off the ear of one of the soldiers. Jesus tells him to stop. He says to Peter, "Put down the sword. Those who live by the sword will die by the sword." What Jesus says is countercultural and counternatural. It goes against every fiber of our being. Fight back, Jesus! Fight back! Imagine how this teaching sounds to gang members.

Forklift is a giant of a man. He committed his first violent crime at nine years old, and he spent most of his teenage years locked up in prison. He joined a gang "on the inside" and earned his position as "the enforcer." His many tattoos tell the tale of his commitment to a life of violence. I don't know how many people he has killed, but he has hurt many more. He hangs around Joe's Addiction off and on for several years and we do our best to love him. Mostly he thinks we are crazy, especially when after hearing the Jesus story about the soldiers, people in Joe's start saying the same thing to one other. Someone gets angry, stands up and puffs out his chest. Then someone across the room hollers out, "Put down the sword!"

Forklift grows to love our family, and we love him. He is especially fond of our daughter, Jewel, who is nine years old when Forklift starts coming around. Despite his tough exterior, he is a teddy bear inside, and he loves children. Over the years, Jewel becomes Forklift's conscience. He comes to me more than once, frustrated that he was about to do something "bad," and he heard Jewel's sweet, lilting voice in his head saying, "Now, Forklift." He wants her to be proud of him, so he starts coming to church to show her he is trying to do better.

I receive a call from Marilyn. Forklift has been shot in the head. A friend who followed the ambulance to the hospital told the doctor that Marilyn is his mom and gave them her number. Forklift's real mother lives in another city, far away, and they have not seen one other in years. Marilyn steps in and becomes Forklift's mama. Surprisingly, Forklift survives the gunshot wound. Part of his brain is damaged, and he suffers a long recovery. He works hard. He learns to walk again and regains the use of his hands, those strong hands that have hurt lots of people.

Sitting with Forklift at a table in Joe's, he tells me, "I cannot understand why God would let me live. I'm a bad person. I've done so many bad things. I do not deserve to be here." Forklift decides he is finished with gang life, and he announces his intention to follow the Way of Love. He understands this to mean he will leave violence behind, learn to turn the other cheek and love his enemies. He tells me, "It's the dumbest thing I ever heard. But I'm done. I can't do it no more. I'm tired of livin' with the nightmares of people's faces I have hurt. I wanna change." We tell him we will do the best we can to help him.

You cannot simply leave a gang. There are commitments, responsibilities and the people you harmed do not forget what you have done. Revenge and retaliation await around every corner. But Forklift is committed.

One afternoon, Forklift approaches me agitated. He says, "I fucked up, Jamie. I punched him right in the mouth." He shakes his head in shame, so I ask him what happened. He tells me a story of an antagonist coming at him again and again. "He just wouldn't stop. I couldn't help it. My fist had a mind of its own. It just flew out and punched him."

"What happened next," I ask.

"He dropped to the ground. Then he got up and took off."

"And what did you do after that?" I ask again.

"Nothing. I just stood there."

"You didn't chase him? You let him go?"

"Yeah. I just let him go."

I smile. "That's progress!" I announce.

"But I hit him."

"Yeah," I say, "but you only hit him once. In the past, you'd have beat the crap out of him, and you would never have let him run away. That's progress, my friend. You're changing."

He grins. "Yeah. I guess that *is* progress."

No Good Deed

A woman who is also part of our community at Joe's Addiction has come to hang out for a while. She is experiencing homelessness and sleeps wherever she can find a place for the night. Sometimes a couch. Often outdoors in the weather. She had been pushing her cart alongside a road and was hit by a car. The driver didn't even stop. A passerby called an ambulance.

Still recovering from broken bones and contusions, she comes back to Joe's Addiction. Her most difficult struggle is an infection that began in her leg. Imagine trying to keep wounds clean when you have no place to wash up. The hospital doesn't house patients after the critical period has passed. She comes to Joe's to have her dressings changed, and we remind her to take her antibiotics.

Several people are sitting on the front sidewalk smoking when she mentions she is hungry and that she still has food stamps on her card. Forklift offers to walk to the convenience store to buy some things for her. He knows how painful it is for her to walk. She is grateful.

A few minutes later, an ambulance and police cars race down our street. She pokes her head in the door and shouts, "Jamie, it might be Forklift! He went down to the store for me and he's been gone too long. Will you go see who's hurt?"

I jump in my car and race the short distance down the street. There he is, lying unconscious in a pool of his own blood. I push my way through the gathered crowd, catching the eye of one policeman, and announce, "I know this guy. I have all his information."

After a cursory investigation and a half-hearted attempt to interview gathered witnesses (who saw who did it), the policemen stand around chatting and joking while the paramedics roll my friend into the ambulance. I ask what they will do about this and they shrug. "Transients fighting with each other. "Gang violence," the officer in charge says to me. In other words, "Nothing. We will do nothing."

I get it. The violence just is. The drugs—it just is what it is. Maybe it's not even worth their time, effort and money to track down the culprit but the injustice of it all has me steaming mad. The next day in church at Joe's, we have an open, community discussion. We remind one another of our intention to love our enemies, as Jesus taught. We agree together to look for ways to love the enemy who attacked our friend. Enemy-Love. We believe it is the Better Way. We dream of "us" and "them" becoming "we." We believe it is God's dream. But damn if it isn't hard. And sometimes the cost of following the Way is a high price to pay.

Forklift survives this baseball bat beating to his head. I know. Unbelievable. This man is indestructible. But lying there recovering in the hospital the doctors inform him he has lymphoma. His time of following this New Way is not over. The path takes a new turn, a new opportunity for living out the things Jesus taught.

Marilyn and the Bullshit

Marilyn comes to me in the coffee shop. I can see something is wrong. Her face is red. I can practically see the steam coming out of her ears. Marilyn's anger isn't surprising. She feels things deeply and doesn't put up with much from anyone.

Marilyn says, "I'm outta here and I'm not comin' back." I ask her what happened and she won't even look at me. She grabs her things, walks out the door and squeals her tires as she drives out of the parking lot.

I know her well enough to know I had better give her some space. Chasing her down would only make things worse, but I am worried I have offended her. I think she would tell me if I have but maybe it is something big.

I try not to, but I fret for three days before I finally call her. When she picks up the phone, I ask if I can come over. She says, "Yeah, I think you better." When I pull into the driveway, her husband is in the yard tinkering with an old lawn mower. He says, "I hope you can help her. She's a wreck."

I find Marilyn sitting at the table in front of a laptop computer. The table and the surrounding floor are littered with empty beer cans. I ask if I can sit down. She doesn't take her eyes from the screen and her finger keeps clicking the mouse, but she nods, so I sit. I wait for a few moments wondering if she might just talk, but she doesn't, so I ask, "What is going on, my friend?" She puts her face in her hands and sobs.

Out pours the story. Pastor-Wanna-Be, Foster, said something to her that hurt her feelings— terribly. That was it? I am confused. This is not the Marilyn I know. Nothing hurts her. Of course, I knew things must, but she never "gives a damn" what other people think. Why now? Why this?

I tell her this and ask her why it hurt her so badly. She says, "I see him as a mentor. I care so much what he thinks about me. If what he said is what he thinks. . . ." and another flood of sobs overtakes her. I am surprised. I had no idea she felt that way about Foster. For a moment, I bristle. I thought *I* was her mentor (damn ego). Foster *was* the one who had invited her to become a barista. *He* had trained her. But *really?* Many people in our community had trouble liking Foster. He is authoritarian. Sometimes he loses his temper.

Ahhh... *now* things are making sense. She *understands* him. And she hopes he understands *her*. She, too, is a tough cookie. She likes order, fairness, and obedience to the rules.

But Foster is growing. He is changing. Becoming more gentle, more tolerant of people's shortcomings. Laughing more. Loving more. He has even begun to wear a light blue, button-down shirt occasionally—a jolt for us, in light of his usual all-black attire. She sees in him the hope for her own change. She admires him and he is someone she can emulate. She is changing too. I soften.

I tell her I am so sorry he hurt her. She looks at me with daggers in her eyes and says, "Look at what you've done to me!"

"Me? I thought you said *Foster* was the one who hurt you."

She sobs, "I'm weak. Even my son says I'm weak now. He told me I'm a pussy now. You did this to me! I used to have walls up around me, so no one would ever hurt me again. It's your fault! I can't find my walls! I hate this!" She is slur-yelling at me.

I try to talk to her about the difference between vulnerability and weakness, but none of it matters. She doesn't care. What difference does it make? Both amount to the same thing—you get hurt. So I say, "It seems to me you have three options here:

1. "You can just leave. Never come back. That's a legitimate choice."

2. "You can come back and just go on. Act like nothing has happened."

She cuts in and says, "I don't think I can do that. I can't be in the same room with him. I'll kick his ass."

Or, 3: "You can forgive him."

She shudders. I say, "Of course it probably means you'll need to sit down and talk to him about what happened. Tell him he hurt you. Work things out with each other."

She jumps in, "I can't do that. What if he thinks it's stupid I'm hurt and he says more things that hurt me?"

I tell her I don't think Foster would do that—that's not who he is—but it is definitely a risk.

We sit there in silence for a long time. She goes back to clicking her mouse. Finally, she turns and looks me in the eye. She says, "This following Jesus thing is bullshit." I burst out laughing. "Yes, it is, my friend. I agree."

After a few more minutes of silence, she says, "I can't leave. Joe's Addiction is my life now. I love it. I love what I do there. I love the people. I can never go back to who I was before I came to Joe's . . . I'm stuck."

"So, what do you want to do?" I ask.

She says, "Will you go with me to talk to Foster?" I tell her I will.

The three of us meet together, and wouldn't you know? As is so often the case, the offense was a simple misunderstanding. Foster had not *at all* meant what Marilyn thought he had meant, and when he hears Marilyn's perception of his influence in her life, it strengthens Foster's own perception of his role in our community.

I can't help but hear the voice of Jesus' own disciples when he asked them, "Are you going to leave me too?" They responded, "Where would we go? You have the words of life."

CHAPTER 8
INTEGRATION

"When I let go of what I am,
I become what I might be."

— Lao Tzu

A man in our community told me a story. He was at work. His boss knows all about Joe's Addiction. She asked him, "Do you ever give altar calls at Joe's? You know, so people can ask Jesus into their heart."

He told her, "No. We don't do that."

She responded to him, "Well, you can talk all you want to about Jesus but at some point you have to close the sale."

He was a confused, so she went on saying, "There's something people need to do, you know, so they can go to heaven."

So . . . I just want to declare some things.

First: I am not selling *anything*. Except coffee and sandwiches, sometimes a brownie or a muffin. But I mean, really?

Years ago, when John and I first came to Oklahoma City, we were new in town, new in our church. We had no friends. We had just come from living overseas and knew no one. The first Sunday at our new church, a couple invited us to come to their home for dinner. We were excited. New friends. We felt so grateful they wanted to know us.

The meal was lovely. They were nice. We exchanged questions and answers. We were having a good time. Then, somewhere in the middle of the baked apple crisp, our host asked John, "What would you do if you had a million dollars?" We were missionaries who lived on donations from Christians who believed in what we were doing. Were these people about to offer us a million dollars? John gave some kind of answer about how we would use the million dollars in ministry, and then the man said, "Well, you could have that million dollars." He pulled out a plastic binder, opened it, and explained the program of a "Christian," multi-level marketing company we could enter at the "silver level," then move up to "diamond" and ultimately to "gold," when we, too, could achieve millionaire status.

It all happened so quickly. I still remember the confusion, the realization, the disappointment, and then the wave of embarrassment. These people didn't want to be our friends. They wanted to sell us something. They wanted to make money off of us.

This was not the only time this has happened to me, and I have become cynical, jaded maybe. I can smell a fake friend a mile away. I bet you can too. And let me tell you, people whom Christians are befriending, in order to persuade them to buy into a salvation plan, can smell a fake friend a mile away as well.

The calling is to Love. To Love without agenda. Without even the agenda of trying to "save" anyone. Love does not include "only ifs." Love does not love "so that." People are not projects. They are not potential converts. And they are certainly are not our customers. People are friends. People are family. People are fellow human beings with whom we share life. Love loves. It's as simple as that.

Jack and Mindy

One afternoon, John is sitting on the couch in Joe's, when a middle-aged, medium-build woman in a tiny miniskirt rushes through the door. Her shoulder-length hair is frazzled from years of bleach, and the deep lines on her face expose the harshness of her life. She looks around the room and asks, "Is there a pastor here? I heard there was a pastor here?"

John follows the woman, who introduces herself as Mindy, outside to the front sidewalk where her boyfriend sits at a table smoking a cigarette. The woman explains that she and her boyfriend, Jack, are arguing, and they need help to work things out.

The gist of their argument is this: Mindy had been dancing in a club for a couple of months. Her job was bringing in enough money per day to afford food and a hotel room each night. But for the last few days, her income had been steadily decreasing. The other girls were offering sex for $20. Who would tip her dancing, when they could have the whole thing for just twenty bucks? They had slept the last two nights under a bridge.

Mindy explains to my husband that if she turns two tricks a day, they would have the money they need. She feels it would be no big deal. She explains, "It isn't me. Just like dancing isn't me. It's just my body, not my soul." Her boyfriend does not disagree with this mind/body separation, or even her dancing, but he cannot accept her having sex with other men for money.

He kneels down on one knee, there on the front sidewalk, takes her hand, and in a deep, gravelly voice that betrays a lifetime of cigarette smoking, he begs, "Baby girl, I don't want you to do it. It will change something between us. I just know it will. I don't care if we sleep under a bridge. I would rather that, than you do this." It is the most bizarrely romantic scene.

The words of Jesus ring in our ears, "I was a stranger, and you took me in."

Now . . . we don't know these people. We don't even have time to find out much about them. We have five children, some of them are little. We know God is not asking us to be foolish. But we had also committed to following the Way of Jesus together as a family.

There is such a thing as an indefinable sense of just "knowing" what you are to do. Doing things together as a team also brings balance and wisdom to impulse. John and I are in agreement.

We invite this couple to live in a tent in our yard. We have a large house, but all the rooms are filled with our children and other guests we have already brought into our home. This also seems like wisdom. The weather is in a comfortable season. They can use our bathroom and we can supervise whenever they are in the house. They accept our invitation with joy and gratitude.

Then we begin to work together on the practicalities of life. Nothing is simple. He has a Commercial Driver's License and can drive trucks. However, he does not have the license in his possession. To get another would be expensive. To make matters worse, his ex-wife is holding it captive, and she is now girlfriend to a leader in the motorcycle gang called The Mongols. You mess with these folks you die. Mindy says, "Since you're a pastor, maybe you can talk to them?"

We put his license on the back burner and we consider how she can make more income. After many applications at diners and many rejections due to her considerable tattoos, she applies at another of the strip clubs—a "classier" club—and she gets the job. Now, I know this may be hard to understand but genuinely this is a step up for her. In church that Sunday she credits God with having given her this new position. We celebrate with her.

I gather a list of low-cost apartments and rentals in our part of town. I want them to be able to stay connected to our community. We go from place to place, putting in applications, and I watch as every manager, every landlord, shakes their head when they read "Baby Dolls" written under "Employment."

Clubs in our neighborhood provide no salaries, no pay stubs, no W-2 forms. In fact, the girls are not paid by the club at all. They are required to pay a cover charge themselves to dance for the evening, and the bouncer will not allow them to leave until the fee is paid. They're considered "lucky" to *get* to dance.

Each time we walk back to the car after being turned down, I can feel the level of Jack and Mindy's despair sinking. I can sense the shame mounting and the humiliation of their position, of their lack of qualifications, of their very existence on the planet mounting. And I can feel my anger rising.

I understand the landlords' positions. They don't want to rent to someone who can't pay. But how are people supposed to move up if they aren't given a chance? There need to be those of us willing to take a risk—a risk of compassion, a risk of Love. After ten rejections, I am livid. We climb back in my car and head toward Joe's Addiction. We have exhausted my list. I don't know what to do next.

We are driving together in silence, when I notice a church on the side of the road. Its marquis cheerfully reminds, "When you have Jesus, you have everything you need." I shout, "No you don't! Dammit! You need a house!" It's the first time I have ever cussed at God. Well, maybe it isn't at God. I'm cussing at the Church. I know not every church is the same but I am still frustrated with my fundamentalist upbringing. Jack and Mindy are surprised and immediately Mindy consoles me. She says, "It'll be all right. Don't worry." Like *I* am the one suffering. I start to cry, and she pats my shoulder.

A couple of miles later, we are almost there—angry and defeated—when Mindy says, "Look at that sign!" Right there on the corner by the coffee shop is a handwritten sign stuck in the ground. It wasn't there before. I had driven through the neighborhood taking down information about rentals. The sign says, "House for Rent" and gives a phone number to call.

The three of us look at each other with eyebrows raised. "It's worth a try," I say.

I call the number and an older lady answers. I tell her our situation, that I am a pastor of the church that meets in the coffee shop. She knows of us. I explain we are helping a couple to get on their feet, that they don't have much, but the church is willing to be their reference, even to back them up if they can't pay. Over the phone, the woman tells me she thinks what we are doing is a noble thing and she wants to help. We go that afternoon and sign the lease.

The little, white house—only a minute's walk from Joe's—
has a back yard, and to Mindy's delight, there are rose bushes
lining the front porch. Church people donate furniture, pots,
and pans, blankets and lamps, and food to fill the cupboards
and fridge. We watch in delight as Mindy and Jack experience
a real-life fairytale.

What is the moral of this story? Maybe cussing at God is
a form of prayer?

Mindy and Jack are in church every Sunday. Early on, she
asks me, "What time does church end?" and I tell her, "Around
noon."

"Good," she says, "Because I told my boss I can't dance on
Sundays til after church is done."

Richard Rohr writes, "You do not think yourself into a new
way of living, you live yourself into a new way of thinking."
One Sunday morning, Jack is sick. They decide to read the
Bible together since they can't come to church. She asks him,
"What part should we read?" and he replies, "Well, when I was
a boy my mama used to read to me from the Book of Jawb.
(He pronounces the word "jawb" with a soft o, not "Job" like
the man's name.) She says, "Okay, then we'll read the Book of
"Jawb." And she reads the *whole* book out loud to him.

Have you ever read the Book of Job? It's long and boring.
Near the beginning of the book, Job loses everything. Then
his friends go on and on explaining why they think God took
everything from Job, and then God basically says, "All they
just said, well, it means nothing. Pay no attention to them."
Through it all, in contrast to me, Job never curses God. Job
remains faithful to God and God blesses him. They read the
whole story.

When Mindy finishes reading she says to Jack, "I think
the point of this story is God is asking us, if he took away all
these wonderful blessings he has given to us—this house, the
furniture, our new friends, everything—would we still follow
him?" And they together decide they would.

Are you kidding me? Most Christians I know haven't read
Job *or* made that commitment.

That afternoon, Mindy goes to her job at Valley of the Dolls. She is so excited about what God has shown her she calls all the other dancers together and announces, "I have to tell you about a story I read this morning in the Bible." She tells them the whole story, then how God has brought such blessing into their life and their conclusion that they want to follow God no matter what. Retelling it to us later, she says, "Five of the girls listened to the whole thing. Only two walked away. I was so excited to tell them!"

Another woman with a bad reputation two thousand years ago, after an encounter with Jesus, ran back to her village calling to her friends to "Come and see" this man who had touched the deepest places of her soul. The Gospel story lives on. The Word is still made flesh. Again and again. By those whose lives are transformed by Love.

Inquisition

Not too long after these experiences with Mindy, some folks ask if they can meet with John and me. They want to discuss some "concerns" they have. We have been in ministry long enough to recognize what is coming and we brace ourselves.

We do our best to listen as they lay out a well-thought-out and articulate confrontation. The overarching accusation is that we do not believe in repentance. Their evidence, from a typed and bulleted list, is we condone unmarried couples living together, women dancing in the strip clubs, and people smoking during the break in our worship service. They claim God is not pleased with our methods, that we are doing damage to the Gospel of Jesus Christ, and God has sent them to call us to repent.

I am flabbergasted. The beautiful story of redemption I see unfolding before us, these "prophets" view as unholy—wrong. They will not accept any explanation or appeal we give. They leave the meeting and relationship with us.

I confess, these kinds of injuries cut me to the center of my identity. I want to please, to be right, to do things well, to be above reproach, and to gain approval from people. And I hate losing friends.

So what about repentance? Jesus' message was, "Repent, for the Kingdom of Heaven is at hand." Evangelical Christians often define this message of repentance to mean something along these lines: "Feel guilty for your sin. Apologize for being a sinner. Pray a prayer accepting God's forgiveness purchased for you by Jesus' death on the cross, so you can go to heaven when you die. And then, do your best to stop sinning, so you can stay on God's good side." But this is not the message Jesus preached. He had not yet died on a cross. No atonement had been made. He made no promise of escape to happy heaven and he freely distributed God's forgiveness.

Here is what I have come to know about repentance from our experience. The Greek word Jesus used when he called people to "repent" is *metanoia*. It literally means to "change one's mind." It can mean to change direction. This change even includes the notion of transformation. When Jesus called people to repent, it was as though he was saying, "You are going in a bad direction. It's harmful. For you and for others around you. In fact, that direction leads to destruction. Now, I'm inviting you to come with me in a *new* direction. It's a Path that leads to life. To wholeness. To freedom."

Jack and Mindy are on this new Path. They have decided to go in the Jesus Direction. And little by little, they are being transformed.

Jack's wife has left him for the biker man. There is nothing he can do about it. His divorce is not yet legal, so we can't marry Jack and Mindy. Is God really that concerned about them having sex before a piece of paper is signed? Should we separate each of them from the only companion with whom they have to walk the painful journey of life, until a ceremony can be arranged? Should we confront and require Mindy to stop dancing? . . . And if she won't? Should we cut her off from relationship? Ban her from community?

All of Matthew Chapter 23 in the New Testament is a sad and angry rant Jesus made against the religious leaders of his day. It seems they had similar confusion about what God desires.

"You tie up heavy loads and you put them on people's shoulders, but then you are not willing to lift a finger to help them.... You shut the door of the kingdom of God in people's faces. You yourselves will not enter, nor do you let those enter who are trying to.... You are careful to obey every detail of the law, but you neglect the more important things—justice, mercy, and faithfulness. You blind guides! You strain a gnat out of your soup, but you swallow a camel." (my paraphrase)

Jesus' teaching then explained again and again that this New Direction is opposite of our natural inclinations. It's countercultural. It is a path of Love. A path of kindness. A path of taking care of one another.

I grew up in a form of Christianity in which we believed rules and boundaries would control our behavior, that scolding and confronting one another would stop us from sinning. This kind of practice can be effective for a while. Most of us want to do right. We want to stop doing bad things—even more so, we want the tribe of people we have joined to accept us—so we try really hard. We stop doing the stuff we aren't supposed to do. Some of us have a strong will, good discipline. For a while. But our heart can remain unchanged, unhealed.

Our sins are born out of our wounds. We try to meet our needs, our desires, through whatever means to satisfy that longing or to soothe the ache in our soul. Unless the wound heals, it remains buried under our religious piety—festering and oozing—until it drags us back again into the hell we tried to escape.

Mother Teresa said, "Kindness has converted more people than zeal, science, or eloquence. Holiness grows so fast where there is kindness. The world is lost for want of sweetness and kindness." I don't think she meant that kindness converted them to a religion. Behavior changes, as people feel and know their value. They begin to desire to live from the infinite value of the Divine image inside them. They become free and whole.

Richard Rohr writes: "It is sad that we settle for the short-run effectiveness of shaming people instead of the long-term life benefits of grace-filled transformation. But we are a culture of progress and efficiency, impatient with gradual growth. God's way of restoring things interiorly is much more patient—and finally more effective."

I believe in repentance. One hundred percent. And I am seeing it with my own eyes. Several months after that confrontational inquisition, Mindy announces she has a new job as a waitress at Mama Lou's. Although waiting tables will make her less income than dancing, she explains that she has started having trouble keeping herself "separated into two parts." She says, "It used to be easy for me to turn off my mind when it was time for me to get up there on the stage. I could just go to another place. But I can't do it anymore. It bothers me. I just decided it's time for me to be done dancing."

Isn't this what God desires? Wholeness. Integration of the fragments of ourselves. Fragments we made to cut off the parts of ourselves that brought us shame. Fragments others made of us when they cut our souls with their words and with their actions. This is what Love does. It puts us back together. It restores. It heals. And healing takes time.

CHAPTER 9
POLLYANNA LONGSHOTS

"May the grace of God be with you always, in your heart.
May you know the truth inside you from the start.
May you find the strength to know that you are
a part of something beautiful."

— Alexi Murdoch

When a local ministry calls and asks me to consider opening a food pantry with food they will donate to us, I feel overwhelmed—both in a good and a bad way. Of course. I would love to open a food pantry.

Up to this point, providing food for people in the neighborhood is an adventure of faith. We have no regular source of food. John and I sometimes deliver groceries we purchase out of the offerings people give on Sunday mornings. Sometimes, a north-side follower of Jesus drops by with a few bags to contribute to our Kitchen Table (the name of our Community Center space).

More than once, a very quiet, shy, young ex-convict shows up on Friday night with a big smile and a box of food to donate. (I have no idea where he gets it from, as his income is limited.

He is just getting back on his own feet, having been in prison for 18 years. He delivers the boxes of canned items, instant oatmeal, and dehydrated mashed potatoes in total silence with his head down and a broad grin from ear to ear.)

Whatever the source, we pass on the food to those who are in immediate need. A family with four children who lost their food stamps over some confusion about the paperwork. A husband and wife who are unemployed. A single man who has AIDS and recently lost his life partner to a sudden, unexpected death. A meth addict who is trying to provide for her children.

Every time someone has come asking for food, we have had food to give. The Muse has provided through one of these remarkable means. However, the shelves are now bare. I have been wondering what God wants to do about this. People are in need. So when this organization suggests we open a food pantry, I am thrilled. This is God's answer to the need.

Immediately following excitement and gratefulness, anxiety rushes in. My busy schedule and unending to-do list come up before my eyes, and I want to just lie down in a fetal position somewhere. I am exhausted. I know there is no way I can manage a weekly food pantry. What an opportunity—but no way to take advantage of it.

Unbeknownst to me, Pastor-Wanna-Be, Foster, overhears me talking on the phone about the offer. Foster asks, "Could I take on the food pantry? Could this be my project?" Tears come to my eyes. Foster is a gifted administrator infused with abundant energy that comes from the fresh transformation Love has brought to his broken life. He could do it. He could manage the whole thing—with fresh faith in God, hope for provision, and love for needy people.

Over the next few weeks, I watch as Foster grabs the bull by both horns. He goes to the other organization and learns the very detailed process for bagging the groceries. He creates flyers to advertise in the neighborhood and organizes a door-to-door knocking campaign to get the word out. Then he recruits volunteers to help.

He finds a volunteer to paint the windows at the Kitchen Table (at the other end of our building) with a sign announcing May 1st as our opening date. He makes announcements every Sunday in church. He creates and posts a sign-up sheet for volunteers to help bag groceries, transport food, and to work the day of food distribution.

During the weeks leading up to May 1st, Foster resembles Tigger from *Winnie the Pooh*. He meets with me once a week to let me know where we are in the planning. He comes bouncing in with his papers and his lists and his ideas. His two areas of concern are transportation of the food (we will need a BIG vehicle), and what if we have too many needy families and not enough food? The organization has allotted groceries for twenty-five families per week. Foster is worried this might not be enough.

My worries go the other direction. Two days before the BIG DAY, I ask Foster how many people he thinks we will have. His eyebrows lift high and he says, "We're going to have a *lot* of people." I ask him if he has heard people say they are coming, or how does he know lots of people are planning to come. Without a beat of hesitation, he responds, "God told me we are going to have a *lot* of people!" My heart drops. Oh, no. What if The Muse didn't really say that to him? What will it do to Foster's faith if people don't show up? I throw up a quick prayer, "God, you know . . . please show up. For Foster's sake."

Friday night, Foster meets with me to go over the plans for Saturday. Everything is arranged. Volunteers are set to bag groceries, to transport the bags, to welcome people, to gather their information on a computerized form, to load the groceries into cars, to carry groceries home for people, if needed. He has even arranged a Prayer Volunteer to be available to offer to pray for each person who comes to receive food.

MAY DAY—spring. A day of fresh, new beginnings. I arrive at Joe's Addiction at around 1:30 p.m.. The food pantry was to begin at 1:00. When I walk in, there are people everywhere. Regulars are drinking coffee and playing cards. Folks are chatting. Foster has situated chairs into a "waiting area," where several people wait their turn to register. Behind the computer is a lady I barely know as new to the neighborhood. Foster has recruited her to help, and it is only her first week in town. A volunteer is praying with an old man who holds his cap in his hand and bows his head. A group of children sit at a low table doing craft projects. As each person registers, Foster hands them a voucher to go down to the Kitchen Table and retrieve their bags of groceries.

I walk down there to see the kitchen organized with bags and boxes of groceries and a mountain of pastries. We are even giving out dessert. Three volunteers are loading groceries into trunks and back seats of cars.

Foster grabs me and says, "What are we going to do with all of this?" The organization has given us the allotment for 25 families, plus extra—extra bread, extra pastries—AND they have given him the very strict policy that we must distribute ALL the food today. I can see Foster's faith is wavering. What if we don't have enough people to take all the food? I assure him we will find people who need it, pat him on the shoulder, and then head out to run errands and pick up a lady I know could use some food.

I arrive back at 3:45 p.m. (15 min. before the closing of the food pantry). Foster is still sitting at the registration table. I lead the woman over to the table to register. She sits down and gives her information, including her prayer request. I look around the room. The flurry has died down. The children's activities are finished. There is a group of regulars playing cards, and there sits one old man in the "waiting chairs."

I go to him and ask, "Are you getting everything you need, sir?" He mumbles that Foster told him to come back at 4 p.m. to see if we had any leftover food. "Did you receive food earlier?" I ask. "Yes, Ma'am. I did. But I know someone else who needs some."

The man tells me he lives down the street in one of the trailer parks. As I ask him questions, he slowly tells me about his life. He is an air conditioner/heating repairman. He tells me about getting old and selling his business to a partner in

California. He tells me of his hopes and dreams to move to Oklahoma to be near his children and grandchildren, only to have had an unwelcome reception from them which amounted to him living at the City Rescue Mission for a while.

Tears fill his eyes when he tells me how the humidity here wreaks havoc on his body. He misses California. But he is here now and he receives enough Social Security to make payments on a trailer. He says the food he received from the food pantry is sure going to be a big help.

I ask him how he likes living in the trailer park. He relays how the people there have discovered his skills. They don't have money to call someone to come and fix their heaters, so many times during this last winter, people had knocked on his door. He says, "I don't have money for parts, but I have the skills, so I help them. I've lived a pretty blessed life, and it's the least I can do to give back."

He's lived a blessed life? He worked hard all his life. Sold his business for little to nothing. Lost relationship with his kids. Lived in the City Rescue Mission. Now lives in a trailer park. But, he's lived a blessed life.

He then goes on: "My ex-wife lives in a senior citizens home. Most of the people there are on a low, fixed income from Social Security. They always need food. If you have any food left, I want to take some over to those folks."

At 4 p.m. Foster comes to us and announces, "The food pantry is now closed for the day, and we do have leftovers to send to your ex-wife and her friends." I ask Foster, "How many families did we serve?" With tears in his eyes he says, "The girl you brought in made twenty-five."

Free Store — Faith Comes Through Them

People keep bringing stuff to Joe's Addiction. Stuff for "poor people." Clothing. Small household items. Blankets. People are kind, and they want to help, but I don't know how to get the stuff from them to the people who need the stuff—and I do not have time to figure it out. So the pile grows in a corner.

One day, during a barista meeting, someone asks, "What are we doing with all that crap over there in the corner." I explain to them what it is and grumble about the complexities of finding the people who need this stuff. Ideas tumble out.

"Someone is going to have to sort it." "Who?" "People here need clothes." "We need to at least hang the clothes on a rack. That pile. God." "We could have a garage sale. We always need more cash." "We could start a thrift store." "Hey, the space at the end of the building is empty. We could rent it!" "Then people could donate stuff all the time!" "A thrift store would be cool!"

Excitement is building, and then someone says, "But didn't Jesus say, '*Give* to those who ask of you?' not '*Sell* to those who ask of you?'"

Deflation.

Tisha says, "Well, then it will have to be a *Free* Store. Everything will be free."

Excitement once again. "A free store. That's a great idea." "Just sharing with each other what we have." "I've never heard of such a thing." "It's perfect. Let's do it!"

Then I say, "Well, we'd have to pay the rent and utilities somehow. The space isn't free." *Duh*. Deflation and looks that communicate, "We don't appreciate your gift of pragmatism, Jamie." We table the discussion and the pile in the corner continues to grow.

A month later, my cell phone rings. It is the landlord. I rarely talk with the landlord. I have only spoken to him when we originally signed the lease and once when, out of curiosity, I asked if he would be interested in selling the whole building to us. ($500k was his answer. Ha! The building isn't worth half of that.) He lives in another state and if we ever have trouble, his father, who lives in town, swings by to fix whatever the problem is. The landlord has *never* called me before.

I answer, and he says, "Hi. I'm calling to find out if you guys would like to lease the space at the end of the building."

"Yes. Yes, we really would. But we don't have any money."

He asks, "If I drop the rent from $500/month to $400/month, could you do it then?"

I answer him, "We don't have $400 any more than we have $500."

He replies, "Well, let me tell you what happened."

He says he had already agreed to lease the space to someone else. He had even drawn up the contract, and he was walking out his door to put it in the mail to them when he heard a voice. The voice said, "You need to give that space to those church people." He says, "I don't know what that voice was but I thought I'd better call you . . . So I'm offering you the space. I'll give you twenty-four hours to get back to me, and if you can't lease it, then I'll give it to these other people."

I tell him I will let him know. I call up our community leaders. I tell each of them the story and ask what they think. One says, "It's our Free Store!" Another says, "I think we should go for it." The last one I call is the newest at following the Way of Jesus. He says, "Are you asking me if we should trust God?"

I sigh and say, "I guess I am."

He asks me, "Do we have a choice?"

I call them all back and tell them, "Look, I am going to sign this lease. My name will be on it, but you guys are the ones with the faith. You will have to believe for this money every month because I have no idea where it will come from." I sign the lease and seven years later, we are still operating a Free Store.

It is so much fun to hear people ask, "How much does this cost?" and to answer, "It's free. Everything is free." There is a sign on the wall reading, "There's no such thing as stealing in a Free Store." More than a handout to "poor people," the Free Store has become a form of recycling for the neighborhood. People bring in things they no longer need and exchange them for things they do need. We practice sharing.

We have paid the bills every month. Faith is not merely blind belief, but it also amounts to lots of creativity. A donation box sits on the counter in the store, and people contribute to pay the bills. When we have an overabundance of clothing that people don't want, we take it to a factory where they pay us by the pound for the fabric they use to make cleaning rags.

One day, I pull into the Joe's Addiction parking lot and see a TV News van parked in front. "Oh no," I mutter, "What do they want to say about us now?" But when I go inside, I discover someone has nominated us for a Pay It Forward gift, and they are donating $400. News Channel 4 paid the Free Store rent that month.

We may step out in faith to start a Community of Hope, but often it is the faith of those who have received Hope that carries the community forward.

Thanksgiving

A Sunday in November, one of our ladies raises her hand in church and asks if we will be having the annual Thanksgiving dinner and what are the details? She says, "People have been asking." It is time to be honest. I have been sitting on this situation for a few weeks now. Sometimes when I don't know what to do, I become paralyzed. I guess this is why I have not said anything yet but now I am forced to make the announcement: "Well, I just don't know what God wants us to do."

For three years, we had hosted a Thanksgiving Dinner serving the neighborhood around Joe's Addiction. A large church in Oklahoma City had given this event to us. The first year, people from this church brought food and fed about a hundred people.

The next year, our own people came to me and said, "We don't want to just be on the receiving end. We want to bless the community." So we invited the neighborhood. We dreamed up a menu. The people from the large church cooked the food at a country club and brought it, but our own Joe's Addiction folks dressed in white shirts and neckties (scavenged from the Free Store) served as hosts and waiters, asking "How many in your party?" to each group arriving to enjoy the meal, bringing plates, filling drinks, and delivering pumpkin pie.

The year before this November, we had done the same and served over 400 people from the surrounding neighborhood. That was 22 turkeys, 30 pies, a mountain of stuffing and potatoes, an ocean of gravy. It took 20 outside volunteers to pull it off. This is what the neighborhood has come to expect.

But about a month before this Thanksgiving, I receive a phone call from the people who helped with this event in the past. They won't be able to do it this year. That means the outside resources are not available. There is no way we can feed 400 hundred people by ourselves. It is just impossible.

Standing on the stage, I tell them, "We don't have the people coming to help us. We don't have the connections to the chef and the location where the food was cooked, and we don't have the money to do it." They all just look back at me. I am supposed to have the answers. Not this time—and the day for the Dinner is only two weeks away.

I say, "Okay, how about we all just pray about this situation over the next few days." (To be honest, I was stalling.) I suggest maybe The Muse will show us what we are to do. Maybe we are to plan something smaller—like our regular community dinner—just for us in the Joe's Community. "I really don't know," I say, "but let's ask together what God has in mind." I tell them if Spirit shows them anything to let me know.

Then I promptly go out of town—for the whole next week.

While I am gone, I receive a text from Foster that he has called the country club chef. The chef is willing to help with the cooking, if we can pull all the food together and find him some helpers.

When I arrive at church, as usual, I am swarmed with people greeting and hugging me. Then the lady who raised her hand the week before pulls me aside. She says, "I need to talk to you." Now, this woman is tough—I mean tough—but her eyes are full of tears. I feel concerned.

She says, "Last week you told us to pray about the Thanksgiving Dinner and so I did. Every time I prayed about it Phillip's name came to my mind. So I talked to Phillip." (Phillip is new in our community.) She says, "I sat down with him and told him all about the Thanksgiving Dinner and our situation. He said, 'I know just what to do.'"

She takes me to Phillip and he says, "Oh yeah. I've been working on it. I called KFC and they've donated cups and plates and flatware. I called Crest and they have given us $100 in vouchers. I also have some turkeys donated already. I know how to cook and I'm sure we can round up more people who can help."

She grabs my arm and says, "It works! It works!"

The service is starting and other people come to hug me and give me reports of how they are doing—things God is doing in their lives—another, and then another. "I got a job." "I got accepted into school." "I started the GED class yesterday." The music pounds from the stage, "I Will Wait, I Will Wait for you!" and the crowd claps in rhythm. There is a new guy I don't know, tears rolling down his cheeks. Pressure is building in my chest.

Following the break (for snacks, coffee refills, and cigarettes for those who can't make it through the service without one), I stand to make the announcements and facilitate our Prouds and Sorries. I begin by telling them it looks like we will have the Thanksgiving Dinner after all, but we aren't yet sure how big we can go. It depends on how much food we can acquire and how many people want to help. A low rumble of muttering voices begins.

A man stands and asks, "How many turkeys do we still need?" I look at Phillip. He says, "I guess we need another thirteen." The man responds, "I'll buy the thirteen turkeys. I'll have them here this afternoon." This man is homeless. He is doing well, and we have all been rejoicing with him. He has just been hired for a job, but he has not yet started working. We all know the turkeys will require most of his food stamps. The rumble of voices grows louder.

I jump in, "Wait a minute, now. If you bring thirteen turkeys this afternoon, we don't have freezer space to hold them." A woman breaks in, "I have room for six turkeys in my freezer." Another man adds, "I have room for some in mine."

I look at John and he shrugs. Still pessimistic, I say, "Okay well, we'll need to have all the other food for side dishes."

People start popping up, "I can bring green beans."

"I'm sure I can get some potatoes."

Foster stands and says, "Okay everybody, if you want to help with set up and serving the meal, please see me after the service."

Phillip hollers, "If you want to help get food or go to the country club to cook, please come to me after the service."

Everyone is talking now.

Then a toothless, old woman, who sits on the front row and is usually on some other planet, raises her hand and yells over the din of voices. "Are we talking about turkeys? I can bring a turkey!"—and I lose it. Everything is out of my control—the Thanksgiving Dinner and my emotions. I dive off the stage and try to find a seat while John shakes his head looking at me with tears in his eyes.

Tisha, our resident prophetess raises her hand. She says, "God has not only said we are to do the Thanksgiving Dinner, but God will supply everything we need—GENEROUSLY."

The atmosphere is charged as people share their prouds and sorries from the last week. Some with great news, some with prayer requests, and some with deep confessions and apologies. All are rejoiced with, prayed for, and forgiven.

John's message for the day calls everyone to join Jesus in drinking from his cup—joining him in his Way of Life, in his community, and in his sacrificial service—and we all share communion together.

After we have washed the dishes and put the coffee shop tables and chairs put back in place, Foster and Phillip come to me. They say, "We have everything we need. All of it has been donated and people have committed to serve. We just need you to do one thing—make a flyer we can take door to door to invite everyone to come to Thanksgiving Dinner."

"Then the master told his servant, 'Go out into the highways and hedges, and compel them to come in, that my house may be filled.'"

— Jesus

CHAPTER 10
PLODDING

"Salivating for success keeps you from being faithful,
keeps you from truly seeing whoever's sitting in front
of you. Embracing a strategy and an approach you can
believe in is sometimes the best you can do on any
given day. If you surrender your need for results and
outcomes, success becomes God's business.
I find it hard enough to just be faithful."

— Fr. Gregory Boyle

Many years before Joe's Addiction, John and I had just completed another training class of wannabe missionaries. They
had graduated and some of them wanted to go to Taiwan to
study Mandarin. Because of our experience in Taiwan, we
decided to go with them to help establish them in language
study and provide support as they settled into a new place and
a new culture.

During our first week there, a typhoon made landfall on
the side of the island where we were living. Everyone made
preparations, battened down the hatches on every building,

and on every window. We were all waiting it out together in our narrow, three-story, concrete house in the city.

The rains fell and the winds blew. The rains fell some more. Water began rising in the streets. Our house was positioned on a little mound, raised back from the road, so we were not worried about flooding in our home. We opened the downstairs walls (large metal grates) and watched the cars slowly driving through the increasing puddles. The water flowed like a stream down our street. Then it became a river, a mighty raging river. We watched as a car stalled out in the water and then floated right past our house. The driver escaped and made his way to the edge of the road, onto a porch.

Suddenly, we noticed shoes floating in the water. One shoe, and then another, and another. Different kinds of shoes. A high-heeled pump, a boot, a tennis shoe. We looked down the street and saw the shoe store on the corner was now sitting *in* the river. The "mom and pop shop" was losing all their inventory to the flood. The shoes would be wet, but maybe we could salvage some of them. We started, from our front porch, trying to fish shoes out of the water as we saw them floating by.

We realized then if the shop on the corner had flooded, maybe some of our neighbor's homes were flooding as well. They all had large metal grates for walls, like ours, but most of them were seated right at road level. The walls opened directly onto the street. John made his way up the side of the road scooting from porch to sidewalk, from post to doorway, checking on our neighbors. We watched from our porch as he went.

Then he started waving frantically for us to come and help. I couldn't go. With three small children to care for, I stayed in the safety of our higher ground. But some of the brand-new missionaries scrambled to where he stood. It was the home of an elderly couple. The river flowed in front of their house, but whenever a car tried to make its way through, the waves caused by the car diverted the flood right into their living room.

For hour upon hour, John and the new missionaries stood in their home scooping water with plastic buckets, tin cans, any kind of vessel they could find. When a car came their direction, John would call out a warning. By this point, there were no drivers in the cars. They simply flowed along with the torrent, bumping into buildings, careening into other cars, as they went. The missionaries would brace themselves for the deluge, and as soon as the car passed, they started scooping water and dumping it out the door. Again and again.

By the end of the day, the rain had stopped, and the river had receded. The little old couple was so grateful. They wept as they thanked the young people for their help. John and the missionaries dragged their weary bodies back to our house to rest and dry off. As I fed them some dinner, one of the new missionaries, a strong, young, energetic woman said, "I love it here! I was made for this!" We laughed.

I learned something that day. Yes, there are adrenaline-filled days. There are days when you feel you are making a difference. There are days when the people you are serving express gratitude, and the work feels worth every bit of sacrifice you are making. And then there are days when none of that is true. In fact, the non-adrenaline filled days are much more frequent than the exciting ones.

William Carey was a missionary to India in the late 1700s. He accomplished remarkable work there, including putting a stop to the practice of burning living brides on the funeral pyres of their dead husbands. When someone praised him for his work, Carey said, "If he gives me credit for being a plodder he will describe me justly. Anything beyond that will be too much. I can plod. I can persevere in any definite pursuit. To this I owe everything."

We spend most of the days in our community at Joe's Addiction plodding. We open in the morning, sometimes to no customers at all. Sometimes people are waiting on the front sidewalk when I arrive, waiting to be let in. It is unpredictable. You would think cold weather would drive people in, but not necessarily. When you are warm and dry in your thick sleeping bag, you don't want to venture out, even for a cup of coffee.

We open the shop, put the coffee on, and people trickle in. Mornings are quiet, just like they are in most homes. Our people live by the proverb that says: "A loud and cheerful greeting in the morning will be taken as a curse." Customers stop by and pay for lattes or steaming hot cups of joe, but we always have a large percolator pot ready for those who cannot afford to pay. It all runs on the "honor system," and it has become understood by peer accountability that if you have money, you should pay (it helps to keep this place running). If you don't have money, you're welcome to take a free cup.

Whoever is serving as barista gently says, "Good morning" and greets each person. Some of our people who live outside make a beeline to the bathroom. Peeing outside can land you an indecent exposure charge. Some of them already bear those consequences, so they would rather be safe than sorry.

We almost always have toast, peanut butter and jelly available for breakfast. We receive a weekly donation of leftover bread from Panera Bread Co. Some mornings a nice man who lives nearby delivers day-old donuts to us. Folks eat quietly while we watch the morning news on the large television screen. I love mornings at Joe's Addiction. It feels like family.

The rest of the day can feel pretty mundane. Making drinks, putting together sandwiches, giving sugar packets for people's coffee, washing dishes, playing *another* round of cards.

Hypocrites and Crooks

Sometimes Percy comes in. He is disabled. He takes a bus from across town and rides his electric scooter to the back door (the only handicapped access to our building). When we hear pounding, we know it's Percy. We open the door and he drives across the room to a table in front of the television.

Percy has been coming to Joe's Addiction for many years now. He really comes to Valley Brook to go to a strip club down the street, but his bus arrives at around 10:15 a.m. The club doesn't open until 11:00 a.m., so he waits out the difference inside Joe's. He always asks us to turn the channel to "The Price is Right," so now when he arrives, without him even asking, someone in the room reaches for the TV to change it to *his* show.

Percy wears thick glasses. His speech is slurred and he carries a towel he uses to wipe the drool that often pools and spills out of his mouth. His hands shake and his fingers curl stiffly. He can walk but it is very difficult for him. And Percy is rude. He is gruff and demanding. Sometimes he wants a glass of milk to go with the package of honey buns or cupcakes he has brought with him. He does not say please and sometimes he forgets to pay. One day, a barista says, "You know he goes straight to Fancy's when he leaves here. Right?" I tell her, "I know, but that is not our business. We'll just be kind to him while he's here."

Percy has come to Joe's Addiction several times a week for more than three years, when I finally quit coddling his meanness. One day, he demands I bring a napkin for him. I do, and when I set it down on his table, I say, "Thank you?" He looks at me with a scowl, but says, "Thanks." Another day, as he is leaving, holding the back door open for him, I say, "Have a good day, Percy. I hope those ladies over there are nice to you." He whirls and looks me in the eye. He says, "What ladies? I don't go over there." I say, "Okay, Percy. Whatever. It's not my business. I just hope they're nice to you when you're there." He huffs and puffs and scoots out the back door toward Fancy's.

One morning, Percy motions me over to his table in front of the TV. He says, "Can you help me with something?"

"Sure," I say, "What's up?"

He shows me his cell phone. Some person has been texting him hateful threats. He wants to know if I can help him block this person from texting him. I ask him who would say such mean things to him. He will not tell me, but I can see he is upset. I scroll through his phone and block the number. He thanks me again and again.

One of the guys pokes his head in the front door one afternoon and says, "Hey, Jamie, Percy's out front. He wants to talk to you." Strange; this isn't his normal pattern. I go out front where Percy is sitting on his scooter. "What's up, Percy? You don't wanna come in?"

He says, "I wanna talk to you about something."

"Okay?"

Percy says, "Some of these people I see sitting here all the time are bad people. They shouldn't be here."

I ask him what he means. Who is bad? He says, "Well, just some of these people. They're homeless; they've been to prison. Why do you let them hang out in your shop? You even let some of them work behind the counter."

I tell him this is what we do here. We are a community of people who love and take care of each other. I explain the circumstances of some of our people, tell him some reasons they have been to prison, the factors of drug addiction and mental illness that make it hard for some of them to find work.

He says, "Well, I don't like them. I don't think you should let them hang out here."

I say, "Well, that isn't really your call, is it? Since I own the place, I get to be the one to decide."

He bursts out laughing. I have never even seen Percy smile.

Percy and I have a lengthy conversation. I sit down on the curb next to his scooter, and he tells me about his life. He is the youngest of eight children and spent most of his growing-up years in a residential facility for disabled kids. Percy adores his mother and has no animosity toward her for putting him in a "home." He says, "She had all those other kids to take care of. I was just a little too much for her. She came to visit me every week though."

He has a job he has held for sixteen years. He is the mail delivery person in a tall office building in downtown Oklahoma City where he starts work at 4:00 a.m. He sorts all the letters and then spends the morning, scooting into every office in the building to deliver their mail. When I ask him if he likes his job, he beams. He says, "I love it, and the people are *nice* to me there." He winks at me, and I laugh. Percy remembers what I said about the girls at Fancy's, and he is funny.

Then he becomes serious and he says, "I think you should know I hate church, and I hate preachers." He is forceful.

I say, "Okay. Why is that?"

"They're hypocrites and crooks," he spits. He tells me his thoughts about TV preachers and some infamous preachers in Oklahoma City history who were exposed in financial improprieties and marital infidelities. He says, "They tell you you're going to hell. Then they tell you if you give money to their church, God will bless you. You don't want to go to hell, and you want God to bless you, so you give them money. Then they put it right in their pocket and walk away. "Charlatans, the whole lotta them." I have to listen closely and piece together what Percy is saying as the more angry he becomes, the more drool garbles his speech.

When he finishes his tirade, I say, "Um, Percy, you know I'm a preacher, right?"

He blusters, "Yeah. But you're not like them. You're helping all these people here."

I say, "Then you don't hate *all* preachers. Right?"

He throws back his head and howls. When he has wiped his mouth with his towel, he says, "You're funny. I like you."

Percy continues to come to Joe's several times a week. He becomes more pleasant, sometimes even offering a "thank you" without being prompted. He becomes friends with my younger kids, Jewel and James. He knows their names and asks them about school and their activities. He has become a bit of a grumpy uncle to them.

A few weeks after our long conversation, I notice Percy scooting up to the front sidewalk. I go out to greet him and immediately I can see something is wrong. "Percy, are you okay? What's the matter?"

He bursts into tears, covering his face with his towel. Percy's eighty-year-old mother and his aunt had taken a trip. They had driven all the way from Oklahoma to California to visit some of Percy's siblings. They had a wonderful trip, but after days of driving, when they had just entered Oklahoma City, a semi-truck had hit them. His aunt was killed instantly, and his mother was in the hospital fighting for her life.

Over the next few weeks, I come to know Percy's brother through conversations over the phone. His mother has several surgeries, improves and is finally moved to a rehabilitation center about an hour away. Percy asks me to help him dial the numbers on his phone to speak with his mother for the first time since her accident. Oh, the joy as he hears her voice. Sitting on the curb next to his scooter, tears pour down my face. Three years of plodding, and now Percy is my friend.

Waves

Sometimes life at Joe's does feel like a typhoon. In one day, we experience this:

One of our men is standing at the bus stop in front of Joe's Addiction and collapses. It is hot, and I am afraid he has overheated. I run to check on him. He is conscious and slurring his words. He tells me he has taken all the pills in the bottle he is holding in his hand.

When the paramedics come, they won't listen to anything I am trying to tell them. I have information for them. I know this man. They disregard me, put him on a gurney, and wheel him into the ambulance.

I don't have time to lick the wound to my ego. I am more worried about him anyway, but it's frustrating.

I call the man's probation officer to let her know he will miss his meeting. That is where he was headed when he went to the bus stop. His P.O. yells at me over the phone, telling me she has restricted him from hanging out at Joe's Addiction, because we frequently have children in our place. "You shouldn't even be involved in his life in the first place!" How would I know she had restricted him? One of my most hated personal injuries is being accused of something I didn't do or my intentions being misunderstood. My ego winces again.

A few minutes later, some leaders of a big church in our city arrive to meet with me. It's a scheduled meeting, and I had known they were coming. I hate this kind of meeting. I always feel intimidated by the size and success of their churches. I have a hard time just standing my own ground and being who I am. I can do it. But it takes a lot of concentration for me. No time to prepare. Adrenaline still pumping from the overdose guy and his P.O., I rush into the meeting.

I answer their questions and give them information about what we do. They use lots of superlatives in their vocal praise and then make promises about financial help and guaranteed invitations to have me come speak at their church. (Neither of these happen, by the way.)

Ten minutes after the big-church men leave, one of our guys flings open the door and shouts, "Big Bob just face planted on the concrete!"

Big Bob is very tall and very big. Hence the name. I run out the door and down the sidewalk. There he is lying face down on the ground in front of the large Narcotics Anonymous symbol painted on our window—a rolled up joint on the ground next to his face.

"Bob! Bob? You okay, man?" He is conscious, sort of. He mumbles and tries to push himself up. Blood is pouring from a wound on his forehead. Some of the guys help me lift him to a sitting position, leaning against the wall, while someone else dials 911. Again.

I hold the joint up in front of him and ask, "Is this yours, dude?" Knowing the police will arrive with the ambulance, I think he might not want to have it on his person.

He says, "That's not mine. If it was, I'da smoked it."

I ask the guys standing around what happened. One says, "He's on Fake Bake. He's been smoking it a lot." I ask if they think that's what is in this joint. One of them says, "Prolly."

It is a synthetic marijuana. There are lots of names for it. Spice. K-2. Our people call it Fake Bake. It has been around in various chemical compounds over the years. Lawmakers rule it illegal, so the drug makers adjust the compound by a molecule or two, and then it is no longer illegal. The problem is it has become more lethal with every adjustment. The latest stuff on the streets is killing people. It causes seizures, brain bleeds, and erratic behavior.

I drop the joint on the ground. I know the police can't charge him with possession of Fake Bake. I am out-of-control angry.

For two years, I have been building relationship with the man who owns the convenience store near us. He buys a daily latte from me; I buy ice from him. We chat about life. I am making friends with his wife, whom he verbally abuses. She cries to me about her pain. It has been hard enough for me to love him with that going on. But this? I know he is the one who sold Fake Bake to Bob. Our people have been buying it from him all the time.

The ambulance is on the way and the guys around Bob are keeping him still and applying pressure to his head, so I charge into the convenience store. The owner has seen the commotion outside and he asks me, "What's up? What's going on over there?" I yell at him, "Do you really want to know what's going on? You sold that shit to Big Bob! He passed out and landed on his face! He's bleeding from his head!" I can hear the sirens now, so I hurry back outside to meet the ambulance.

As the paramedics examine Big Bob, they ask him questions.

"What day is it?"

He doesn't know.

"What year is it?"

He answers 2013. That is right.

"Who's the president?"

He says, "Bush."

I chuckle. Big Bob is homeless, and he usually hasn't any idea what day it is, anyway. He doesn't need to keep track. Every day is the same to him. He knows what year it is, but he probably didn't know who is president even before the cement knocked him in the head. I am just glad they are taking him to the hospital. They will take care of him—at least for now.

The ambulance leaves, and I look around on the sidewalk. The joint is not there. I had not heard the police questioning about it. I ask the guys, and they all shrug their shoulders.

Now there is a crowd of people at Joe's. They all want coffee. Their adrenaline is pumping too. I make another pot and sit down to take a breath. In comes one of our ladies with her four children. She has planned a craft night for the neighborhood kids. I help her move tables around and set up the craft supplies.

Cliff comes through the door. He sees the children and cries out, "Sharla! You look so pretty!" Sharla is wearing a dress and has a bow in her hair. She is shy and quiet. It warms my heart that Cliff would so kindly call her out to encourage her.

One of our ladies comes in looking terrible. She is sick with a head cold. I sit her down, make herbal tea for her, and douse her with essential oils.

Pastor-Wanna-Be, Foster, is taking over for the evening shift, so I fill him in on the adventures of the day. I say my "goodbyes" and go home to make dinner for my family.

While sitting in my living room that evening, I receive a phone call from a friend involved in Narcotics Anonymous. We only have one meeting happening per week. She says a guy she attends another meeting with has offered to start up more meetings at Joe's Addiction. He's committed, and he wants to help, so he will run a meeting every night of the week for us. People can attend a meeting every day if they want to! I erupt into tears.

The waves sometimes feel like a giant, tidal wave, and other times a roller coaster is a better description of the ups and downs of the drama at Joe's Addiction.

It can be overwhelming, but not every day, not every week is like this. Most of the time, life is pretty mundane. We make coffee. We wash dishes. We play cards, watch some "Price is Right." But it is the daily plodding, the showing up every day when nothing is exciting, that makes us ready, that has us present when the crises occur. And sometimes amid those crises, we can love in a way that makes a difference.

Praying the Work

Back when my faith had unraveled, I felt gravitationally attracted to the Jesus I saw healing the sick, casting out demons, holding little children, feeding the hungry, forgiving the broken, extending mercy to sinners, loving the outcasts—the "least of these" in society. The Jesus who stood up for them against the religious jerks who made it impossible to feel God's favor. I wanted to be like him, but he seemed so far away, so long ago in history.

I read authors I admired who pointed to Mother Teresa as an example and realized I knew nothing about her. As I researched her life, I felt the same gravitational pull. Here was a woman who sacrificially gave herself to the "least of these" because she heard Jesus calling her to do so. I read of her love for Jesus and her utter devotion to him. I even appreciated her struggles, the doubts that came to light in her journals, as I could now totally relate. I respected her perseverance in her call, and I think most of all, I admired the simplicity of her love—the Love God gave to her—with which she loved the people she encountered.

My one regret: I found her after she had already died. How I wish I could have seen her in action. I had known about her, but because she was Catholic, the Evangelicals I hung around didn't consider her "Christian." Such a shame.

When my daughter, Jessi, and I took a trip to Kolkata (formerly Calcutta), I was determined to spend at least one day volunteering at Mother Teresa's Missionaries of Charity in the Home for the Dying and Destitute. This was the place where her ministry began by picking up dying people from the streets of India, cleaning them, feeding them, loving them, and offering them dignity as they died.

I only had one day there. What could I really do? Not much. Other volunteers from all over the world who had been there for months or even years gathered in a hall for a simple breakfast of bananas, bread, and chai, and to hear instructions for the day. I stood there among these experienced world travelers and long-term volunteers, as that old, familiar insecurity of my youth snuck up on me.

What am I doing here? I don't know how things work. I'm only here for a day. What can I really do? These other folks probably think I'm wimpy for only coming one day. Perhaps they even think I'm selfish—coming to have "an experience," rather than genuinely to serve the poor and needy. Oh, I hope that's not what I've done. What if that's really why I'm here?

The nun is giving instructions about things that do not apply to me as a short-termer, but the part I hear for me stands out, "The Sisters are all very busy; don't bother them with questions. Just ask another of the volunteers. There's plenty to do. They will help you."

I follow the crowd out the door onto a bus to the Home for the Dying, the whole way second guessing and reconsidering this perhaps foolish thing I have done. What if I can't handle the sights? What if I can't take the smells? What if I cry? Oh God, what if I end up standing in a corner watching everyone else do the work because I don't know what to do with myself? This is an old insecurity that sometimes plagues me.

A French lady on the bus tries to make pleasant conversation. She asks where I am from and how long I will be staying. When I tell her I am just there for a day, an awkward silence now adds to my fears.

The bus stops and we file into the home. We walk through a long room full of low, cot-like beds, each one occupied by a thin, Indian man. The room smells of disinfectant. I glance around, but then keep my eyes ahead on the volunteers, who go upstairs to lockers to put down their bags. People are taking off their jewelry and rolling up their sleeves. I do, too.

A young girl in her early twenties smiles at me. She looks nice, so I file into line behind her. She heads down the stairs, and I follow. We enter a room where there are large tile basins full of soapy water. Piles of soiled sheets, pajamas, and blankets cover the floor. People grab items and stuff them in the basins and begin to scrub.

Okay. I can do this. I know how to wash. I step up beside the girl and put my hands in the bubbles. We scrub and rinse, wring and hang things for two hours. An assembly line of cheerful volunteers.

A lady pokes her head in and says, "We need help making beds." I know how to do that. The girl I had followed dries her hands too, so I shadow her into the women's ward. The room is filled with rows of the same low beds. A thin, fragile-looking woman lies on each one. A volunteer sits next to one bed, holding a nebulizer to a woman's nose and mouth, helping her to breathe. Another volunteer massages the hands and arms of a woman who lies still. Another combs the tangled hair of a frail and tiny lady.

The German woman who called for help thrusts a pile of linens at me and says, "We'll move the ladies. You make the beds." The girl and I get busy. They lift a woman and lay her on the next bed while I remove the sheet and blanket. We work together to wipe the plastic covered mattress with disinfectant and then tie up the corners of the sheets volunteers must have washed the day before. They return each woman to her bed, and we move to the next one.

Some ladies smile. Some speak words I cannot understand. Many stare with no expression at all, perhaps even unaware they now have clean sheets.

Beds all finished, I look at the girl and ask, "What's next?" I follow her upstairs to a table piled high with bulbs of garlic. We sit down with a few other volunteers to peel hundreds of cloves for the evening meal.

Soon it is time for lunch, and a call comes for help downstairs. Someone puts full plates in my hands, and I follow others who take the food to the women in the beds. Some can feed themselves. The long-term volunteers know who needs help, and they sit down to spoon-feed the ones who are too weak.

Plates all distributed, I stand watching, not sure what to do next. "Oh, no. Here's that feeling. Only here for a day. What was I thinking? The long-term volunteers have this totally under control. Maybe I'm just in the way."

I spot that girl going into the kitchen, so once again I follow. No time for thinking, as basins have been filled, and once again my hands go into soapy water. I know how to wash dishes. Again, an assembly line of cheerful volunteers—doing the work.

Suddenly I remember something I read, something Mother Teresa told a discouraged volunteer many years ago. She said, "You must learn to *pray* the work."

The crisis of faith I experienced years earlier left me reeling. After twenty years of serving God, I was not even sure God existed. And yet . . . I could not deny the personal spiritual experiences I had known. God has gently and lovingly been rebuilding for me the foundation of faith that deconstructed. A new—and I hope better—faith has been growing in me.

I still struggle with prayer. I pray. I can't help myself. It is so much a part of who I have been my whole life. But I have watched many a fervent prayer go unanswered. These are prayers from godly people, about things that most certainly are God's will—and honestly . . . I just don't know.

I am comfortable with meditative prayer, for peace, for centering, for transformation of myself. What I struggle with is petitioning prayer. I no longer know what prayer does. Do we convince God to do things God otherwise would not have done? Why do some prayers receive answers and others don't? Does God intervene? If so, why sometimes and other times not? Why for him and not for her? Why for Americans and not for Indians?

These are the struggles of my own walk of faith, but with my hands in the dishwater, suddenly I understand what Mother Teresa meant.

So many times at Joe's Addiction, I face overwhelming need. I don't know what to do. The needs are so often not simple. Layers of issues complicate. Not enough money. Not enough food. No home for this person. Can't seem to help this one find (and keep) a job. Can't help this one stay sober.

In the ever present sense of helplessness, I often look at people and say, "I don't have a house for you, but are you hungry?" Sometimes I say, "Can I take your dirty laundry home and wash it for you?" These are my favorite things to do at Joe's—because I can *do* them. I sometimes don't know what else to do, but I can feed and I can wash.

Mother Teresa must have lived in the despair of helplessness. The poverty of India overwhelms me. But somehow, she found solace in "praying the work." The work of serving, of practically loving and caring for the least of these is a connection with the God of the Universe. Perhaps it is a most precious place of communion with God, because as she said, we see the face of Jesus in the poor and needy. "Whatever you've done to the least of these, you've done it unto me."

Dishes done and put away, the volunteers disperse. Small groups pick up their bracelets and bags and head for the door. I look at the girl I have been following and ask, "Are we done? Is that all?" She says, "Yes, the Sisters take care of the afternoons. We only work until after lunch."

As we go upstairs to gather our things I thank her. "Thanks for helping me today. I looked for someone who seemed like they knew what they were doing and I decided to follow you."

Her eyes widen and she laughs out loud. "I just got here yesterday! Today was my second day!"

This is the way of The Beloved Chaos. None of us has any idea what we are doing, really. We are each just doing our best to follow the Way of Love. We look around and we see someone who looks a little farther along the road ahead of us, so we jump in behind them and start following. Praying the work together. An assembly line of cheerful volunteers.

"What we would like to do is change the world—
make it a little simpler for people to feed, clothe,
and shelter themselves as God intended them to do.
And, by fighting for better conditions, by crying out
unceasingly for the rights of the workers, the poor,
of the destitute—the rights of the worthy and the
unworthy poor, in other words—we can, to a certain
extent, change the world; we can work for the oasis, the
little cell of joy and peace in a harried world. We can
throw our pebble in the pond and be confident that its
ever widening circle will reach around the world. We
repeat, there is nothing we can do but love, and, dear
God, please enlarge our hearts to love each other, to
love our neighbor, to love our enemy as our friend."

— Dorothy Day

SECTION 3
HARD STUFF

"The blues aren't pessimistic.
We're prisoners of hope, but we tell
the truth and the truth is dark."

— Cornel West

CHAPTER 11
LICE, COCKROACHES, AND SHIT

"Listen with ears of tolerance!
See through the eyes of compassion!
Speak with the language of love."

— Rumi

During Prouds and Sorries one Sunday, a man stands and comes forward to use the microphone. People usually call out their prouds or sorries from their chairs. Sometimes they stand at their seats. I breathe a sigh as I see him make his move. Handing the microphone over to anyone can mean a long recitation or excessive attention grabbing. Emceeing Prouds and Sorries can require skills in diplomacy.

It is difficult to talk about these uncomfortable things, and I hope I don't sound mean, but I think it is important for me to be honest. Bad smells are a difficult thing for me. Maybe I have overactive olfactory glands, or maybe it is a manifestation of my own emotional issues. I notice the slightest offensive odor. I can walk in the front door and know if our cat has peed somewhere in the house. It works the opposite way for me as well. Beautiful smells can change my mood, bring peace, or even delight.

Because many people in our community live outside, have inadequate heating for water in their homes, or are simply lacking social skills, body smells are common, sometimes over-powering—and difficult for me. Love demands I hold my breath. I find some comfort in my shame from Dorothy Day, who lived with and loved people living in poverty. She said, "There are two things you should know about the poor: they tend to smell, and they are ungrateful."

This man who approaches the stage is particularly odorous. He lives in a sixteen-foot travel trailer with four dogs. Add a cleft palate that has eliminated his own sense of smell and some mental illness. Let's just say he is pungent.

As soon as he takes the microphone, I can see this is serious. He begins to cry. This man is not generally very demonstrative. The whole room feels the intensity, and concerned silence settles in. I place my hand on his shoulder to offer some empathy and suddenly realize I just placed my hand in dog shit. A smear. Still moist.

Don't react. Don't move. Just stand here. When he gathers his composure, he talks about some very painful interactions he is experiencing with family members. His parents are elderly and ill, living hours away. His relatives are not including him in care decisions or even in communication. He is hurting.

I keep my hand still on his shoulder, paralyzed. When he finishes talking, I take the microphone from him and invite everyone to bow their heads. I pray for him and for his parents. When I finish my prayer, he turns toward me. Oh, no! He leans in for a hug.

He goes back to his seat, and because I am to preach, the service continues nonstop. There is no way for me to exit to the bathroom without an awkward and abrupt interruption to our normal flow of service. A half hour later, when I am finished preaching, I am finally able to wash my hands.

Jesus touched the lepers. Did they smell? Infections. Rotting wounds. Did the smell vanish the moment of a miracle? Or did their clothing and bandages still retain the stench? Needy people sometimes smell. They just do.

Toenails

Chuck can't reach his feet. He hasn't been able to for years. He is overweight and even though his belly makes the distance hard to breech, osteoarthritis in his hips makes bending that far a painful impossibility. Chuck whispers over the counter that he needs help with something "kinda gross." When I ask what it is, he says, "Well, I need help cutting my toenails."

Okay. I can do that. I know he lives outside, but Chuck is clean. He uses the bathroom at Joe's Addiction almost every day to take what he calls a "bird bath." I wonder about his feet though. If he can't cut his toenails, can he wash them?

We go to the bathroom to hide from the view of customers and people eating food. He sits on the toilet seat while I sit on the floor. Chuck has brought a good set of toenail clippers. He is prepared, and so am I. Groaning and grunting, with a combination of reaching and leveraging one foot on the other, he pulls off his shoes. No smell. No problem. I can do this.

Off come the socks, and I discover that Chuck has not cut his toenails in years. You know the pictures of the guy who won the Guinness World Record for the longest fingernails? Chuck's toenails are like that. They have twisted over the ends of his toes, into curly-cues.

I ask, "Dude, how have you lived with them like this?"

He says, "I just wear shoes that are too big for my feet. They haven't really bothered me until recently."

I examine them and find one has taken a wayward turn and pierced the skin on the side of his toe. It has buried itself in a festering, red hot blister.

I take a deep breath and tell him this will take a while. "It might even hurt, but I'll be as careful as I can."

He says, "It's okay. It's got to be done."

My tools are woefully inadequate. The thickness of Chuck's big toenail is deeper than the width of the clippers. I have to chip and carve away bits and pieces, a little at a time, until I can make his nails into a reasonable shape. The whole time I work, Chuck apologizes, again and again. "I'm sorry. I know this is so gross. I can't do it by myself. Thank you so much for helping me."

Cleaning House

One of our ladies invites me over to her house. I always feel it is a privilege when someone welcomes me into their home. It feels like welcoming me into their life. But sometimes the mess I find is overwhelming.

One young woman asks me for help. She says, "I grew up with cockroaches. Having them was normal. But the roach problem in my house now is just too much. I can't seem to get it under control."

My teenage daughter, Jessi, offers to help me clean out her kitchen, and what we find is the basis for a horror film. Every drawer, every cabinet we open is swarming with roaches. They are even inside the refrigerator and the freezer.

We don rubber gloves and duct tape them at the top to our sleeves. I imagine bugs climbing up into my clothes. No. Just no. Then, we dive in. We open a drawer and scoop *everything* into a heavy duty trash bag. Each compartment we open reveals hundreds of swarming roaches startled by the light and movement. We don't stop to think. We open another cupboard and swipe everything into the bag until we have removed them all.

Later, I learn that glue in the construction of cheap furniture attracts roaches. You know, the kind made from particle board, the kind that poor people can afford to buy. We remove all the shelves and the wooden microwave cart from the house as the roaches are hiding in every crack and crevice. Everything goes. We bomb the house with bug killer, then help find new furniture, kitchen utensils, dishes, and food. She starts over, with that wonderful sense of "newness," but also with the awareness that the little devils live all over the neighborhood and will find their way to her house sooner rather than later.

Naughty Woman

While his disciples had gone to look for something to eat, Jesus was sitting at a well by himself. A Samaritan woman came to the well to draw water. The Jews despised Samaritans because they considered them "unclean" and "unholy" people.

Jesus asked the woman to draw water for him to drink. This surprised her. Not only was she a hated race, but she was a woman. Jewish men did not speak to women—especially women who were alone, and even more especially, women of her reputation.

Jesus held an interesting conversation with this woman about Living Water. He told her that there is a kind of water that when you drink it, you never thirst again. She responded to his cryptic metaphor with a bit of a sassy comeback:

"Okay, then give me this water so I won't ever get thirsty. I won't ever have to come back to this well again!" Drawing water from a well is hard work.

Here's more of the story:

Jesus said, "Go call your husband and then come back."

"I have no husband," she said.

"That's nicely put: 'I have no husband.' You've had five husbands, and the man you're living with now isn't even your husband. You spoke the truth there, sure enough."

"Oh, so you're a prophet! Well, tell me this: Our ancestors worshiped God at this mountain, but you Jews insist that Jerusalem is the only place for worship, right?"

Jesus told her that was true in the past, but now it does not matter what you're called or where you go to worship. He went on:

"It's who you are and the way you live that count before God. Your worship must engage your spirit in the pursuit of truth. That's the kind of people the Father is looking for: those who are simply and honestly *themselves* before God in their worship. God is sheer being itself—Spirit. Those who worship God must do it out of their very being, their spirits, their true selves."

The woman said, "I don't know about that. I do know that the Messiah is coming. When he arrives, we'll get the whole story."

"I am he," said Jesus. "You don't have to wait any longer or look any further."

Just then his disciples came back. They were shocked. They couldn't believe he was talking with *that kind of* woman. No one said what they were all thinking, but their faces showed it.

The woman took the hint and left. In her confusion she left her water pot. Back in the village she told the people, "Come see a man who knows all about the things I did, who knows me inside and out. Do you think this could be the Messiah?" And they went out to see for themselves. (John 4:16-30 MSG)

Growing up in church, I always saw this woman as sinful. She was naughty, right? Promiscuous. She had been married five times, and now she didn't even bother to have a wedding ceremony. She had just shacked up with a guy. I also saw Jesus as a bony-fingered prophet calling her out on her sin. This is what religious leaders do, right? It is their job to point out the ways the people are failing and call them to righteous living.

After the meltdown of my faith, I began to feel that this couldn't be what Jesus was doing. He was supposed to be the model of Love. My pictures of that scene didn't feel like Love. I did some research, and what I discovered changed everything for me.

Why was this woman at the well in the middle of the day? People went to the well in the morning to draw water for the day's needs, or they went in the evening to draw water for the next day's needs. They avoided the middle of the day. It was hot.

She was there because she was an outcast. At that time of day, she would not have to endure the critical gazes, the awkwardness, the comments. Yes, she was a "sinner." But the term "sinner" applied to anyone the majority rejected because of their differences. Sick people were even called "sinners," because people believed if someone was sick, God was punishing the sinner.

Jesus pointed out the woman's "sin," but he did not call it "sin." He told her what he knew about her. She had been married five times, and the man she was currently with was not even her husband.

Women of Jesus' day could not divorce their husbands. Women did not have equal rights with men. They had no rights. There was even discussion among the religious leaders of the day about whether women had souls. The Jerusalem Talmud notes the opinion of Eliezer ben Hyrcanus, the Tanna: "Women's wisdom is solely in the spindle." He added, "The words of the Torah should be burned rather than entrusted to women."

Divorce was the right of a man, and he could divorce his wife for any reason he desired. Because he didn't like her anymore, because she had become old and not as attractive, or because she wasn't satisfying him (by her poor cooking or her poor love making). He simply needed to state his right three times to make it so. "I divorce you. I divorce you. I divorce you," and the marriage was over. He was free to move on, and he left her with no place in society whatsoever. She would have no way to provide for herself. Social norms did not permit women to conduct business of their own. How would she undertake to begin a business, even if she was permitted? Her only means to survive would be prostitution—or remarriage. If she could find someone to marry her.

Five times. Five men had divorced this woman. Five men to whom she had entrusted her life, to whom she had given her heart. She had believed these five men would love and take care of her. Five men had used her and then abandoned her. No wonder she had not even married the one she was with.

When Jesus told her what he knew about her, he was *not* confronting her. He was not the bony-fingered prophet saying, "Ha! I know your deepest, darkest, secret sins."

No. With overflowing love and compassion, Jesus was saying, "I see you. I know you. And I feel your deepest pain." Can you just see the eyes of Jesus as he is looking at her? "I know you. I know how you have been betrayed. I know how you have been abandoned. I know how everyone in your community has rejected you."

This is why she was drawn to Jesus. She told everyone she knew about this Jesus, this man who had looked into her soul and told her everything about herself, this man who knew her deepest pains and loved her with so much compassion.

It was not because he was the man who pointed out her sin. Has anyone ever been drawn to you because you pointed out their sin? Yes, we have all sinned. We are *all* ashamed of our sin. I have never met a single person who doesn't experience the darkness of shame. But more shame does not draw us to the Light.

Love does. Compassion does. Kindness does.

Isn't it interesting that as we read the story of this woman at the well, as people for *so many* years have read her story, just like the people in her own community we considered her a whore? Who Jesus was, what he came to say, what he came to do—we missed the point. And I am afraid that we are still missing the point about who *we* are to be, what *we* are to be saying, what *we* are to be doing.

Bonnie's Hair

Bonnie is a beautiful woman. She is in her mid-forties and has long, thick, wavy hair. She is shy and she has no idea she is so pretty. She keeps her head down, rarely looks us in the eye, and speaks only when spoken to.

Her husband has gone to another part of the state to work, or so he told her; but he is not communicating and he is not sending money back for Bonnie to pay the bills. Eventually the landlord evicts her from her trailer, and she and her two teenage boys become homeless. One family in our community already has a full, small house with four children of their own, but they invite Bonnie and her boys to live in a tent in their backyard until she can find a job.

It is hot. Oklahoma summer hot. But a tent is better than nothing, and a back yard is better than sneaking onto a stranger's land, so Bonnie is grateful.

She begins to look for work. The only work for women right nearby is bartending or dancing in the clubs. "I'm too old for that," she tells me with an embarrassed smile. She applies at several fast-food places within walking distance, but they don't need her. She finally finds a job in another part of the city cleaning houses. She has to ride the bus every day to go there, but she is glad for the work.

Life at Joe's Addiction is busy and we aren't in everyone's "business" every day. As far as I know, things are going better for Bonnie. She is putting aside some money, hoping to afford a deposit on a place to live in a couple of months. Time goes by.

The woman in whose yard is where Bonnie is living comes to me one day with the quiet whisper, "Bonnie has lice, and she lost her job because of them." Now, for me, lice is a big deal. Once, my sister's children (all seven of them) had lice, and it was the very end of the world. So much work. Washing and drying every linen in the house. Treating their hair. Killing the lice. And then combing *every single* egg from *every* hair on *every* head. Ain't nobody got time for that.

Plus the stigma. Yes, everyone knows if you have lice, it's because you don't bathe. That is what we all fear people will think if our kids are the ones who have lice. But my sister's kids were the cleanest kids I know. She is a meticulous housekeeper and an organized mother. Lice travel. Her children could have picked them up by sharing a hairbrush, or even by sitting next to a kid whose lice crawled the distance from one shoulder to the next.

And then there's the misery. I bet since I mentioned lice, you have at least once reached up and scratched your head.

For many in our community, lice is a common experience. Stigma is not the big problem. It's just the lice. How to get rid of them is the problem. Lice treatment shampoo costs money. Wash all the linens? No washer and dryer, and the laundromat is several miles away. How will you carry all that laundry? And laundromats cost money.

The easiest way to get rid of them is to shave off all your hair. You can kill the bugs, and the eggs have no hair in which to hide. No problem if you're a guy, right? If the children are little, they don't mind. Or if you're an adventurous, young twenty-something who doesn't mind the punk-rock look, you don't mind. But Bonnie? Her beautiful head of hair?

I talk with some of our volunteers at Joe's. "We have to help Bonnie with her hair." Heads nod slowly, then one young man says, "I'll help." I go to the store and buy some of every kind of treatment I can find. Shampoo, spray, powder, and a lice comb. Two rounds of shampoo later, I start combing for the dead bugs and their eggs. The problem is that Bonnie's long hair has matted into dreadlocks. Combing is impossible.

We decide we will have to cut it. I promise her I will leave as much length as I can. I comb, then cut, then comb some more. Each time I cut into a matted clump, live lice fall out. I reach for the spray and shoot 'em with a chemical death ray.

I start this project with my own hair tied up in a bun, short-sleeve shirt, long pants, and latex gloves on my hands—careful to not touch my own hair, in case of transferring an egg to myself. But the lice are everywhere. Falling on the tile floor. Crawling on my arms. Eggs? Normally, you pick an egg or two. Maybe ten. There are globs of eggs the size of marbles. There is no hope of finding every egg, and no hope of preventing the lice from discovering my own scalp.

Then there is the pain. Bonnie sits quietly while I work, but those chemicals burn. Open wounds on her scalp ooze from the bites and scratching. Every once in a while, she winces. Several times I see a tear roll down her cheek. She tells me it doesn't hurt too badly, and I tell her that when we have killed all these nasty buggers, we will take her to the beauty salon for a stylish, new hair cut. She mumbles, "Thank you."

I am not telling this story, so you can know of what *I* did for Bonnie. This is just the set up so you can see what Love *really* looks like. Not the romantic notion but the nitty gritty.

I have done about half of Bonnie's head (and when I say half, I don't mean that all the eggs or even the bugs are out of that half, but that I have completed a good first round), when in walks the young man who volunteered to help.

Nate is a calm guy. It takes a lot to ruffle his feathers, and he often deals with the stress of chaos at Joe's by making dry, witty jokes. His slow grin is the tell for you to guess that he is being sarcastic. He is a recovering drug addict, and he has come to serve and be a part of our community for a while. The idea is that in serving others, he might find more healing and freedom himself. And serve he does. He makes coffee, leads NA meetings, wraps bread, builds shelters for guys who are homeless, gives rides. You name it, he jumps in to help. And now here he is, offering to comb lice out of Bonnie's hair.

He strides into the room, announcing that it is his turn to take over. Bonnie asks him, "Are you sure you want to do this?"

Standing behind her, I try to catch his gaze with my eyeballs wide, telepathing, "Not sure you know what you're getting into here."

He laughs and says, "Of course! Bonnie, you are looking absolutely beautiful!"

Bonnie looks at the floor and says, "Not really."

Nate responds, "Well, you *are* gorgeous, and we're gonna have you *feeling* gorgeous again in no time."

Over the next week, Nate works tirelessly washing and combing every bug and every egg from Bonnie's hair, and all the while he teases her and compliments her. One afternoon, I step in to check on the progress, and Bonnie is talking. She is laughing. Still shy and tentative, but true giggles. "He's funny," she says, "and so nice." The poet Galway Kinnell writes, "Sometimes it's necessary to reteach a thing its loveliness."

Later I thank Nate for his kindness to Bonnie. He says, "Awww. I just decided to shamelessly flirt with her. She doesn't know she's beautiful. She is, and she needs to know it." There was nothing lustful or seedy in Nate's flirtation. It was pure and it was kind. Lust is selfish. Love is kind. Nate saw the deepest pain in Bonnie's soul—not merely the loss of job and embarrassment of lice—but her husband's rejection and her fear that no one would ever want her. His gentle kindness was Jesus to the woman at the well lived out all over again.

Helpless

The most difficult thing I face at Joe's Addiction is an overwhelming feeling of helplessness. Sometimes the Love we give heals and fixes a life, and sometimes it doesn't. Sometimes it is not enough or not soon enough.

Alec comes to our community wounded. He has grown up in the foster care system changing homes at least once a year for most of his life. He lived in 23 different families by the time he turned eighteen and graduated to an adult life he was completely unprepared to face. When we meet him, he has just been released from a three-year prison sentence for having a sexual relationship with a teenage girl. He was nineteen when he committed his crime.

His felony brands him as a sex offender for the rest of his life, printed on his ID in red letters for everyone to see. He cannot find a job. He is living outside, and he cannot even imagine hope. We begin to love Alec. We welcome him into our community. We make sure he has food to eat and transportation to his probation meetings. It takes a few months for Alec to warm up to our friendship and to share his story with us, but when he does his mood seems to improve. He sometimes smiles. He sits and visits with some of us, sometimes. We are glad he has come around.

One day, Alec comes into the shop with his head down. I can tell something is bothering him. When I ask, "What's up?" he tells me he has just learned that his girlfriend—the relationship that had sent him to prison—had his child. Unbeknownst to him, she had been pregnant when police arrested him. He says, "I am a dad." I put my hand on his back, while doubled over in his chair, he sobs his grief. "I'm a sex offender. I'll never be allowed to see my child. I can never have a relationship with her, at least until she turns eighteen. Even then, she might not want to know me." He sits up, looks off into the distance, and says, "I have a daughter. I'm a dad."

I do my best to comfort Alec. Several of us do. But the next morning, one of the guys in the camp comes in with the news that Alec hanged himself from a tree. We are devastated. We earnestly loved him, but in Alec's greatest sadness, no person could offer hope.

CHAPTER 12
ADDICTION

"The Gospel takes away our right forever,
to discriminate between the deserving
and the undeserving poor."

— Dorothy Day

Luther is a very big, very beautiful, African American man who comes to Friday night open mic nights at Joe's Addiction. He towers over everyone and his bright, smiling eyes glow, set against his dark black skin. His smooth voice melts souls. Having grown up in southern black church, he loves to sing gospel music. Luther asks if he can sing in the band on Sundays, and we give him the opportunity.

Luther has spent many years in prison for armed robbery and drugs. His drug of choice is crack cocaine. In prison he stayed clean. He exercised, built his muscles and his focus, and he gained a reputation as a "good guy." He has a winning smile, and the other guys followed his charismatic leadership. I'm sure his size has something to do with his influence as well.

He gets a job soon after he is released, makes monthly payments on his fines and meets responsibilities. Though life after prison is difficult, Luther seems to have the determination it takes to make it on the outside. He works hard. We see him as an example to others and mark him in our minds as leadership potential.

About six months into our relationship with him, on a cold afternoon in December, Luther shows up at Joe's high. He is pacing and ranting words I can't understand. Sweating profusely, big drops run off his face. Sweat has drenched his shirt. He walks in the door and then turns right around and goes back out. He paces the sidewalk, looking up and down the street, paranoid as though someone is after him.

I go to him and ask if I can help. "Is there anything I can do?" He looks at me, eyes piercing, and says, "No, sister. I fucked up. I just fucked up." A few regulars sit drinking coffee and playing cards. They don't need me, so for a while I join Luther's pacing, trying to keep stride alongside him. He talks and talks, but he isn't making much sense except to say again and again, "I fucked up. I fucked up."

It is cold, and I begin to worry about him. I have never dealt with someone in this condition before. I don't know what to do. He is sweating so much, I wonder if this might be an overdose. I don't want him to die. I am in over my head here.

I call 911. I don't tell the dispatcher anything about drugs. I simply describe his condition and say I need assistance. Somehow by the time the paramedics arrive, I have convinced Luther to sit down at a table near the window inside. He keeps watching the cars and looking up and down the street, but he is at least seated.

The paramedics recognize drugs and they are immeasurably kind. One quietly asks Luther directly, "What are you on? What did you take?" and Luther answers straight-faced, "Crack cocaine, Sir." I cringe at his automated response to a uniformed white man.

The paramedics take his blood pressure and measure his pulse. They ask him more questions, and then they tell him they would like to take him to the hospital where doctors can monitor him until he feels better. Luther says forcefully, "No.

I don't want to go to the hospital. I won't go." Again, they try to convince him to go, but he refuses. Calmly, but with eyes flashing, he tells them, "I'm not going to the hospital. The sister here will take care of me."

The paramedics look at me, eyebrows raised. I look at them and then back at Luther. The one who has been so kind pulls me to the side and explains, "We cannot take him to the hospital if he is refusing to go." I ask if Luther is in any danger. He tells me that because he is sweating so much, they are most concerned about dehydration and then hypothermia. I look back at Luther who still sits, a little calmer now, sweat still rolling off his nose, and I say, "Okay. I'll take care of him, but I don't know how. You'll have to tell me what to do."

He tells me to give Luther water, lots of water. "Do your best to make him drink it. And make him walk. It's important he keeps moving. It will help the drugs to move through his system more quickly. Make him walk and drink. Can you do that?" Can I do that? How did I get here? I cannot count the times I have wondered this question. I tell the paramedic I will do my best and I thank him for his kindness to Luther. He promises they will sit outside in the ambulance until they receive another call to go. "If you need us, we'll be right outside."

Somehow, I help that big man to his feet and we start walking. My arm in his, my hand on his massive bicep, I lead him. We pace the room—back and forth, around the furniture, front to back. He holds the glass of water I hand to him. Every few minutes I push it toward his mouth, reminding him to drink. He talks and he talks. More and more makes sense. What had happened?

That morning, he had been watching the news when he saw a report of a robbery at a convenience store on the other side of town. Right there on the television Luther saw the booking photo of his own teenage daughter. His big shoulders hunch, and holding his face in his hands he sobs as he tells me, "She's on the same road I took. I wanted so much more for her. I tried. I was doin' my best to show her I could do it. She didn't have to go down the same road I did. But I couldn't stop her.

What's the use? It don't matter how hard you try. I said, 'Fuck it,' and I went and bought some shit."

He talks. Then I talk. We cry together. And we walk. At some point I notice the ambulance is gone. I don't know what I am supposed to do next. How will I know when he is safe? How long does this kind of thing take?

Then Luther tells me, "I have a rock right here in my pocket." "Cocaine? Right here? In your pocket? In Joe's?" I talk with him about his future, about the choice he has in front of him. I speak hope. I speak plans and dreams. I acknowledge his failure but encourage him to get back up and start again. He becomes quiet. I hope he is listening. Finally he says, "Let's go to the bathroom and flush it right now." I am thrilled. Victory.

As we walk through the door into our tiny bathroom, it crosses my mind this might not be the safest thing for me to be doing. There are other people in the shop, but they could never make it in time if he attacks me. There is no turning back now. We are there. I pray, "God, help me" (I had not stopped praying since the moment Luther walked in a couple of hours before). I want this. I want to be a part of helping this man flush his drugs, to start his life again.

In one swift and nimble motion, Luther pulls a loaded pipe from his pocket, puts it to his mouth and clicks his lighter. He puffs two times, takes a deep breath and leans his head back. I am confused. It happens so fast I'm not sure what is going on. Then suddenly I am overwhelmed with emotions. Anger replaces any fear I had. He has tricked me. He had no intention of flushing his drugs.

I step back from him and open the bathroom door. Standing in the doorway, I say, "If this is what you have decided to do, that is your choice, but you cannot do it here." "Aww. Come on, sister." "No. You cannot do this here." He stands up, and for a moment I think, "Here it comes."

Then he puts the pipe in his pocket. As he passes, he puts his hand on my shoulder and says, "Thank you for everything, sister. I love you." He lumbers out of the bathroom, out the front

door of Joe's, down the sidewalk, down the street. I crumble
to the floor and bawl.

I only see Luther once after this day, months later. He is
downtown, miles away from Joe's Addiction. He still towers
above, but his muscles are gone. His skin hangs on his bones.
He smiles and asks, "How you doin', sister?" I tell him I am
fine and ask how he is. He answers, "Well, you know."

The day of Luther's drug crisis, I cry out to God, "Don't
send me any more drug addicts, if you won't send me help for
them!"

Two weeks later, a lady calls me. She says she has heard
about Joe's Addiction and is a leader in a Celebrate Recovery
group at a big Southern Baptist Church nearby. She wonders
if we might need some help for addiction recovery.

The woman explains how the group works. She tells me
about the materials and that they require the participants to
purchase the books ($30/person). They would also need to
come to the meetings once a week at their church. She says
everyone is welcome, and they would love to have people from
our Joe's Addiction community attend.

I tell her I am grateful she has called and I believe she is
the answer to my desperate prayers. I then explain to her that
most of the people who need her program are living outside
and have no means of transportation. It would be difficult for
them to make it to a once a week meeting at their church. She
responds, "Well, we're only a few miles away from you. I'm
sure they can walk if they're serious about their recovery." This
church is an eight-mile-round-trip walk from us.

I then tell her, because most of them are unemployed, that
they cannot afford the books the program requires. She explains
it is an important piece of the program for the addicts to pay
the cost. It provides accountability and tests their resolve. "I
understand," I tell her, "Truly I do. We agree. We do our best to
help people help themselves, and we understand codependency
and enabling." I suggest perhaps they could reduce the cost.
She responds that would be up to us. If we want to purchase
books for our people and then offer them at a reduced rate, we

can do that, "As long as you charge them something. It's really important they pay for the materials themselves."

I thank the woman for her offer and then I ask her, "Out of curiosity, are you an addict, ma'am. Are you in recovery?" She says, "Oh yes, I am. I am a recovering workaholic. One of the great things about CR is that it is open to people with *any* kind of addiction. It doesn't just have to be substance abuse."

I would like to be able to say I hung up the phone simply deflated, but that is not who I am. I was livid. I may have dropped a few F-bombs. My addicted friends would rather use drugs than eat. Walk four miles each direction to attend a meeting? That's not going to happen. A pack of cigarettes costs $4. There is no way they can stay sober without their cigarettes. Pay for recovery study books? Where would they store them even if they bought them? Keeping their clothing dry is a big enough task.

We since have hosted Narcotics Anonymous meetings, but drug addiction continues to be one of our most difficult and frustrating challenges. It is hard for those of us who have not experienced addiction to empathize with the struggle. Judgment often shouts, "Just stop! Quit!" I have even heard a pastor say, "It's not that hard to quit. Just don't put it in your mouth." The ironic thing is that this pastor was obese. I restrained myself, but I wanted to shout at him, "Just don't put it in *your* mouth!" Addiction is a killer. If the substances don't themselves do the killing, more often than not futility and shame do the job. The suffering is worse than any illness I have encountered.

House of Hope

A young woman comes to church and sits through the whole service, only because she wants to speak to me after. Her boyfriend has brought her to ask if I can help her. As I ask about her life, she points to the back of the room and asks if we can go where others cannot hear. She then says, "I heard you could help me get into rehab." She is a mess. Fidgeting. Can't stand still. The unmistakable sores from the picking of buggy, crawling skin cover her face and arms. And those hollow eyes.

As I begin to look for the phone numbers of rehab programs in the city, I ask her questions.

"What is your name?"

"Jamie."

"That's my name too," I say.

"How old are you?"

"Twenty-five."

"What are you using?" I ask.

"Meth."

"How long?"

She says, "Years."

"What makes you want to stop now?"

"My daughter," she says, "I promised her."

"How many children do you have?"

"They're 8, 6 and 4." she says. "One is in this city, one is with these people, the youngest is in another place."

"Do you think you'll ever be able to get them back?" I ask.

"I signed them over. . ."

"Oh girl."

Then the tears fall.

"Do you have a place to stay?"

"No, I'm sleeping outside."

"Some of these rehab programs require you to go to Detox before they'll take you," I explain. "Do you think you'll need to detox?"

"Yes."

The problem is, Detox only has a few beds available for indigents. The best of these programs require potential participants to call them every morning for five days in a row before they will enroll them. They do this because people often call while they are on a terrifying drug trip, begging to be admitted, only to not show up after they come down. Understandably, treatment programs want to be sure a person is serious about getting clean. I know there is absolutely no way this girl could make a call every morning. She has no idea where she will sleep each night, maybe outside, maybe in a "trap house." She won't even know what time it is. She wants to get sober now, but if she is actively using, her resolve will fade with the next high.

Once the faucet has turned, Jamie cannot stop crying. She says, "It's the paranoia. I just keep thinking they're coming to get me."

"Who?" I ask.

"I don't know."

I make sure her boyfriend sees the list of numbers I'm giving to her and I ask him to help her make the calls. I tell them to please come back if she needs a ride, or if we can help make sure she gets in. Hugging her and thanking me, he says he will.

I never see Jamie again, but I post her story on Facebook, along with a dream I have of purchasing the house that sits behind Joe's Addiction. The "for sale" sign went up in the yard more than a year before, and I had told John I wanted to look at it. The realtor had given us a tour of the small three-bedroom house, and John had asked me what I wanted to do with it. I had told him I didn't know, but I knew it should be part of our Joe's Addiction community. He had smiled and said, "Well, how 'bout we wait until you have a little clearer picture before we start trying to figure out how in the world we would get the money to buy this house."

Months have gone by now. The sign still stands in the yard. Every time I see it, the feeling grows. It is ours. I just know it. The day I meet Jamie I know what it is for. If we can provide a place to stay, even if only for a few days while she waits for a rehab program, maybe—just maybe—her chances of success will be that much greater.

John is in India, so I can't even ask him what he thinks. I post her story, and within twenty-four hours, $10,000 has been donated for the house. A week later, I am teaching a class in a large church in Texas. My lesson topic is God's heart for the poor. I tell stories of Joe's Addiction and hope to inspire good church people to move out of their comfort zone and into relationship with people who live in poverty.

At the end of the class, a man asks me, "What do you need?" I think he's offering to help me dismantle my resource table, so I point at a box he can help me carry. He says, "No. I'm saying, I have money. What do you need?" I tell him Jamie's story and my dream of buying the house. He says, "I am an architect. That is what I do, create buildings. Tell me how much you need, and the house and any money you need for repairs is yours."

I have many dreams. Lots of them are hair-brained ideas I could never pull off. Some of them might be God's dreams, but the timing is just not yet here. One way to know for sure if your dreams are God's is if the resources fall out of the sky right into your lap. We buy and fix up that little run-down house and dedicate it as our House of Hope.

Newbies Enter the House

Two years later, we are having a house meeting. Once a week, the staff, recent graduates and the current HOH girls meet together for dinner and to talk about life, how we're doing, concerns, plans, etc. Two new girls have spent the week moving in, attending two NA meetings a day, visiting doctors and counselors and becoming adjusted to the daily times of meditation, chai making and garden weeding. It's been a busy week, and I am sure they are more than a bit overwhelmed by the newness—of place and people.

We fill our plates and take our seats in the crowded, little HOH living room. Marilyn and I choose the chairs, our recently graduated girl scrunches together with the two newbies on the couch, and Ren, our House Mom, takes the floor, saying, "I wanna be able to look at 'em." Silence hangs in the room, as we stuff our faces with drippy, chicken tacos and ice cold soda. Nervousness. These new girls don't know what to expect. They don't know us yet. And we don't know them. Who are these ladies? What will they do? What will they expect from us? Someone breaks the awkwardness with a light story and a joke, but we can all feel the uncertainty in the air. What's coming?

When our plates are mostly empty, I start the serious talk. I welcome them and tell them how glad we are they are here. Then I ask the two new girls to share with us anything they would like us to know about themselves. I assure them they don't have to tell anything they don't want to tell.

One of the newbies, shrugs. "I guess I'll go first." She bluntly confesses her IV drug addiction to heroin and meth, her previous attempts to get clean, and her run-ins with the law. She has only spent two months sober in the last ten years. "The longest damn months of my life!" This go around she only has eleven days clean, and those are because she was in jail before she came to us.

She tells these parts of her story as a matter of fact, and even with hardened smiles, but when she speaks of her children, her tone softens. She pauses. Tears fill her eyes. Then she tells of their daddy, an abusive, fellow drug addict, her attempts to run from him, and the many times she went back because she needed him, and the tears begin to fall. Around the room, heads nod and knowing looks are exchanged. "I only wanna be a good mama," she cries, and five voices declare, "You will be."

She continues, and now the words flow quickly, "This is my last chance. I don't even know why the judge gave me another chance. I think God must have a purpose for my life. I'm so grateful for this place and for you ladies. You're all so beautiful and so strong." She turns to the other newbie and says to her, "You are included in those here who are beautiful and strong!"

Taking this as her cue, the second girl begins. It is a tale of the last two years of living on the streets, being taken advantage of by her own children who steal her money for drugs, her own drug use and mental health struggles. The night before she came to HOH she slept by the train tracks. She says, "This is a new beginning for me."

Our recent graduate is shy. It took months for her to open up, but oh, she has come a long way. She jumps in to tell her tale of "been there done that" and her own recovery through House of Hope. She says, "If it wasn't for this group of ladies here, I'd maybe be dead. I don't know where I'd be." She tells the girls they are now her sisters, and she will be available to them, and in fact —she needs them. Then she asks, "So when are you comin' to my house for dinner?"

When the girls have said all they want to say, I explain to them this is a safe place, not that we will never hurt one another—this is met with "Oh, we wills!" from other girls in the room—but we are committed to love each other no matter what. We will be here for one another and help each other through.

Marilyn tells them soon she will share with them her own story, that it is a story of terrible abuse and many years of running away from God. "I only decided to come back to God about three years ago." She expresses our need for honesty, the only way to recovery, and she thanks the girls for their openness with us.

Ren, their new advocate and best friend, finishes our meeting by telling the new girls a parable. "You have just been dropped off in the middle of the desert. You have no idea where you are. You don't know how to get home. You are totally lost. Suddenly, two men appear before you. One is dressed in a fancy suit and tie. He has slicked-back hair and a briefcase in his hand. He says, 'Come with me. I will show you the way.' The other is a wild eyed, crazy looking, tribal guy. He has a bone in his nose and a spear in his hand. He, too, says, 'Come with me. I'll show you the way.'" Ren asks, "Which one do you follow?"

One of the ladies blurts out, "The guy in the suit will just pimp you out! Go with the crazy tribal guy!" Everyone laughs.

Ren says, "Yes. That's the one you should follow. He has been there; he knows the terrain. He looks like he belongs. He knows the way home. These women here have been through similar things. Some the abuse, some the addiction, some the crimes. They have received healing and new life, and they will lead you to new life. They will show you the way home."

Two years later, after creating a home of her own and reunification with her kids, one of these women posts on Facebook:

"Someone said to me the other day, 'You'll get back in the swing of things.' They were talking about parenting. Only I never had a good swing of things as a mom. Only time I wanted to go to my oldest son's school functions is if I had a handful of tabs before. I didn't want to sit and do homework unless I had a bump first.

"As far as my other three are concerned my addiction only got worse after they were born. I mean, I had three babies in diapers and I needed to be awake 24/7. So I started shooting up five times a day. Before they woke up, after breakfast, nap time, when my mom got home, dinner time, bedtime . . . And then when they weren't busy, and I was hiding in the bathroom. Meanwhile I never had a job, but I always managed diapers and dope. I was a happy, functional addict and a somewhat decent mom, until I wasn't anymore. And that's when they were taken out of my care.

"Even that didn't stop me. I showed up to visitations detoxing, and I was high as soon as I got home. Couldn't pass a UA, couldn't hold down a job, was in an abusive relationship, because I needed someone to love me, and I truly believed that was all I was worth. I realized either the drugs were gonna kill me, or he was, so I finally left.

"I've been trying to learn how to be a functional human being again, and it's really hard some days. But I promise you I don't wanna get back into the swing of things. I want a new way of life! I desperately seek it when I feel like I do today.

"I am so grateful for everyone's faith in me. It builds my own. I don't feel like I deserve anything. I feel just about worthless. But God has trusted me to take care of his kids, so I have to suit up and show up. They definitely deserve everything good this life has to offer.

"God, show me the way. I'm ready to do the footwork."

We are finding the key—maybe the only hope—to recovery from addiction is community. Without the support of a group of people, addicts cannot make the journey to recovery. How I wish it was enough for them to pray a prayer or be bopped on the head by a spirit-filled preacher, but it just isn't. We believe in the twelve-step programs of Alcoholics Anonymous and Narcotics Anonymous. The meetings provide not only accountability, but a safe, nonjudgmental place where people can be real. It is in this safety where the roots of addiction can be acknowledged. The twelve steps are a proven and profound process that address each person's addiction at its deepest source.

We also have found that Love heals. The craving of every human soul is to be loved unconditionally. An environment of no-matter-what Love provides a foundation that gives both the freedom to mess up (which is guaranteed) and the support to get back up and start again.

Angela

Angela comes to House of Hope with the goal of getting clean from drugs and regaining custody of her children. She is an outgoing, charming Hispanic beauty. Angela's vibrant energy lights up every room. She is loud and boisterous. She loves to sing and dance, and her humor keeps all of us laughing. Many times, her jokes lift sadness and depression from the House.

We walk with Angela through her recovery and the many requirements placed upon her by Drug Court. Community members give rides, hold her hand, supervise visits with her kids, take her to drug tests and classes. Angela works hard. She fights her addiction by focusing on her love for her children. Angela moves into her own house. She is working and paying her own rent. She is granted overnight visits with her kids—at her own home—and she is headed toward full reunification with her family.

Then Angela is diagnosed with cervical cancer. It is bad. We watch as Angela sinks into depression. Drugs had once robbed her of life; now chemotherapy steals her physical and emotional strength. The question, "What's the use?" becomes her mantra, and she returns to the drugs. She quits attending meetings. Quits jumping through state-required hoops. Angela's cancer metastasizes to her brain, where a large tumor swells her head.

Many in the Narcotics Anonymous community attend Angela's funeral. As we gather at her gravesite, the sadness is not only the grief of Angela's death, but the awareness of the millions of souls who have battled addiction. Angela fought hard. We cheered her on. We loved her to the end, and we will never forget her shaking her booty, keeping us in stitches, as she sang at the top of her lungs, "You know I'm all about that bass, all about that bass."

"If you want to understand the good news that Jesus offers for the poor in a particular place, you first have to discover what the bad news looks like."

— Joyce Rees

CHAPTER 13
SLOUGH OF DESPOND

"It is not enough for us to talk about love,
Love is one of the pivotal points of the Christian faith.
There is another side called justice.
And justice is really love in calculation.
Justice is love correcting that which
revolts against love."

— Martin Luther King, Jr.

Melvin comes to us fresh out of prison where he has been locked up for eight years. He is young, too young. The state suspended his sentence and released him on probation, which means he is under supervision and owes regular fees for his probation costs. Gaining employment is difficult. Few companies hire felons, and because Melvin can't pay rent, he is living on the streets.

Melvin hears about Joe's Addiction from other folks living outside, and he starts hanging out with us. I am happy to have another African American join our predominantly white community. His toothy smile and cheerful demeanor not only make him pleasant to be around, but his presence also helps bridge racial tensions. He appreciates the food and friends and he helps out, washing dishes, sweeping floors, carrying out trash. He jumps first when something heavy needs carrying. Melvin attends church at Joe's every Sunday. He likes the music, and he bows his head and folds his hands when we pray.

Melvin decides he wants to apply for a job at Burger King. He has heard they might hire felons, and the walking distance is about a mile and a half from his camp. He can manage that. But Melvin has no ID. No birth certificate and no Social Security card. The state releases people from prison and expects them to pay court costs and fines, but gives them nothing to start the process of looking for employment. Identification papers cost money, take time to receive, and one has to know how to apply for them. Prisons in Oklahoma are privately owned. Someone is making money off of housing each inmate. Making it likely for people to go back to prison is "good business."

The Joe's Addiction community helps Melvin track down and pay for his papers. Then he goes to Burger King and asks for an application. The manager tells him all applications need to be filled out online and gives him a web address.

Melvin has never heard of such a thing as an online application and he has no access to a computer. I know people reading this might comment that there are computers available for public use at the library. Melvin wouldn't know this, and even if he did, finding the library would not be an easy task and would mean money for bus fare.

I give Melvin access to our computer at Joe's to fill out an application and it becomes clear he has no idea what to do. Melvin's family could never have owned a computer and the inner-city school he attended did not have computers for student use. He looks at the screen with a blank stare.

I sit down at the keyboard and walk him through the long process. He answers the questions, and I type for him. The "test" part of the application takes half an hour to complete. Questions about whether he thinks it is okay to steal from an unfair boss, how he would handle conflicts with fellow employees, and what he would do if he doesn't know how to do his job. These questions elicit adamant responses from him.

He belts out his answers with no doubt in his mind. He does his best, and, at one point comments, "I think their tryna trick me!" He shakes his head and thanks me, saying, "There is no way I coulda done 'at by myself."

The next day, Melvin walks back to Burger King, where the manager tells him she has received the application and now there are forms to fill out online so she can hire him. She assigns him a username and password, which he writes down and brings to me. We sit down again to fill out the forms in a list of eight different links. Green check marks appear beside each one we complete. Until we get to the last link. It is a PDF. I know how to download the document, fill in the blanks and save it, but there is no way to upload it back to the website. No green check mark appears. I don't know what to do.

I suggest he call Burger King to ask the manager. He does and is told she is busy and can't help him at the moment. The next day he walks again. She tells him she cannot process his application until he completes the online forms. He tells her it doesn't work, the last part won't finish. He doesn't know how to explain the problem to her.

Discouraged, he comes back to Joe's Addiction, and I am not there. He borrows someone else's computer, and since he saw me doing it, he thinks he knows how to get back on there and try again. He can't make it work.

Another day passes and the next time I see Melvin I ask him about his application. He says, "I don't know what happened, but now the whole thing is missing." How could that be? I log back in, and sure enough it is gone. This time, I go with Melvin to Burger King. We speak with a nice lady employee. She says the manager is out but gives us some advice about the website.

Back at Joe's, we try her suggestions to no avail. He calls Burger King again, and the exasperated manager gives him a phone number to call for help with the website. We call. Somehow, Melvin has created a second account. It is an internet/technical mess. After fifteen minutes on the phone, the woman suggests we just start over.

When I hang up the phone, I let out a few choice cuss words. Melvin laughs. "Pastor! Don't be angry. It'll be okay." I sigh, and we start over.

There are even more details, but I will just say it takes us two whole weeks to finish and submit a completed application to Burger King. Melvin grins when he finally comes through the door with the announcement he got the job. He can start whenever he acquires black pants and black, non slip shoes. The community at Joe's Addiction supplies them. When I say, "the community at Joe's Addiction," I mean the folks who hang out and do life together. Many of these people live on next to nothing, but when a need like this arises, they pool their funds and help one another.

Melvin goes to work. He is a good worker. He is punctual. He works hard. He smiles at both customers and bosses who tell him what to do. It is great to have money in his pocket. He is still living outside in a tent, and life is still hard, but he can pay for bus fare to and from his probation meetings, and life starts to feel hopeful. His hope inspires some of the other guys to look for work. Melvin carries himself with pride, and his joy brings life to our little community.

About two months into his new employment, Melvin wakes up late on a Saturday morning. He looks at the time. He is going to be late for work. He feels awful. He remembers when he went to sleep last night, he wasn't feeling so good. Now, his body aches, his head hurts, and he is pretty sure he has a fever. He is supposed to be at work in ten minutes.

He calls Burger King and tells the manager he is sick. He says, "I can still make it there if you want me to. I'll be a little late, but I don't know if you want me to come. I'm really sick, and I think I have a fever." The manager replies, "Don't bother to come in. I told you when I hired you if you were going to miss a shift for any reason you need to call at least two hours ahead, so we have time to find somebody else. You didn't do that. So don't bother coming back at all."

I watch as Melvin descends into the darkness of depression. Several times I offer to help him with another application, but

Melvin just shrugs. He says, "It's not worth it." His probation officer becomes angry with him because he isn't paying his fees. She puts extra restrictions on him and tells him to get a job, or she will send him back to prison. He quits going to the meetings.

He comes to Joe's Addiction less frequently, and we miss him. When I ask the other guys in the camp about him, they fill me in. He has started using drugs and is running with some bad dudes. The last time I see Melvin, I ask him, "What's going on, man? What are you doing?" He says, "I don't know. It's just stupid. I don't give a shit. They can come get me if they want me." And "they" do. The police arrest Melvin as he is walking down the street one night. He is back in prison where he will sit for more years.

I did not know Melvin when he committed his original crime. I do know he was twenty-two when he was convicted. How many of us did stupid stuff when we were young adults? I am not excusing Melvin's behavior. I believe we should hold people accountable, and we must keep society safe from future harm. But I also know Melvin was a child when I met him. He had never grown up. He didn't know how to do adult life. Who knows what Melvin's parents did or did not teach him? Melvin spent eight years in prison. Then the conditions of his "life on the outside" made it impossible for him to succeed.

Sometimes the hole of despair is just too deep. Hope cannot reach that low, or maybe a person cannot hold on to the edge of Hope from inside the crater of despair. Martin Luther King Jr. said, "It is a cruel injustice to tell a bootless man to pull himself up by his bootstraps." Dr. King also inspired us with a dream, but we are still so far from his dream being fulfilled.

The ATV Incident

Otis has both physical and mental challenges that have made life difficult for him. He cannot work and receives a disability check which helps. But life is complicated.

Police arrest Otis for cruelty to animals. Otis would never harm an animal. Quite the opposite. He adores them. The problem is he has taken in so many stray dogs his small travel trailer has become—well, foul. Quite literally, uninhabitable. For dogs and humans. The neighbors in his RV park report him to the police. The time in jail and defaulting on his lot fee cause him to lose his home. It takes months to pay off the fines. Putting together deposit money and showing enough income make new housing impossible for him. He moves into a tent outside.

Because he pays no rent and no utility expenses, his monthly allotment of food stamps is $16. His disability check doesn't go very far. He buys a four-wheel ATV and trailer to help transport the aluminum cans and other metal he recycles. We tell him again and again not to ride that thing on the street. We explain to him it isn't street legal, and the police will give him a ticket if they catch him. He says he understands.

One night he becomes confused. His mind sometimes doesn't process things well. He is pushing the four-wheeler through the long parking lot which is an okay place to ride. When he comes to the intersection of two main streets, he climbs on it and rides it through the intersection. A police car is sitting right there.

The officer asks to see his driver's license. He pulls ID out of his pocket. When the officer sees it is expired, he arrests Otis, impounds his vehicle and then charges him with four criminal misdemeanors. 1. Driving an ATV on the street. 2. Driving without a valid driver's license. 3. No insurance. 4. No working headlight or taillights.

Otis sits in county jail for a week, and then they let him out. I ask him about the possibility of fines. He tells me they didn't give him any paperwork or tell him he owes anything. Probably not accurate, but life at Joe's Addiction is busy. Lots of daily urgencies. We all forget about his case.

A couple of months later, the police arrest him. He has not paid the fines associated with this ATV incident. Again, he sits in jail for a week, and they let him out. This time I look through all his paperwork. Nothing in the paperwork states the amount of fines, but there is a date to appear before a judge. Otis says, "I want a public defender."

"Otis," I tell him, "It won't do you any good."

But he insists. It is his right, right? He feels some of these charges are not fair, and he wants to contest them. I understand. I help him fill out all the paperwork.

He goes before the judge who deems a public defender unnecessary. He removes two of the charges and requires Otis to pay a $110 fine. Okay. He can do this.

But there is one more piece. Jail fees. A person should be able to either pay the fine or do the time. But no. When someone sits out a fine in jail (which counts as $78/day), the county then charges the Town of Valley Brook for housing their inmate. That charge amounts to $42 per day. From the city's perspective, why should they have to pay for his crime? That is not just. So the city then issues a bill to the criminal. If he is not able or forgets to pay, they will issue a warrant for his arrest. Otis owes a $110 fine plus $294 in jail fees for the ATV incident.

Poverty breeds poverty. People in our Joe's Addiction community are in an endless cycle of going into and out of jail. Homelessness intimidates and threatens the housed, and for those who are already experiencing homelessness, the climb to permanent housing is impossibly high to reach. They have no ability to plan or save for the future. The struggle for hope is hopeless.

Equal Housing

The systems of injustice infuriate me. Justice and fairness are values that rank as some of the highest for my personality type. I want to see people treated fairly, and when they are not, I find anger rising in my soul. When the injustice comes from "good church people," it is all the more maddening. Christians sometimes fall on the wrong side of the line of justice.

A young family in our Joe's Addiction community faces a crisis. A family with four beautiful little children. When you have grown up in poverty and drug addiction, all you are qualified to do is minimum-wage work. One parent only has a third-grade education. (Where were the truancy officers to require her to go to school?) The other parent went to high school through junior year, but never finished. One minimum-wage salary at Pizza Hut is just not enough to pay the bills. It's just not.

I know it can be frustrating to help folks who don't want to "help themselves." I get that. But this little family is not like that. There are so many life skills they want to gain—from parenting to financial management, from marital conflict resolution to GED studies. They are a joy to pastor.

When the electric bill is too high for them to pay, they come to me and we discuss how they are using electricity. They do not understand leaving the lights on or running the air conditioner is costing so much money. They follow every bit of counsel I give them. And the next month, they rejoice that they can pay the bill. They are learning.

But did I say minimum wage is not enough to pay the bills? It's just not. One of the kids gets sick. They have to buy medicine. They use food stamps to splurge and buy cake and ice cream for the son's birthday. Now they don't have enough for real food. A daughter's shoes get too small. Have to buy new ones. Need to give "So-and-So" some money to pay for gas because he gave a ride to work. Mom has a urinary tract infection, needs an antibiotic. One thing after another. Never enough. And you can imagine the stress.

The plumbing has a leak, and the landlord will not fix it. The water bill is too high. They only make a partial payment, so the company shuts off their water. Next month they will be able to pay the remainder, but they do not have enough to pay the deposit to turn it back on. Plus the landlord will not fix the plumbing, anyway. They have to move out.

A relative takes them in with the caveat it only be while they look for another place to live. A family of six at the mother-in-law's can't last long. They have to find a new place.

We search with them. They will need help with the deposit money. Some places we find require evidence of monthly wages being three times the amount of the rent. Are you kidding me? And places they can afford? . . . the environment . . . drug deals and stabbings happening right next door.

There is one more piece to this story. What I have not told you is that this family has two mamas. A lesbian couple with four kids? Yes. They have a story. We all have a story. What I can tell you about these mamas is they are some of the best mamas I have ever known. The kids are well-behaved, kind, clean, obedient. I watch them put their children to bed, read them a bedtime story, pray for them and speak a guided relaxation meditation that helps the kids calm down to go to sleep. They rise early and put their kids on the school bus, attend parent-teacher conferences, help them do their homework. They hang a chore chart on the wall in their living room, teaching their kids responsibility and accountability. These are good mamas, and they love their babies.

In the search for housing, again and again, we watch landlords start out saying "Yes, we have available units," but then change their minds when they discover the family wanting to rent is a lesbian couple. Some give no explanation, just deny their application. But others openly say, "We don't want your kind here."

These are stories you might remember from the Jim Crow era: black families who could not find housing, interracial couples who were denied. Landlords used the same reasoning back then. "The Bible says mixing races is wrong. The government can't make me violate my religious convictions." We think back to these conditions as appalling, but here we are again. Laws and petitions are before state congresses and federal courts appealing for the rights of religious people to deny housing to families with four little children. And Christians are proudly defending these laws. A coalition of pastors contacted me, asking me to sign a petition and to help them advocate for this law in the State of Oklahoma. They assumed I would be on their side. Strange, when Jesus was always on the side of the oppressed.

It is easy to hold to and demand the "religious right" to discriminate, until you know this beautiful family. The discussion remains theoretical, distant, a theological truth to stand for, a conviction to die for. Until "they" become people to you. Until "they" become your friends. Until "they" become your family. More than all of this, until we belong to each other we will always be "us" and "them." In the Beloved Chaos—the Kingdom of God—there is no "us" and "them." There is only us.

God Shows Up In Court

Forklift, who was shot in the head, then beat in the head with a baseball bat, and then began fighting lymphoma, has to go to court. He ran a stop sign three years ago and never paid the ticket. A few months before this, Foster (Pastor-Wanna-Be, Now Full-Fledged Minister) took him to court to face a warrant that had been issued for this ticket. Seeing his disabled condition, and hearing he had applied for Social Security Disability, the judge issued an extension. Now the date has come for him to return to court and pay his $439 fine.

Foster is not available to take him this time, so we meet Sunday night to exchange all the paperwork, debrief about his case, and find out the details of when and where I am supposed to go. Foster tells me I should be at the courthouse before 9:00 a.m., when the morning session will start.

I have to back up . . . we have helped Forklift apply for disability. He was shot in the head. He lives disoriented, outside, doesn't know what day it is, requires help to find his way to the coffee shop every day, is practically blind and in constant pain. His condition was well documented in the application, along with multiple testimonies given from medical personnel. However, Social Security denied his application in a letter that stated, "We believe you are still capable of doing certain kinds of work."

I have been around this block quite a few times now. This is standard procedure. They almost always deny the initial application. The disabled person must hire an attorney to make an appeal, who will, of course, take a percentage of the first check when Social Security awards it.

This day, I awake early and drive to Joe's Addiction to find Forklift. I have told him to meet me at 8:00 a.m., and he has asked some of the other guys in camp to make sure he is up and ready. When I pull into the parking lot, he isn't there. I'm not surprised. I slowly drive around the neighborhood until I find him. He is lying on a sidewalk. I pull up next to him and jump out of the car. He immediately sits up and begins to apologize.

"Oh man," he says, "I'm sorry. I even put on my Sunday shirt, but now I got it all dirty." Forklift has just received his second round of chemo. Somehow, he has awakened at the right time, put on his best clothes and started the walk to Joe's Addiction, but he is just too weak to make it. The dude is living outside. While in cancer treatment. (You might wonder why. Why hasn't someone taken him into their home? I know it is hard to understand, but his past gang affiliation as an enforcer makes it impossible for any of us in our Joe's Community to take him in.)

We drive to the courthouse, park and begin the slow walk. I laugh to myself at how we must look. Forklift is an enormous man. I am a tiny woman. As we walk, I keep my hand on his arm, to support him and to guide him in the right direction. I wonder if he stumbles and falls, what am I expecting to do? There will be no way for me to catch him. He will crush me.

We make it to the check-in counter, and I present his paperwork. The woman says, "His appointed time for court is this afternoon at 3:30 p.m. in Courtroom 1." Really? Seriously, Foster? It is right there in the paperwork. I should have looked at it myself. All that effort to get here, and we are here at the wrong time.

Then I remember Forklift has a blood work appointment in the afternoon. I ask the woman, "Is there any way he can see the judge this morning?" I explain his medical situation.

She tells me to go to a different courtroom downstairs, to wait our turn, to explain our situation and see what they can do.

After a long, slow walk, we make it to Courtroom 2, but the door is locked. A lady on a bench tells me they will open soon, so we sit down. We wait forty-five minutes. The doors finally open, and they let the now small crowd enter. When they call our number we go forward to a court clerk. I think, "Hmmm. He looks familiar."

The court clerk is not curt or short with us. Just doing his job. I explain our time problem, and he says, "So you need to ask the judge for an extension, because you can't pay your fine today." I start to explain more, and he repeats, "So you need to ask the judge for an extension, because you can't pay your fine today." Again I think, "He looks familiar," and I look at his name tag. I say, "Marcus Johnson, I know you."

He tilts his head, looks at me, and says, "I don't think I know you."

I say, "I'm Jamie Zumwalt."

"JAMIE ZUMWALT?! You don't look the same at all!" (which kinda hurts my feelings).

I have not seen this man in over twenty years. We attended the same church back then. He starts loudly inquiring, "How have you been? What's goin' on? Are you still running that coffee shop?"

I tell him, "Yes, I am. In fact this man right here is from our coffee shop community."

He opens the banister gate and says, "Come right over here and sit down."

We sit down with him at a desk where after hearing our story and looking through the paperwork showing Forklift's Social Security appeal, he says, "There is no reason this man should have to pay this fine. I'm gonna help you." He takes out a piece of paper and asks my friend detailed questions.

"Do you have any income?"

"No."

"Do you own a car?"

"No."

"Do you have any credit cards?"

"No."

I interrupt and remind him Forklift lives outside. He is homeless—he has nothing.

He says, "I know, but I have to be thorough here." He continues with his questions.

"How much do you think your belongings are worth?" Forklift looks at me. I shrug.

Marcus Johnson says, "Okay, how 'bout this? If you were to sell all your clothing in a yard sale, how much do you think they'd sell for?"

Forklift says, "I have three pairs of clothes, and to be honest I think one of them might be moldy now from getting wet."

Marcus says, "Okay, so zero," and he writes it down. He points at my friend's size thirteen feet and asks, "How much do you think your shoes are worth?"

Forklift says, "These are my buddy's shoes. He loaned 'em to me for court today."

Marcus says, "So those shoes aren't even yours?"

"Nope."

"Okay, so zero," and he writes it down.

"How about your tent and sleeping bag?"

Forklift says, "My tent got burned down and all my stuff got burned too. I sleep in the tin can."

Marcus smiles and says, "So I'm assuming that means you don't have any appliances either," holding his pen over a check box on the form. Forklift and I burst out laughing.

After he has asked all the questions, Marcus tells us, "Now you gonna go back upstairs to Courtroom 1, and when the judge calls your name, you go and stand in front of him." He looks at me and says, "You approach the judge with him. I can't guarantee what the judge will do. He may decide when he receives disability, he will need to go ahead and pay this fine, so he'd give an extension. But I'm hoping when he sees all I have written here, he will just waive the fine and dismiss your case."

Then Marcus starts to talk. He catches me up on the last twenty years of his own life, tells me of some current challenges he is facing, and asks me to pray for him. I look up several times at the other people in the courtroom. The whole room is waiting while Marcus chats with us. We thank him again and again, and I promise to pray for him.

Upstairs in Courtroom 1, it is quiet and intimidating. Before the judge enters, the court clerk solemnly explains the rules. No cell phones. No conversations. Go out in the hall if you need to talk. Respect the judge.

"All rise."

By the time Forklift works his way to his feet, the judge has already said, "Be seated," and we are the only ones now standing. I help him sit back down, and then we wait, as the judge hears multiple cases before ours.

Did I mention Forklift has brain damage? Even before his injuries, he was not the kindest person, and he certainly did not have any social etiquette or charm. And now . . . Forklift cannot whisper. He has opinions and comments about each person who walks past us to approach the judge. "Wow. That woman has broad shoulders." He looks at her and then looks right and left at his own shoulders. I nod and put my finger to my lips, reminding him to be quiet.

A woman in front of us is holding a tiny, newborn baby. The baby begins to fuss, and Forklift says, "I love babies." He begins "cooing" and "awwing" at the baby. The woman is three rows in front of us. He says, "Your baby is so cute." She doesn't know whether to thank him or to glare at him. I keep looking at the judge who is speaking quietly to the person standing in front of his bench, wondering if he might at any minute scold Forklift.

The court clerk calls the next name. Jessica Something. The woman stands and walks to the front, and Forklift says, "Oh my god. I thought that woman was a man." I know the judge is going to throw us out of court. But he doesn't even look up from the papers in his hands.

Finally, the judge calls Forklift's legal name. We go forward. Forklift does his best to appear respectful. When the judge asks him his name, he remembers to put "sir" on the end of his answer.

The judge looks at me and asks, "Who are you?" I tell him I am this man's pastor, and I am here to help him be in the right place at the right time. I also explain when Social Security awards him disability, either I or another leader in our church community will be his payee, and we can ensure he pays this fine.

The judge turns the pages that include his Social Security appeal, evidence of his disabilities and current cancer treatment, and the document Marcus filled out downstairs. Then he looks up at my friend and says, "I see no reason why you need to pay this fine. As of today, your balance with this court is 'zero.'"

Forklift thanks the judge and then turns to me and bellows, "Why does this kinda stuff happen to you all the time?"

The day before this, Forklift had been contemplating suicide. He told me he could see no reason he should keep going. And honestly, I had no good answer for him. As we drive back to Joe's Addiction, he says, "I don't know why God still has me here. God keeps doin' stuff for me. Doesn't make one bit of sense. But I beat the gunshot wound. I beat the baseball bat. And now I'm gonna beat this cancer."

Sometimes God shows up as a merciful judge because that is precisely what God is like.

CHAPTER 14
NOT RIGHT UPSTAIRS

"The wrong idea has taken root in the world.
And the idea is this: there just might be some
lives out there that matter less than other lives."

— Fr. Gregory Boyle

Cliff comes to us homeless and drunk. He tells me he has started the day with half a mug of whiskey every morning since the Vietnam War.

Orphaned as a young boy, a kind couple adopted Cliff from a "boy's home some place in Texas." He remembers his parents fondly, but no longer has any living family. His first prison sentence was in the seventies when he was arrested for marijuana possession. He has been in and out of prison several times over the last forty years.

Besides alcoholism, Cliff has paranoid schizophrenia. The combination creates challenging experiences both for Cliff and for those who hang out with him at Joe's Addiction. Sometimes Cliff talks to himself. He easily becomes frustrated. Sometimes he blows up and yells at people, and when he is drunk Cliff becomes a little grabby with the ladies. We often have to ask Cliff to leave until he sobers up.

To complicate the difficulties in his life, Cliff has severe cataracts that render him nearly blind. His paranoia is aggravated by wondering through squinted eyes if the fuzzy group of people at the next table is talking about him. He has trouble relating to and trusting anyone in the Joe's Addiction community.

We feed Cliff and encourage him to obey the rules of his probation, help him apply for Social Security Disability and then help him manage his money. He is grateful for everything we do for him. He wants to thank us, so he washes dishes, sweeps floors, and carries out trash.

The faucet in the kitchen leaks, so Cliff offers to fix the sink. I'm not sure he knows how to do it. I have no one else, so I let him take a shot. Leaning in close to the faucet, Cliff diagnoses the problem and says, "We'll have to go to the plumbing store for parts."

Cliff and I jump in my car. Now I have to tell you about my car. It is a 2004 Buick LeSabre. A sweet, older man in Arkansas, who heard we needed a reliable car for traveling to speaking engagements, donated it to us. It is fancy—way too fancy. It has leather seats, automatic climate control, a nice stereo, and it is champagne colored (I told you a sweet, *older* man owned it). We had graciously accepted the gift, but thought to trade it in for something more appropriate. I could not drive this fancy car in the poverty of Valley Brook. I was embarrassed.

We looked at other cars, but I kept thinking, "How would the nice man who gave it to us feel if we trade his gift in for something different?" It is a great travel car. John has problems with his back, and it is comfortable for long distances. Hadn't we asked God for a reliable car? Reliable, yes. But fancy, no. The more we looked, the less peace we felt. One day John said, "I think God might be asking us, 'Why are you looking my gift-horse in the mouth?'" We decided to keep the car.

So this is the car Cliff and I jump into to go to the plumbing store. Immediately, Cliff begins pushing buttons, lowering and raising the electric windows, changing the radio station. He leans in close to the dashboard to see what the lighted words and numbers mean. He is fascinated with all the gadgets.

It's hot outside, over 100°, so I start the air conditioner. We have not traveled far, when Cliff says, "It's hot in here. Doesn't the air conditioner work in this thing?" I push the button to cool the temperature.

A few minutes pass and Cliff asks again, "Damn, it's hot! Doesn't the air in this fancy thing work?" I lower the temperature again. Cold air is blowing nicely now.

A couple more minutes and Cliff says, "Dammit! I'm burnin' up in here. You'd think this fancy car would have decent air conditioning!"

By now, I am freezing. I tell him, "The air is on, Cliff. It seems like it's working to me."

He is fidgeting in his seat now, wiping sweat from his face, and cussing under his breath. I think, "Oh man, I'm in trouble here. He might freak out on me right here in the car."

Then I look over and notice the yellow, lighted letters near his right knee: HIGH. In all his button pushing, Cliff turned on the heated seat.

Still driving through traffic, headed to the plumbing store, I try to explain to him the seat is heated and how to turn it off.

"What? Heated? Why? It's a hundred degrees outside, why would you heat the seat?"

"No, Cliff. You accidentally turned it on when you got in the car."

"What? I didn't turn it on. I didn't even know this damn car has heated seats. Are you kidding me? Heated seats?" He is becoming more and more agitated.

I pull the car over, climb out and walk around to his side. I open his door and push the button to turn off the heat. "Here's the button. See, it says HIGH. You have the heat on."

He leans in close and looks at the button. It sinks in. "Oh my, God! I thought I was goin' crazy! My ass was on fire!"

Gary

Most of our friends who live outside are relatively clean and relatively healthy. Relatively. We actually have some of the best-dressed homeless people in the city, because of our Free Store. However, a friend named Gary, whom I have not seen in a few months, shows up one day. He is filthy. Dirt and grime in every orifice. Hair matted in unintended dreadlocks. His clothing reeks of bodily fluids. Immediately it is clear to me that he has not been taking his medication. He rattles off stories about having been in California and New York and the people he has seen there, the thousands of dollars he owns, and the stuff he has done. I just listen. His bright blue eyes sparkle as he tells his tales.

When his words trail off into mumbles, I ask him if he is warm at night.

He says, "I have a cellar."

I know the place. A stairwell where he sleeps. It's a good wind break. I ask if he needs hand warmers.

"No," he says, "I'm fine." He ducks his head low, and then whispers, "I could use something to eat though."

As I turn to go make him a cheeseburger, I nearly run into Irish, a new guy who has just begun hanging out at Joe's. He is standing inches from me. I look at his face wondering, "Dude! Why so close?" Then I realize he has been standing at my elbow to protect me. (Gang members call it "shouldering up.") Gary concerns him, and he is watching out for me. I smile and thank him. He says, "I'm right here, Miss Jamie. You let me know if you need anything."

I serve the burger on a nice plate with a pickle and a bag of chips, but Gary wraps it in the napkin and shoves it in his pocket. He heads out the door, mumbling as he goes. We might not see him again for days or even weeks.

My husband was working in Haight Ashbury in San Francisco at a drug detox clinic back in the 1980s. He remembers the day when under Ronald Reagan's Administration, the federal government cut funding for residential mental health facilities. That day, bus after bus rolled into the city and unloaded their mentally ill patients into the city park, where they left them to fend for themselves.

In Oklahoma, the only residential treatments available for those with mental illness require payment of astronomical fees, some more than $1000 per day. Only the very wealthy, or those with expensive health insurance can afford residential treatment. Of course, this does not include my friend, Gary.

Over the years at Joe's Addiction, we have developed good, working relationship with some outpatient facilities that provide case workers, counseling, addiction recovery support, classes, and some psych medications. But people who are mentally ill have a hard time functioning. That is the problem. Some of my friends don't even know what day of the week it is, or which bus to take and when. Remembering to go or making it to counseling appointments are not easy tasks.

And the meds. The meds sometimes work, and sometimes they make things worse. If you have ever paid attention to any of those television commercials for depression medication, you've heard it yourself. Some of them can make you suicidal. You take them because you are depressed, but they can make you want to die. A middle-class person with a supportive family network will go back to the doctor and say, "Doc, this is not working. We've got to do something else." My friends who are mentally ill either keep taking the medicine because the doctor told them to and kill themselves, or they decide the doctor is a quack and quit taking meds all together.

One day a couple in our community comes for counsel. Well, actually, she drags him to me for counsel. Okay, it is more than for counsel. His face is swollen so much I can barely see his eyes. I say, "Dude, I think you need to go to the hospital. Looks like you're having some kind of allergic reaction."

"No, Jamie," she says, "it's an STD. He's been havin' sex with other women and got hisself an STD. Serves him right. He don't need a doctor. He needs Jesus. And I've about had it with him. Can you help us?"

I try hard not to smile, and I say, "Um... Swelling of the face and eyes isn't really a symptom of any STD I've heard of."

She starts pacing around the room, muttering about his infidelities and what kind of preacher could I be if I can't help her boyfriend get saved?

While she paces, he leans in close and says, "Ma'am, you know this ain't no STD. It's really motor oil that done it."

My eyes widen. "Motor oil? What do you mean?"

He goes on, "Well, I could feel the bugs crawlin' on my head. It's cuzz'a those damn birds 'at hang out at the dump. You know, they pick up all kinds of diseases from 'at garbage. Then they shit all over our trailer and our yard. We got no screen door. I think all 'at shit air has been comin' inta our house carryin' bugs with it. I could feel 'em bugs crawlin' on my head."

I ask him, "But what about the motor oil? What's that about?"

He says, "I done poured a bottle of motor oil over my head yesterday. I figger'd the bugs couldn't live in 'at oil. I guess some of it got down in my eyes and made my face swell."

I take him to the Emergency Room where they flush his eyes and give him some Benadryl. If I had known that was all he needed, I would have given it to him myself. Now there is a medical bill that he will never pay. Both of the people in this couple are mentally ill and drug addicted. Most likely, the bugs crawling on his head were a sensation that is a symptom of methamphetamine use.

One of the more frustrating elements of life in the Joe's Addiction community is the complexity of the roots of problems. Daily we encounter people who have the dysfunctional family backgrounds and emotional woundings found in average church congregants, plus we encounter the worldview and value system inherent to generational poverty. Add the additional ingredients of drug addiction and mental illness. Now, otherwise simple needs become recipes for extreme frustration. We struggle to know whether to hope for improvement or simply to recognize one another as family and love each other in the condition we are in.

I attended a training at an outpatient mental health facility that helps many people in our community. Something the teacher said helped me a lot. "When people are suffering from mental illness, they have symptoms not character flaws." She then said, "Medicine makes it possible for them to work on character flaws. If someone is addicted and experiencing mental illness, you must deal with both. If you only deal with one, then you're wasting time." It is a constant challenge for us at Joe's Addiction to encourage treatment for the whole person.

Statue of Liberty

Henri Nouwen, who after two decades of teaching in ivy league institutions, spent the last years of his life living and serving among a community of mentally and physically disabled people at the L'Arche Daybreak community in Richmond Hill, Ontario. He wrote, "In their poverty, the mentally handicapped reveal God to us and hold us close to the gospel."

Trena believes she is the Statue of Liberty. She often comes to Joe's Addiction holding a rolled-up newspaper over her head and talking about her boss, President Obama. She tells of her job with the Secret Service, how important she is to our government, and how much money the president pays her to be the Statue of Liberty.

Other days Trena believes she is Pamela Anderson and talks about how abusive Tommy Lee is to her. Sometimes she is Michelle Pfeiffer and is soon to embark upon a professional career as a singer. Needless to say, conversations with Trena are always surprising and often humorous.

When Trena begins to hang out at Joe's, some of our regulars—some of our ministers—are afraid of her. Frankly, she is more than a handful, and her occasional outbursts are frightening. Sometimes her delusions become loud, cussing tirades. Ironically these tirades often are about the "immigrants who are destroying our country." (Lady Liberty, you're supposed to welcome the immigrants.) But then it isn't funny because the look in her eye sometimes makes our hair stand on end.

Regular customers tell me I should run her off. She is bad for business. She bothers and frightens paying customers. But I can't dismiss her. She is so obviously "the least of these" about whom Jesus spoke. Besides, how can I make her leave without calling the police?

I ask local folks from the neighborhood about her. Everyone knows her. Years ago, a man she was married to beat her head in with a hammer. He left her bleeding, dying. Someone found her and took her to a hospital where they saved her life, but Trena is brain damaged.

So the regulars at Joe's Addiction become accustomed to Trena wandering around the shop, muttering her rants, and some of them even become helpful at calming her when she is overwrought. Little by little, she warms to our smiles. I ask if she is doing okay, and she usually mutters she is fine. She occasionally lets one of us hug her. Sometimes she stands right next to us, looking over our shoulder, wanting to be near but not wanting us to acknowledge her. Much of the time, she is just there, kind of like the comfy armchair. She becomes a feature of the shop.

I have a difficult conversation with one of our men who is homeless. He has come to Joe's in a drunken stupor more than a few times, each time being increasingly dangerous to others in the community. I have to tell him we are restricting him from coming to Joe's until he enrolls into a rehab treatment program. I tell him we will help him, but we cannot let him endanger the other regulars.

He is angry and says hurtful things. I cry. I know the things he is saying are born out of his own pain, but I cannot help but feel hurt by his hateful comments. After he leaves, several of the other regulars speak kind words to me and assure me I am doing the right thing. Then the afternoon continues as normal, serving coffee, making meals, cleaning up messes, etc.

About a half an hour later, I am sitting at a table working on my laptop computer when Trena pipes up from over on the couch by the front window: "Jamie, are you doin' okay?"

She knows my name! She is looking directly at me, eyes clear and filled with concern. She is checking on me. She saw the whole scene with my alcoholic friend. She saw my tears, and she is concerned about me.

I tell her, "Yes, Trena. I'm doing okay," Then I ask if she is all right. She smiles and says, "Yep. My Liberty butt is doin' just fine." She turns her head, and the distant look returns to her eyes. Just for a moment, she had been there and then she is gone. I live for such moments.

We don't mean to, but when we decide to love Trena and make her part of our community, we communicate a message to every single other person. The message is that it doesn't matter who you are or how big your issues are, we will love you, no matter what. Welcoming her tells everyone else they, too, are welcome. Because if we aren't running her off, we won't run them off either.

Working together with Trena's aunt, we help her enroll in a mental health program. She starts to take medication and a team of doctors visits her home once a week to make sure she continues to take her meds and check on her physical condition. Trena improves. The lucid moments come more frequently. She expresses her gratitude and love for many in our community.

One day, Trena talks to me about a friend of hers. She tells me her friend is always with her, that the friend's voice, which she hears in her own head, tells her what she should and shouldn't do. Trena tells me her friend's name is Bezel. Bezel sometimes encourages Trena to run into the street, into oncoming traffic. Bezel instructs Trena to turn on the broiler and stick her head in the oven. I tell her, "Jesus said the devil's job description is that he steals, kills, and destroys. It sounds to me like Bezel is not your friend, but really your enemy." She changes the subject, then walks away.

Over the next couple of weeks, Trena's condition worsens. She is anxious and angry. She wanders the coffee shop muttering threats of violence. I call her aunt to ask if she knows of any problems at home or with the medical program. Her aunt tells me she is taking all of her medications. Except—in the bottom of each daily pill compartment lies one, solitary, green pill. The green pill is for anxiety. I ask Trena why she is not taking the green pill. She says, "Bezel told me if I take the green pill, I will die." I try to explain the importance of this green pill to her and convince her of her need to take it, and she then decides I must be trying to kill her.

One afternoon, Trena becomes out of control. She is pacing and fuming, yelling and cussing, threatening to beat people in the shop. I try to talk with her, but she pushes me away. I am afraid she will hurt someone. I can't handle her, but I don't want to call the police because I'm afraid she will know I did so, and her feelings will be terribly hurt. I call, Foster. In the past, he has had success at calming Trena. Maybe he can help.

"Foster, Trena is out of control. I'm afraid I'm going to have to call the police for help." He says, "I'll be there in thirty seconds," and slams down the phone.

Foster' family heritage is German. He even speaks German. Maybe it comes with the genes. I don't know, but Foster has the ability to put on a dictator-sort-of air of authority. He shoves open the door, marches in and barks, "Trena, I want to see you in the backyard immediately."

She freezes. She looks at me, eyebrows arched, and asks, "Am I in trouble?"

I say, "I don't know, but I'll go with you." I have no idea what Foster has in mind.

We go together out the back door of Joe's Addiction and stand on the wooden deck outside. Foster points and shouts in drill sergeant tone, "Trena, what color is the grass?"

She says, "It's green."

Foster points again and bellows, "Trena, what color are the plants?"

She says, "They're green."

Again he points and barks, "What color are the trees, Trena?"

She says, "Well, they're green, Foster."

Then Foster comes close to Trena. Quietly, he says, "Trena, Bezel has lied to you. Green is the color of life. You need that green pill to live. You must take the green pill."

Trena stands still for a long moment. She looks at Foster. She looks at me. Then she says, "That ol'e Bezel has been lyin' to me. Drive me home and I'll take the green pill right now."

Foster drives her home, where she takes the green pill, and we never hear from Bezel again. At the writing of this book, it has been six years.

Trena becomes one of our most beloved in our Joe's Addiction community. She asks me for a job. "Everybody has a job here. I need a job." I hand her the fly swatter and ask if she might help me rid Joe's of the summer flies. (Remember, we're near the city dump.) She takes me seriously. Instead of wandering around with a rolled-up newspaper raised in the air, now it is a fly swatter. And she tells people in the neighborhood she works at Joe's Addiction.

One day Trena comes to me in a panic. This is not a delusion. Her fear is current, and it is real. Her ex-husband, the one who beat her head in with a hammer, is bringing her sixteen-year-old daughter to see her. Why he has custody of their daughter, I will never know. She has agreed to meet with them at Joe's Addiction because it is a safe place, but she is terrified. She says, "I really want to see my daughter, but I don't want to see him."

Several of us lay hands on her shoulders assuring her we will keep her safe. She paces back and forth, watching the front window. When a truck pulls into the parking lot, she says, "That's him." Every man in the coffee shop stands to his feet. They form a semi-circle, "shouldering up" behind her, as Trena faces the man who took so much from her. Her ex-husband enters with her daughter, but when he sees the group of men standing with her, he says, "I'll just wait outside in the truck." Trena spends an hour hugging and crying, catching up with her daughter who looks just like her mama.

Lady Liberation

On a Sunday, not too long after, I preach from Matthew 18. Jesus told a story of a servant who owed a large amount of money to his master. The day came when the money was due, and he could not pay. He begged his master for mercy, and the master forgave his debt. The servant

soon encountered a friend who owed him a small sum of money. His friend could not pay, and begged for mercy, but he refused to forgive his friend and threw him and his whole family into debtors prison. The master heard of what the servant did and became incensed. He ordered the servant to be arrested and turned him over to the torturers. When Jesus finished the story, he told the listening crowd, "This is what my father will do to you, if you don't forgive your brothers and sisters from your heart."

I tell our people at Joe's that I don't believe Jesus is talking about sending people to hell. I share with them how bitterness works in my life. My mind returns again and again to the injury. I not only think about how someone has hurt me, but I relive it—in my mind, and sometimes even in my body. I can feel that pain again as though it is happening right now. It's torture. It really is hell. This is the natural consequence of unforgiveness. When we don't forgive, bitterness turns us over to the torturers, to be tortured again and again, as we hold on to our pain. Forgiveness frees us from the pain.

At the end of my sermon, I allow time for quiet reflection. I ask for everyone to consider if there is anyone who they need to forgive, any pain they need to release, rather than live it again and again.

From the back of the room, Trena cries out with a loud voice, "I need prayer! I want to forgive my husband for beating me in the head. I don't know if I can do it, but I want to. I need to!" Community gathers around Trena, lays hands on her and prays with her. Many weep great tears of compassion and then tears releasing our own bitterness. If Trena can forgive her ex-husband, then we, too, can forgive those who have hurt us.

And we see God, "God with Us," in the tear-stained face of Lady Liberty.

CHAPTER 15

FEAR

"Because of a great love, one is courageous."

— Lao Tzu

My younger kids, Jewel and James, are with me. Sometimes, people are waiting on the front sidewalk for us when we arrive in the early morning, but this day no one is around. I unlock the door, and we start the opening procedures. I flip on the lights, turn on the Wi-Fi, and take the cash drawer out of the safe, while Jewel brews the coffee, ties back the curtains and fills the drinking water cooler.

I think I hear a strange sound, but then nothing. We continue busying ourselves with setting out bread and peanut butter and turning on the ice machine. Again, I think I hear a sound. I tell Jewel and James to hush for a second, and we listen.

From outside the back door, we hear what sounds like a monster. Deep growling and grunting with intermittent spaces of silence. Jewel looks at me with wide, terrified eyes. What in the world? We stand and listen for a couple more minutes. "Grahww, grahww, grahww... rahrrrr... RAHRRR." Could it be a dog? More like a wolf. But it sounds creepily human, rhythmic, and too evenly spaced to be a creature. Images of the Demoniac of the Gadarenes that Jesus encountered come to my mind.

I start for the back door. Jewel whispers, "Don't open the door, mom."

"I have to, Jewel. We have to find out what it is."

She hides around a corner while I unlock the deadbolt and turn the knob. I crack the door and peak outside.

There, standing on the back deck, is Skinny. He looks as scared as we feel. I startled him. I open the door wider and ask, "Skinny, what are you doing out here? Everything okay?"

He says, "Yeah. Everything's fine. I was just practicing for karaoke tonight. Warming up my voice."

"You were singing back here?"

"Yeah," he says, and then he belts out in his best screamo growl, "Let the bodies hit the floor! Let the bodies hit the floor!"

Fear is a natural emotion. We all experience fear. I think it is most magnified when one doesn't know what there is to fear. The fear of the unknown can even become debilitating. Imagination plants a seed, and before you know it, you can't even function.

A student of mine, who became a missionary in India, noticed the men looking openly and directly at her when she would go to market. She was a foreigner. Different. Of course, they would look. The thought entered her mind that she was in danger. It was not an irrational fear, but a reasonable one. Although not common, foreigners are sometimes attacked in India.

However, the thought became thoughts, and each time she went to market became more difficult for her. Images of "what-if" played in her mind. Nightmares filled her sleep. It became increasingly difficult to leave her house. She and her family finally had to leave the mission field and come back to the States, where religious guilt pummeled her for "quitting" her calling. Fear is painful, and it can paralyze.

There was much about Valley Brook that we did not know, and thus much to fear. We did our research. We examined crime rates, read stories on the internet. There was no natural location for hanging out somewhere in the neighborhood, besides the clubs, to get a feel for the atmosphere, so we drove the neighborhood at different times of day, observing. But there wasn't a lot to see to make us fearful. People were mostly inside their houses. So we didn't know what there was realistically to fear. We simply had to step out and put our toe in the water.

People often ask me, "Weren't you afraid to take your children into this place?"

We had five kids. They were 14, 12, 10, 4 and 2 years old. We had been in ministry for eighteen years. We spent our first years in Taiwan, and we enjoyed watching our kids go to Chinese kindergarten, learn to speak Mandarin, and develop international skills. When we came back to the States, our life became about training others.

Over the years, without even knowing it, we had allowed ourselves to move up in the "multi-level marketing scheme" of the American Church. You know, as you move up, you train others to do the work, who train others to do the work. We spent all our time with Christians. Planning meetings with Christians. Conflict resolution meetings with Christians. Worship meetings with Christians. Even most of our meals were really meetings with Christians. We said we were all about helping people who knew nothing about Jesus, but we didn't even know anyone who didn't know Jesus.

In the midst of our own faith crisis, we realized this is not what we wanted for our kids. We did not want them to grow up thinking life is a series of meetings with people who think the same way they think. We wanted to bring them along on this Grand Experiment to see if this Jesus thing is the real deal, and, at the least, we wanted to model for them parents who are actually out there doing the stuff. Looking back, I had absolutely no idea what "the stuff" was, but I decided that whatever the dangers might be, they were worth the risk.

Rick

Rick fought in Vietnam and returned from war an angry young man experienced in violence. One night, drinking in a bar, a fight broke out. It ended with Rick killing a man with his fists. Rick went to prison. He murdered another man while he was in prison, which landed him on Death Row. After appeals, the court determined the prison murder was self-defense. Rick has the scars to prove it. Prison tats cover his arms, and his shaved head speaks of alliances he has made on the inside. He is a dangerous man. When we meet Rick, he has just come out of prison where he has spent thirty years.

Rick went into prison strong and young, but the man we meet is physically spent. The self- assured way he holds his head and the tattoos scream, "I don't need no one!" But Rick walks with a cane due to a knife injury that damaged his vertebrae. Bullet wounds have atrophied his leg muscles, and his lungs wheeze from a lifetime of chain-smoking.

In the first weeks he spends with us Rick opens deep parts of his life to us. Sometimes he confesses he feels tempted to commit another crime. He does not know how to do life out here. Although prison was rough, at least he understood it. He doesn't know if he can make it on the outside.

Rick has a daughter he has not seen since before he was locked up. She lives in California, and, though he has contacted her, she wants nothing to do with him. He missed her entire childhood, and she sees no use in bringing him into her life now.

When Rick comes to Joe's, he sits next to our youngest daughter, Jewel. Maybe he thinks of his own daughter. Jewel likes him too. They sit and talk together. He tells her stories of when he was a kid, and she tells him about her day at school. If Rick comes in and Jewel isn't there, he asks me, "Where's my baby girl?" and often when he sees her, he hugs her and sometimes gives her a kiss on the top of her head.

We have not seen Rick for a couple of weeks, and I start to worry about him. One day he comes in, sits down and explains. "I'm sorry I ain't been around in a while. I wasn't doin' so good."

"It's okay, Rick. We missed you. I'm glad you're back."

He goes on, "I got really depressed. I'm just in constant pain, and it really wore me down. I was done. I just wanted to be done." He tells me he took out a gun and held it to his head, but as he sat there searching for courage to pull the trigger, Jewel's sweet face came to his mind. He slumps over on the table. As sobs shake his broken body, he sputters through his tears, "I couldn't do it. I thought about what it would do to her when she heard what I had done. I couldn't do that to my baby girl." Sunday, in church, he tells the whole community Jewel saved his life; the love of a child saved him.

Children love. It isn't hard for them. They don't see race or economic class, ex-con or homeless person. They only see people they love. It is a risk to take our children into the mess, and we think we are teaching them how to minister there, but in reality they are the ones who teach us to love because they *are* Love. And perfect Love casts out fear.

Angel Eyes

Oscar has taken a taxi to Joe's Addiction. He doesn't live far away. It is within walking distance, but Oscar is still recovering from a recent hip replacement surgery. He takes slow, baby steps supported by a walker from the taxi to the front door.

The place where Oscar is living is a well-known drug house where many people stay. Oscar is a veteran who receives a check from the federal government, along with the PTSD he suffers for fighting their war. He numbs his pain with a mixture of drugs and alcohol. Oscar is a pleasant drunk. He often comes to church high as a kite. His shouts of "Praise Jesus" and "Glory to God" add an element of joy and, honestly, entertainment to the service. We like Oscar, and he is easy to get along with. Since his surgery we have not seen him much, and I am glad to see him. He hangs out for the afternoon, drinking coffee and "shooting the breeze" with some regulars and me.

The time comes for my shift to end, and another barista arrives to take over. As I am gathering my things to leave, Oscar motions me over to where he is sitting. He asks, "Would you mind dropping me off at my house?" I know a taxi ride will take more of his money, and it is just around the corner. Of course, that is no problem.

I help Oscar to my car and into the front seat. His pain meds have worn off. He winces and moans all the way down to the sitting position. I scold him, "Oscar, you shouldn't have come out today. You should have stayed home and rested."

He says, "I hadta get outta there for a minute. You know."

I don't know, but I can imagine what things are like in his house.

We drive the short distance down the street, around the corner and pull into the driveway. I go around to open his car door. He is lifting his leg out of the car with his hands when the front door of the house crashes open. Two disheveled and wild-eyed men charge at us. It's obvious they are high on drugs. They're cussing and threatening, raising their arms. They reach the car door and lunge around me, into my car, toward Oscar.

I grab one of their wrists and look the man in the eye. I yell, "Back away! Back away now! This man is injured! He just had surgery, and I am helping him. I don't know what you want with him, but you better back away now!"

Both men freeze. Then the one whose wrist I still hold in my hand cries out, "Look at her eyes! Look at her eyes! It's an angel! Oh my god! It's an angel!" He tears his wrist from my grip and the two of them run, stumbling and falling across the yard, back into the house.

I turn to Oscar and he is staring at me. Then he howls. "Ha! Those guys thought you were an angel!"

"Well they were high out outta their minds," I say, "It was pretty easy to fool 'em."

Gangs

I am serving coffee and sitting and chatting with folks amid the crowded coffee shop. The 110+° heat of the Oklahoma summer brings in all those who live outdoors or have no air conditioners in their homes. Joe's Addiction provides a cool place to be and a meal or three-a-day for some of these folks.

This particular day, the crowd includes gang members from two different gangs. The rivals don't interact with one another. They mostly just watch the television and drink cool water. I know these guys. Some have told me their stories. Others haven't revealed much; they simply appreciate the AC.

I am hanging out listening to the chatter when suddenly, near the front of the shop, chaos erupts. Young men, with fists clenched and chests arched, shout cuss words and vile names. Instantly, lines are drawn. Around the room guys stand, fists ready, scrambling to their respective sides to defend their "brother."

I jump from my seat and run toward the commotion shouting, "No! We're not gonna do this! Stop!"

They shout at me: "He called me Punk! He called me Bitch! No one calls my brother a Punk! I'll beat the shit out of him!" I ask questions of the one so many of them are pointing at. He won't answer and starts pushing buttons on his cell phone. "I'm calling the police!"

I appeal to him, "Don't call the police. We can work this out. Tell me what happened."

He jumps up and charges out the front door. Several of the guys take off after him, followed by me hollering, "Stop! No!"

I chase down the one on the phone, asking him again to not call the police. Two of the guys bolt into the neighborhood as a police car pulls into the parking lot.

The policeman steps out of his car, and the young man who had called breathlessly rattles his complaint. "These guys are gonna beat me! They threatened to hit me! I didn't do nothing to them, but they're gonna kill me! Some of them are Juggalos and some of them are Crips. They're gonna kill me!"

The policeman looks at me, so I start in: "It's okay, Officer. These boys are all stressed out. It's so hot. Many of them are living in tents. They can't sleep at night. They are angry and hot and tired. I think we can work this out." I don't want anyone to be arrested.

He looks around, surveying the situation, and then asks, "So you don't need me?"

I tell him, "No, I don't think so. I think we can work it out."

He responds, "Okay," with that raised inflection at the end that says, "I'm not so sure." He returns to his car and drives away.

The young man, with terror in his eyes insists, "They're gonna kill me. They'll come to my trailer tonight while I'm sleeping and kill me."

I ask him why.

"They're sayin' I was texting one of their girlfriends."

I assure him we will not let that happen. I will talk with all the guys, and no one will kill him. Inside I am praying, "Oh, God."

I tell him he probably ought to go on home and take a break from Joe's for the rest of the day to give the guys a chance to calm down. I will let him know when it is safe to come back. He heads down the street, periodically looking back over his shoulder.

When I turn around to walk back to the shop, here comes a pack of guys toward me. As they approach I say, "Boys, we gotta talk about this." They come up in a semicircle around me, fingers pointing and bodies posturing. They all speak at once: "He was disrespectful to you. You told him not to call the police, and he did it anyway. He was disrespecting this place and disrespecting you."

I breathe a sigh of relief. They are not angry at me ... and inside I smile that they are trying to deflect their own blame in another direction.

Then they tattle their tales, "He did thus and such, and I told him thus and such, and he threatened thus and such." Then it gets to the heart of the matter for them: "He called me a punk," and, "Nobody calls my boy a punk! I'll kill anyone who calls any of my homies punk!" Some of them bear the tattooed evidence of their kills.

I ask them, "Are you in a gang? Who of you is a Juggalo? Who is a Crip?" They nod, raising their hands and acknowledging their different affiliations. I say, "Okay. I don't understand a lot about gangs, but one thing I know is you guys feel like your gang is your family, right?"

"Yeah. We are family. I would die for my boys. Ain't nobody gonna mess with my homies."

I explain to them, "I can't stop you from doing whatever you're gonna do when you're away from here. But here at Joe's Addiction we are a family. You know how you guys have each other's backs?" They all nod. "We here at Joe's have each other's backs. Not the Juggalos have the Juggalos' backs, and the Crips have the Crips' backs, but *we*, the family of people who hang out at Joe's Addiction—*we* have each other's backs. I guess I'm saying if you hang out at Joe's, you've joined a new gang."

One of them pipes up, "It's the Joe's Gang!" Another one laughs and says, "Maybe we should call it the Jesus Gang!" We all laugh.

I explain that the young man they had all threatened is a part of our gang. They again start tattling, "But he . . ." I tell them I understand, but this young man has not been in prison like they have. He doesn't understand gang or prison culture. In fact, this young man has spent his whole life in Special Education classes and mental institutions. He doesn't understand what he said and how offensive it was to them. This is exactly the kind of outcast Jesus told us to love as we love ourselves.

The whole time I am speaking, they are all hanging their heads and nodding. Then I ask them to consider him part of our family. They're looking at each other, mulling over what I said.

Finally one speaks up and says, "We understand, Miss Jamie, and we're sorry. It won't happen again." Another says, "I'm sorry we disrespected you and your place, Miss Jamie. We'll be nice to him." And another: "He doesn't understand, but there won't be any trouble from us again, Miss Jamie."

I thank them all, and each one of them gives me a hug as they head back into Joe's.

In about twenty minutes, here come the two most violent culprits of the conflict: one is a young man who has only been out of prison for two weeks; the other has been hanging out at Joe's for about a year. Both are homeless. They are dripping with sweat from their race through the neighborhood in the over 100° temperature. With heads hung low, they both say, "Miss Jamie, I'm sorry. It won't happen again. We really appreciate all you do for us here. If it weren't for you and this place, we wouldn't have anything to eat. We'd be out in the heat all day. We won't disrespect you or this place again."

I share with them the community that is Joe's Addiction, and what it means to be part of the Joe's Family. With eyes staring, the new guy responds, "I've been gang-bangin' for mosta my life. It's all I know."

Smiling, I say, "Well, then how 'bout you join the Joe's Gang, and let us have your back?"

He grins and replies, "Sounds good to me."

A gang council meeting takes place shortly after this day. (I am not invited.) All the gangs make an agreement and designate Joe's Addiction a "chill zone." We have had no gang violence since this day, and word on the street is that if any gang member brings violence to the coffee shop, there will be consequences to pay. Many years later, we find top level mobsters still honoring this code. And we are grateful.

Armor

One afternoon, I am sitting across the table from Biker Clint. He says, "I know what it is about you. You don't wear armor." His eyes twinkle, and he is looking at me intently. I can tell he has been thinking about this. I ask him what he means.

He says, "I wear this leather jacket, you know." (The patch on the back says, "Fuck you. I have enough friends.")

"Yeah, I know."

"Well, it's my armor. People see it and they stay away from me. If people stay away from me, then I don't get hurt. It's my armor."

He says, "But you, you don't wear armor. I have seen you let people hurt you. You know it's coming. You know they're gonna hurt you, and you just let it happen."

Love is vulnerable. Love is family. Love is Life. We hurt one another. We just do. But we also need one another. We all know hurt people hurt people. Wounded people lash out in anger and in fear. I like to call them porcupines. These are people who desperately want a hug, but if you dare hug them, you will probably be stabbed.

The idea of loving and helping "broken" people seems romantic. I'm going to rescue girls from the sex trade. I'm going to see addicts freed from drugs. I'm going to protect abused women. Then you get hurt.

The first drug addict I love in Valley Brook initially loves me back. She is so grateful for my help (time and money). Until I say, "No." Until I say, "I can't do it today." Then she calls and yells at me over the phone, "I hate you. I'm never gonna speak to you again. I want you out of my life!" A few days later, she walks into Joe's Addiction, right up to the counter, and acts like nothing ever happened.

We decide to set boundaries with one man who is homeless and who is hanging out at Joe's all day every day. We try to resist creating a new list of rules, but we deal with each person individually as a family does in relationship. We communicate. We feel we know this guy well enough to know he can work, and we realize our letting him hang out all day is just enabling him to continue his lifestyle of crime and homelessness.

We sit down with him to talk about it and explain our perspective. We feel we are not truly helping him. We want to see him improve his life, to work, hopefully to get off the streets into a house. So we are restricting him from being at Joe's Addiction from 9 to 5, when he ought to be out looking for work. (We might do this differently now, but this was the first time we tried to set this kind of boundary.) We tell him we are happy to serve him breakfast in the morning, and he is welcome to come back after five for dinner and hang out for the evening, but we want to encourage him to go out there and look for work.

He blows up. I mean ballistic. He launches off the couch, paces back and forth, ranting about how much he hates us, and how we have done nothing for him. We should rot in hell. This after countless acts of service we have done on his behalf. The most painful words cut to the core of my intentions and desires: "I thought you were supposed to be like Jesus! You're nothing like him! You're the worst Christian I've ever met. I'm never coming back to this place!"

Pain. I hate pain. So much more than physical pain or death, I fear emotional pain. Perhaps the most painful injuries in my life have come from rejection. People misunderstand or misjudge my motives. I hate it. I want people to believe the best about me, and I don't want them to walk out of my life. We are a family, for goodness' sake. So these words strike to the deepest place in my soul.

Sometimes we have to ask people to leave for the day. If they are not honoring the Conduct Code. If they're cussing out the barista or threatening violence, we might even put them on a restriction for a week—kind of a "time out." And when we do this, it is almost always met with, "I hate this place, I'm never coming back!"

But you know what? They come back. They always come back. Joe's Addiction has become home. It is not just because people know they can receive help here, but they know they will be welcomed back. They know they will not be rejected. They know they are forever and always part of the family. No matter what.

So, they come back—sometimes head in their hands, apologies on their tongue. More often, acting like nothing ever happened. And you know—mercies are new every morning.

I used to just want to curl up and die from the pain when people said these things, because I am committed to never reject them, and I hoped for and wanted the same commitment from them. My feelings got hurt. They still do. But I have found often people cannot give that kind of commitment; they cannot love—because they have never truly been loved.

And so, they wear their armor and they brandish their quills.

But I am no longer floored by the pain of "I'm never coming back!" Instead, I simply say with a smile, "See you tomorrow."

"I've learned that people will forget
what you said, people will forget what you did,
but people will never forget how you made them feel."

— Maya Angelou

CHAPTER 16
STANDING AGAINST OR FOR

"When you forgive somebody,
when you are generous,
when you withhold judgment,
when you love and when
you stand up to injustice,
you are, in that moment,
bringing heaven to earth."

— Rob Bell

I experience the most infuriating encounter at the Department of Public Services. Infuriating is the right word. I am helping Norm renew his ID. His old one is about to expire. When we approach the counter, he explains that a person at the tag agency told him he must to go to DPS to renew his. She looks at his ID, and then announces his shame to the entire room, "Yes. If you're on the sex offender registry, you are required to come here."

She then looks up the address he has written on the form. It is the same address on his current ID, and the one he has used for several years. She says, "This address is not on the registry." He explains to her that he is homeless and the address he gives to the Registration Office is an intersection. He knows you can't put an intersection as your address on an ID card. She tells him, "I can't give you an ID if you are homeless. You must have a residence to get an ID."

I jump in. "Ma'am, I know that isn't true, because I am a pastor, and I have many people who are experiencing homelessness in my care. Most of them have an ID. I have helped many of them get their ID."

She purses her lips and says, "Well, whoever is giving them IDs is doing it illegally because homeless people are not 'residents' of the State of Oklahoma. You must have a residence to be a 'resident.'" She uses finger air quotes each time she says, "resident."

I say, "Ma'am, there is no possible way what you are telling me is true. I have been helping people who are homeless (including sex offenders) get IDs for many years, and I have never run into this problem."

Again she says, "A person must be a legal 'resident' of the State of Oklahoma, to get a State ID." Again she uses finger air quotes to emphasize "resident."

Standing next to me, Norm is becoming agitated. He huffs and puffs, barking his complaints to the woman. He explains that he has used this address for several years, his previous ID card is still valid with this address. He can usually be found at this address, etc. She keeps saying the same thing again and again. He is furious.

I put my hand on his arm and tell him to calm down. We will figure this out. I am doing the best I can to keep my own anger under control. I say, "Ma'am, just think about this for a moment. How can a person who is homeless ever become unhomeless if they can't get an ID? They can't get a job. They can't get a house. They can't even get into the homeless shelter. In fact, if a policeman stops them and asks to see their ID, they can even be arrested if they don't have one." (Although this should not be the case, it has happened to our people many times.)

She listens to my comments and then says, "I'm looking at the law right here on my computer screen. Only 'residents' of Oklahoma can obtain an Oklahoma State ID."

When she does her finger air quotes again, I take a deep breath and say, "Then we need to see a supervisor."

She says, "You'll have to take a number."

We do. Then we sit watching person after person who came in after we did hear their number called and go to another room. While we wait, we form a new game plan. We look online on my phone for the actual address of the location of my friend's tent. At one point, as we sit watching the TV on the wall, Norm says, "I can feel that energy coming off of you. You told *me* to calm down. I think *you're* the one who needs to calm down." We laugh. We wait for an hour before our number comes up on the screen.

When we sit down with the supervisor, we explain that the address Norm first gave is not the actual place where he lives, and the woman at the front counter had been concerned about that, but we can now give the actual address of where he "resides." (I did not use finger quotations.) Norm explains that he is homeless, but the address we are now giving is the location of his tent.

The supervisor does not say much. She sits at her computer typing and typing and typing for about five minutes. I do the best I can to make small talk with Norm, while we wait, trying to seem nonchalant. Then the supervisor says, "I'll be right back." We watch her go out to the front counter where she stands talking with air quotes woman for about five more minutes. The whole time, I am planning in my head what should be my next move, in case they refuse him an ID.

When she comes back, Norm asks, "Is there a problem, ma'am?"

She says, "No. No problem at all." Then she fills out all the information. We walk away with our piece of paper and make a trip to the nearest tag agency.

While we wait in line to have the card made, I tell Norm they will ask him if he wants to be an organ donor.

He asks me, "Are you an organ donor?"

"I am," I say. "After I'm dead, I won't need my organs anyway, and if my organs can help save someone else's life, I think that would be a pretty great thing to come from my death."

He says, "I'll prolly be cremated, cuz I don't got no money for a burial. But just in case I come into some money before I die, I'd really like to be buried. If they take your organs, does that mess up your body for the viewing?"

I tell him, "They sew you back up, Dude. And they put clothes on you for a viewing, so you'd look just fine."

Then he asks me, "What if they start cutting you open to take your organs, and you're not really dead?"

I laugh. "Well that would be pretty bad. But generally, they make sure someone is dead before they start cutting."

When the woman finishes taking his picture she says, "If you want to be an organ donor, you need to mark this box and then sign below."

He tells the woman, "I'm going to be an organ donor, cuz my pastor here convinced me." He grins sideways at me. While he is signing, he says, "They generally make sure you're dead before they start cutting."

Is God a Pyro?

The Christianity I grew up in, Evangelical Christianity or Fundamentalist Christianity, was often marked by what Christians stood against. When I was a child, the church was standing against the "Godless" hippie, anti-war movement. It stood against the feminist movement. Then it stood against abortion. Today, while the abortion fight continues, they have added standing against gay marriage to the war. "Standing against" seems to be part of the ethos.

Maybe it is in the genes, as the movement started with the protest of the Protestant Reformation. Back when it began, the protest was against religious power and authority oppressing the illiterate and poor population. It was a fight for the right that every person could have personal access to God, without paying money to the church for it and without going through proper, priestly channels of authority. It was a fight for justice.

I was born into this "standing against" culture. Not only was it in my religious upbringing, but as I learned about my personality type, I learned that by nature, I am a reformer. When I see something wrong, I want to make it right.

I have a confession to make. It is something embarrassing, something for which I am deeply ashamed.

Twenty-five years ago, John and I led short-term missionary trips to Taiwan that we called "exposure trips." Our goal was to take average American Christians to places in the world where people had never heard the Good News of Jesus Christ. We wanted to expose them to the realities of life in a people group where there is no influence of the Gospel, no knowledge of the forgiveness of God, and no understanding of the effect of the Love of God upon their everyday life. I am not ashamed of this part of what we did.

On these trips, we also did what we called "prayer walking." As we traveled and observed temples to "pagan" gods, idolatry, and ancestor worship, we prayed that God's Kingdom would come to those people and to those places. I am not ashamed of praying for this either.

However, on these trips we also did something else. Here it comes. . . . We prayed for God to drop giant balls of fire from heaven upon the idolatrous temples. We had read in the Bible of fire falling from the sky when Elijah prayed against idols. We had also heard stories of fireballs landing on temples in Cambodia. Surely God could do this for us as well. Surely this was praying in agreement with God's will. Against the worship of idols. Against the proliferation of other religions. Surely God wanted to see these temples destroyed.

We "prayer walked' the physical territory of major temples, sometimes marching around them like the people of Israel around the walls of Jericho. Temples cover the island of Taiwan, too many to visit, too many to walk. Riding the busses and trains, we saw thousands of orange and red-roofed shrines passing by, in the heart of villages, in the center of rice paddies—temples we saw as "abominations"—ones we could not reach. So we devised an abbreviated prayer. (Oh, I am ashamed to the point of tears.) For each temple we saw, we proclaimed in hushed tones, "Boom! Boom! Boom! Boom!"

Not once did I think about the people the fire would kill if it actually fell on them. I guess I categorized them as collateral damage in the war between God and Satan. They would go to hell anyway, I believed, since they didn't believe the right things, so if they died in a catastrophic judgment of God, for the sake of God proving that Jesus was really the one they should worship? Well, I guess that was just the price that had to be paid. Oh. my. God.

Of course, I never articulated these thoughts out loud. Not even to myself. All of this was simply the kind of religion in which I grew up, the kind of religion I then practiced as an adult. I was a passionate and committed personality, and I believed I was going "all out for Jesus." Although I had grown up knowing the stories of Jesus, somehow I missed so much of his life and teaching. The words of Jesus ring in my ears now, as I remember his disciples wanted to cast fire down on those who had rejected him, and in astonishment Jesus turned to them and said, "You have no idea what spirit you are of."

So that was my background, when in the midst of the disintegration of our faith, we opened Joe's Addiction. When we first drove around Valley Brook, observing and praying about opening this coffee shop, I felt disgusted by the strip clubs. They were the enemy, and their owners must be in cahoots with the devil himself. I was angry about the abuse of women and angry at the men who used them. I dreamed of the day when the clubs would one day shut down. I'm sure my own experiences of abuse from men partly fueled my passion.

Six years after we opened Joe's Addiction, the club next door to us did catch fire. It was an interior fire. No one was hurt, and the building sat empty, locked up for a few months, while we wondered what would happen next. Did they have insurance? Would they rebuild, making it bigger and "better" than before? The bulldozers came and razed it to the ground.

No insurance. No rebuilding. Now an empty concrete slab lay where Valley of the Dolls—the oldest, longest-standing strip club in Valley Brook—once shared a parking lot with us. Instead of rejoicing, I felt sad. I felt concerned for those who had worked there.

I had met many of the girls as they came in for coffee. They had become my friends. I had worked hard to develop a relationship with the bouncer, whose job was to check IDs at the door. I had cleaned up urine from drunks they sent over to sober up. But it had taken me two years of serving, safely behind the counter of our coffee shop, before I gathered the courage to enter the door of Valley of the Dolls.

I was afraid. I had grown up so sheltered. I had never even set foot in a bar, much less a strip club. It would be dark. The music would be loud. The men might be drunk. I wasn't sure what I would see and how I should respond. I would be embarrassed. Where should I look? Would people in there know I was nervous?

The day finally came when I had to push past my fear. A woman who had left that line of work went with me. We opened the door, showed our IDs, walked across the smoky, dark, loud room and sat down at the bar. The bartender, a middle aged, large-breasted woman asked what we'd have, and I ordered a Coke. She recognized me and smiled, shouting over the music, "You own the coffee shop next door, right?"

I now know the people of Valley of the Dolls—and for me that changed everything. That changed me. I no longer believe God is a pyro.

Seeing injustice still makes me angry, and I want to fight against it. It is part of who I am. But often the war in which Christians are engaged feels to me that rather than standing *with* the oppressed and the vulnerable *against* power, Christians are standing in positions of power fighting against those people the system has beaten down. So my fighting has changed. Instead of "standing against," my fighting has now become "standing for."

Officer Jones

Martin Luther King, Jr. asked, "Will we be extremists for hate, or will we be extremists for love? Will we be extremists for the preservation of injustice, or will we be extremists for the cause of justice?" In our fight for justice, it is all too easy to mirror the hatred we encounter. Sometimes we must take a stand for the ones who are being oppressed, but when we do it out of a motive of Love, maybe the world moves one step closer to looking like heaven.

Sunday morning during church, a lady who is mentally ill and often lives in delusions begins to holler obscenities during the service. This isn't surprising to us. Over the years, we have become accustomed to being on our toes, ready for any kind of drama that might break out in the crowded room. Someone goes to her and says some calming things. She quiets down.

But a few minutes later, she yells again. This time it is about seeing angels fighting the devil. She paces and yells, cussing at the devil and his hoards. A couple of people walk with her, trying to ease her anxiety, but she won't listen. My daughter, Jessi, having had success at calming this woman in the past, goes to her and speaks quietly and gently, asking if she wouldn't like to go outside and get some fresh air. Without acknowledging Jessi at all, she moves toward the front door. Jessi looks at me with an "I've got this, Mom" look. I am not too sure.

I continue leading the service with one eye trained on the front sidewalk. Jessi is all of four foot ten inches, full of bravery, and feisty as hell. But this woman is a foot taller and twice as broad as Jessi, and her delusions can make her as strong as the forces of the real hell itself. Thankfully, I see two men in our community have gone out to the front sidewalk with Jessi to help.

I am finishing up the sermon, when I see the woman pull back her fist and swing directly at Jessi's face. In the same moment, one of these dear men bends his head forward into Jessi's space and takes the punch, full force, right in his own face. He grabs her wrist, his glasses broken, hanging from one ear, while Jessi sticks her head in the door and says, "Um, I think we're gonna need to call the police for help with her. She needs to go to the Crisis Center."

I hate to call the police. Flashing police lights don't help our reputation. But worse than that, this woman is afraid of the police. This would not help her delusions, and she might even remember I had been the one who called the police on her, even though we were trying to help her. But she is out of control, and if the police will transport her to the Crisis Center, professionals can offer her some help there. I make the call.

The police car rolls up to our front sidewalk where a small crowd is still trying to keep her contained. The officer asks what is going on, and I explain that she is having a really bad day. She is out of her mind and threatening violence. Can he please take her to the Crisis Center? I know he knows this woman. She has lived in Valley Brook for many years.

He walks to the woman who now stands frozen in fear. He places her arms behind her and puts her in handcuffs.

I am aghast. I ask, "Sir, where are you taking her?"

He says, "She's going to jail."

"No," I say. "She doesn't need to go to jail. No one here is pressing any charges against her. She needs to go to the Crisis Center."

He says, "That's not my job. I don't take people to the Crisis Center. I take people to jail."

I follow him as he leads her to his car.

"No sir. She hasn't committed a crime. You have nothing to arrest her for. You need to take her to the Crisis Center."

"Nope. I'm taking her to jail."

I am standing on the other side of the door, as he places his hand on her head and seats her in the back seat, my back to his driver's door. He closes the back door, and I decide, "I shall not be moved."

I fold my arms and say, "I will not let you take her to jail. She is not a criminal. She is sick. She needs to go to the Crisis Center."

He puts his hand on his stick and says, "That is not my job."

"Yes, sir," I say, "I believe it is."

We stand there in silence. Well, not silence. She is banging on the back window, screaming at me for having called the police on her. I fight back the tears, and say once again, "She needs help. Please take her to the Crisis Center."

After another pause, he then says, "Do you know how to reach her family? If you can find someone to take her to the Crisis Center, I will hold her in the back of my car, until they get here. How does that sound?"

I say, "I can do that. Thank you."

I call a relative of hers, an aunt who I had only met once. She is just leaving a church service at another church across town. She tells me she will be there in about twenty minutes. I turn to the woman in the car and say through the window. "I spoke with your aunt. She is on her way. You're safe. You're not going to jail. Your aunt is coming to help you."

She nods, tears coursing down her face, forehead pressed against the window. She says, "Thank you, Jamie. Thank you."

I suddenly become aware of the crowd standing on the front sidewalk. They have all been watching the drama. The police officer shifts his tone and starts asking me questions about what we do, about how long we have been here, and why we were doing what we were doing. We have a pleasant conversation while the woman sits mumbling in the backseat of his police car. When her aunt arrives, the officer helps move her from one car to the next, and her aunt drives her to the Crisis Center to get her the help she needs.

From this day forward, Officer Jones becomes a friend of the Joe's Addiction community. Not too long after, he comes into the coffee shop and asks me, "Do you know Sonny?" I do. He tells me Sonny got into trouble the night before. He says, "I didn't want to arrest him. He was just drunk and causing a scene. He promised to stay in his house, and he did, so that was the end of it. But I thought I'd come by and see if there is any way you guys might help Sonny."

Another time, Officer Jones comes and asks if I know Brenda, another woman who is mentally ill in the neighborhood.

He tells me he was called to her house for a domestic violence situation. Her daughter made the call. He asks if I have been in her home. I haven't. He says, "She thinks the FBI has bugged her house, and she has pulled all the sheetrock off the walls with her bare hands. Her fingernails are bloodied, and the house is a wreck." He says, "There's no food in their house at all. I thought you guys might at least have some food you could take to her."

Officer Jones works together with us for a few months. He does his job of arresting those who have committed crimes, but he comes to us with any situations he thinks we might be able to help. And then he is fired. The official reason is he was "ineffective" in his position. He was "shirking his responsibilities as a police officer." What it really means is that Officer Jones had not been bringing enough money into the city coffers. Every arrest amounts to a fine. The fewer arrests, the fewer fines.

We see Jesus in the Gospels doing this again and again for the most vulnerable in society. Often he stood for them in the face of the religiously powerful, who used their position to oppress. He even broke the religious laws of the day to heal and care for people at the "wrong" times and in the "wrong" places. Ultimately, the religious elite executed him for standing for "the least of these." Officer Jones lost his job. Perhaps he, too, had become a follower of The Way of Love.

SECTION 4
RLOVEUTION

"The more I get to know Jesus,
the more trouble he seems to get me into."

— Shane Claiborne

CHAPTER 17
SHEDDING MY SKIN

"Creating but not owning, giving without demanding,
controlling without authority, this is love."

— Lao Tzu

Tisha's home church shuts down, closes its doors. Her former
pastor recommends that she come to Joe's Addiction for church
so she joins us, and to be honest, Tisha is difficult for me.
Tisha informs us she has a prophetic gifting. She comes from
a charismatic church where they encourage supernatural gifts
of the Spirit, and she is quite confident in her ability to hear
from God. She is a righteous person who feels commissioned
by God to deliver "God's Word" to whoever God is speaking
through her.

   This bugs me. Because. Well, because this was me. I, too, had
seen myself as a prophet. Much in the vein of Old Testament
prophets, I had believed it was my God-given gift to the church
to deliver correction. In the destruction of the old version of
my faith, I came to see my own motives as self-righteous,
arrogant, and perfectionistic. I spent thirty-plus years living

this way and I am trying to change. So as is so often the case, I dislike Tisha because I see my own shadow in her.

One difference between Tisha and me is that she is much bolder than I ever was. She hears things from God, and she steps right out to do them. She walks over to people in the coffee shop, lays her hand on their shoulder, and prays for them. She comes out of the bathroom and approaches someone to tell them, "While I was in the bathroom, God spoke to me about you." In church, Tisha announces that she has heard God, and then she delivers a pronouncement of God's judgment upon "someone in the room" who has hidden sin in their life. Well, obviously there are people in the room with "hidden sin in their life." Managing her and her gift is a challenge for us.

Many years ago, I quit spanking my children the day I was spanking my son for having hit his sister. I realized I was hitting him for hitting someone else. How could he learn that hitting was not okay, if I was disciplining him by hitting him? That was the last time I used hitting as a discipline. In the same way, I feel myself being frustrated with Tisha for always correcting people's sins and shortcomings, and yet, for me to correct her would be me doing the very same thing to her. You get what I mean? So I am stuck. I don't know what to do with her.

One day, Tisha announces she feels God is "calling" her to serve the Saturday evening shift as a barista. Sigh. I want to say, no. We need someone for Saturday evenings, and she is willing, but I am afraid she will scare people off. We have tried to create a space where everyone will feel welcome. Too many of our people feel rejected and damaged from their past religious experiences. The last thing we want them to feel is that the coffee is just a set up so we can get them to pray a religious prayer so they can go to heaven. In my mind's eye, I can see Tisha aggressively blessing people or delivering "words from the Lord" to customers and them running right out the door.

But as I stand listening to Tisha describe her "God-calling" experience I am having a "God- calling" experience of my own. I know The Muse is asking me, "Do you really think if I am in this thing, Tisha can screw it up?" I am humbled. Who am

I to think I, myself, won't screw it up? I know I am to take my hands off of it, to stop trying to micro-manage and control who is doing what. If the Spirit is really in this place, in this experiment, then the Spirit will give it Life.

It turns out people love Tisha. Yes, she is a little kooky and maybe a little over-the-top. People know this. That is just Tisha. But Tisha is sincere, and she loves people. I watch as Tisha does what Tisha does and see that people feel loved. For a season, Tisha feels God wants her to tell each person who comes into the coffee shop the meaning of their name. Yes. And . . . she doesn't have all these name meanings in her head, so sometimes it is a bit of a wait as she goes to the internet to look it up. I watch as Tisha delivers name meanings more like they are prophetic statements of destiny. Again and again, customers and community members are moved to tears as Tisha calls out the beauty God (and she) sees in each individual.

The corrective words from Tisha become fewer and fewer as she experiences God's love flowing through her to others, and as she herself experiences a place where she belongs. The people of Joe's Addiction become her family.

I suppose we all change over our lifetime. Some changes come naturally; pain forces some changes in us. Still others come as we intentionally set our minds to think differently, to be differently. Joe's Addiction has brought about so many changes in me.

People Over Tasks

In the early days, the coffee shop was not busy. I brought my laptop computer with me. I worked on emails, handled accounting paperwork, or wrote a blog post during slow times. Before long, regular customers frequented the shop. Sometimes people stayed for hours. I asked them about their lives. They talked. I began to know them. Some people were obviously starved for attention. They kept coming back for more.

I was sitting at the counter working on my computer one day when a particularly needy person came up and stood at my elbow. I paused. She asked me a question, and I answered. She went back to her table, and I continued working. A few minutes later, here she came again. This time she did not wait for me to pause. She asked for a refill on her coffee. I stood up and filled her cup. She went back to her table, and I sat down to pick up where I had left off. A few more minutes passed, and again she came to stand by me. She interrupted my typing to ask me another question.

I was annoyed. This woman had no social awareness. She was hogging up my time, keeping me from doing my work. Couldn't she see I was busy? I had stuff to do. Then I remembered. Wasn't she why we opened this coffee shop? Wasn't having conversations with people what I wanted to do? What if all she needed was somebody to listen to her? Was I here to love people or to answer emails?

I put away my laptop, and I decided while I was at Joe's Addiction I would not expect to get anything done. I decided people are more important than tasks. And this doesn't just mean at the coffee shop. Something changed in me. The next time I went to the grocery store, as I stood in the check-out line, I looked at the woman passing my groceries over the scanner. I was not there just to accomplish a task on my list. She was not just there to serve me. She was a person. A person with a life full of who knows what kinds of joys and sorrows. I asked her, "How you doin' today?" She looked me in the eye and said, "It's been a rough one. Thanks for asking." Because of Joe's Addiction, life for me has become all about people, and I have begun to love everywhere I go.

Shy about Sexual Stuff

Sex was an open topic in my house growing up. Although my family was steeped in conservative Christianity, my mother decided she would do a better job than she felt previous generations had done at talking about the birds and the bees. She took each one of her three daughters on an overnight "mother-daughter date" when we were almost twelve so she could have "the talk" with us. My sisters and I still tease her about how she used the same line with each of us: "It's a beautiful thing."

My mom's progressive approach was healthy in many ways and gave me a level of comfort to talk about sex. However, I could never have anticipated how openly people in our community talk about their sex lives and how much I would need to grow in this area.

We offered a basic women's health class that we hoped would also be an opportunity to build the self-esteem of some of our women. We discovered that although sex is such an obvious part of life in the neighborhood, this does not mean our people understood even the basics of the biological reproductive system. Grown women in our community had never seen a drawing of female reproductive organs. Some did not understand why they have a menstrual period each month. Some lived with chronic urinary tract infections, due to a lack of healthy hygiene. Some did not even know how a woman becomes pregnant. Myths and legends abound. Men have told women if they have sex in certain positions they will not get pregnant. They have told them if they do it in various ways, they will be immune to sexually transmitted diseases.

Our daughter, Jessi, who was a midwife-in-training at the time taught these classes. She was kind and gentle. She did not make anyone feel stupid for their lack of knowledge. She also did not assume they knew anything and started from the very beginning. Jessi answered questions and gave information. She wasn't awkward or embarrassed. And neither were they. I was the one who squirmed at the detailed descriptions, and I cried as I watched our women learn about themselves. They discovered their own bodies for the first time.

Jessi included a lesson about body image, and what is so common among so many American women was true for the Joe's Addiction women as well. They thought their bodies were ugly. Jessi taught them about "loving their tree" which is a beautiful image of the female body that gives life.

"Eve, is one of those trees more beautiful than another?
You must love all the trees,
and you must love your tree."

— Leah, a 74-year-old Masai woman:
The Good Body, by Eve Ensler

We laughed about sexual words. We cried about miscarriages. We gave compliments to one another. And I changed some more. No longer is sex a weird topic to be talked about in whispers. Conversations about sex have become a matter of fact. Real. A beautiful thing, yes, but also a thing of lots of confusion and pain for both women and men. A thing I have become comfortable talking about.

Pastoral Advice

A man in our community who is mentally ill sits down with me one afternoon. He is obviously frustrated about something. I ask him what's up. He starts by telling me he went to one of the strip clubs the night before, intending to have sex there. He tells me there is a "VIP" room where the girls take the men. $25 was the price for intercourse. I have been told by both men and women that no condoms are used. One man told me, "But they make us wash off in the hand sink before they do it."

I nod, listening intently. I cannot imagine what upset him. He continues, "I washed and then was ready, but I couldn't do it."

I ask him, "You mean you couldn't go through with it, or you couldn't *do* it?"

He says, "Both." He goes on. "I started thinking about things you have said to me. Like, she has a soul. She's a person. And I couldn't do it."

I can sense his frustration. He says, "What am I supposed do with all this desire? If I can't have sex with prostitutes, then what am I gonna do? I might lose it!"

This man is serious. He is not joking around. This is a real problem. I think fast. He is mentally ill. He has already been in prison for a sexual offense. What is he to do about his sexual urges? All the while, I am thinking, "How did I get here?"

Then I say, "When you feel like that, you need to go to your tent and masturbate. All by yourself. When no one else is around."

He looks at me funny. Then he asks, "Is that really okay with God, you think, Pastor?"

I say, "Dude, you've been having sex with prostitutes. I'm pretty sure God would see this as an improvement."

He says, "Okay, I'll give it a try."

The next day, he walks into Joe's Addiction, straight to me, and whispers, "I met Five-fingered Sally last night."

"Who's that?"

He holds out his hand and counts his fingers, "One, two, three, four, five. You know, Five- fingered Sally."

"Oh! Congratulations. How did it go?"

He says, "I think it's gonna work, Pastor. I think I'll be just fine."

Little Mary

Five years into our time at Joe's Addiction, nineteen-year-old Little Mary changes me down to the core of my being.

She is a tiny little thing, maybe four foot nine with curly, blond hair, a fair complexion and gray eyes like the color of the ocean when it's raining. When Mary first comes to Joe's Addiction, she sits at a table on "the front stoop." That's what I call the cracked sidewalk in front of the coffee shop. On a good day, when the weather's mild, I dub it "the veranda." She smokes her cigarettes and makes quiet conversation with the men. I wonder if they know her, if somebody knows her. Someone tells me her name.

The days are busy at Joe's, always another plate to make for someone or a pastoral "counseling" conversation to have (which mostly just means I listen). In the midst of the busyness I begin to notice that the crowd around Mary is always men. Especially men who have recently come out of prison.

One day, someone comes to me and says, "What are we gonna do? Mary is taking guys out back into the trees. I saw her with my own eyes!" She leans in close and says in a tone that would have been a shout, if she hadn't been trying to whisper, "The guys are paying $5 for a blow job!"

I am angry. Angry at the men who would use Mary. Angry at Mary for bringing that kind of business to Joe's Addiction. The girls in the clubs next door offer those services—but not at Joe's. Some of these guys are fresh out of years in prison. How can they resist that kind of temptation? Impossible. I am mad. I say, "I'll talk to her."

I march out front to the table where Mary sits smoking, take a seat across from her so I can look her in the eye, and I put on what I hope is my most authoritative face. With some forcefulness, edged by my anger, I say, "I need to talk to you." She is startled, and her gray eyes widen. I have never said more than a hello to her before.

I do not wait for a response. I rush on with what I have to say. "Mary, I know what you have been doing with the guys here and it has to stop. There will be no more blow jobs. We cannot have the reputation of Joe's Addiction be that we are a place to get cheap sex."

With the same wide-eyed, shocked expression, she whimpers, "But I gotta have bus fare, 'cause I gotta get downtown to see my P.O., or they'll put me in prison."

The anger melts out of my shoulders, down my legs, and out the bottoms of my feet. I lean over the table, grab Mary's hand and say, "You need bus fare, you come to me. I will give you $5. You don't need to do that to get what you need. If you need something, you come to me. Do you understand?" She nods silently.

I go back inside to answer a phone call, serve another cup of coffee, wipe another table— whatever is next. A few minutes later, as I pull a bulging trash bag from the can, I feel an arm reach around my waist and turn to find Mary's head of blond curls buried in my shoulder. "Thank you," she whispers.

This is the beginning of my relationship with Little Mary. She comes and goes from our community. She hangs around for a few days and then disappears for a couple of months. Mary has family in another part of the city—sometimes a place to stay there. Sometimes she is in jail. Sometimes, when she shows up at Joe's Addiction, she is high. Sometimes she trembles from the need for another fix.

Every time I see her, I make sure she eats something. Especially after she tells me she is pregnant. I play the mama chasing her kid around with another plate of food. I don't know what else to do. I give her a few rides. I ask her how she is doing. I listen to her problems, but I don't know what more I can do.

Little Mary is a sex worker—not the street-walker type— well maybe sometimes, but not the leopard skin, mini-skirt and high heels type you might have in your mind. For Mary, sex is a currency, as is the case for so many women living in poverty.

I don't know what it is about Mary, but she captures my heart. I look for her blond, curly mop every time I drive up to Joe's Addiction. She is so little. So young. So naïve. She puts herself into so many bad situations with the wrong people at the wrong time, doing things she shouldn't. Once she calls me from the jail just to let me know where she is. She has been arrested for stealing a cell phone. I ask her, "Did you do it?" and she responds, "Prolly. I was high."

Both of Mary's parents are drug addicts. Who knows? Her mother may have been on drugs while she was pregnant with Mary. She does not think right. She does not seem to understand cause-and-effect consequences. She doesn't understand who she is or how valuable she is no matter how many times I tell her.

One night, I am standing in the ER next to my dear friend, Foster, holding his hand and restraining my nausea, while they stop his bleeding, reset his broken and dislocated wrist, and prep him for surgery after a motorcycle wreck, when my cell phone rings. It's Crystal, who I know is at Joe's waiting with many others for news about Foster' condition, so I answer. Instead of the question, "How is Foster?" I hear, "Mary is dead."

I can't do this. Not now. It's too much—too much. It is another twenty hours, after we have the assurance that Foster' three surgeries have gone well and he will recover (though it will take many months), before I can track down what happened to Mary. Internal bleeding caused by a miscarriage, complicated by late stage syphilis and AIDS.

I post my grief on the internet with these thoughts and a confession:

I didn't even know she was sick. I didn't know she had syphilis. I didn't know she had AIDS. If she knew, she never told me. If she knew she didn't have long to live, she never told me. What would I have done if I had known?

I have thought long and hard about this. I have been carrying it like a weight upon my chest—a weight that at times has pressed upon me the futility of all we are attempting to do through Joe's Addiction and left me in utter despair. I know "should've, could've, would've" is not a healthy way to think. I know I did a lot. I know I could have done more. I know the problems it would have caused had I brought her to my home—but maybe I could have. I know she would have probably continued in all her same behaviors—but maybe I should have. If I had known she was dying, I would have.

Life at Joe's is always busy. There are so many people, so many needs. Most days only have enough hours to meet a few. Often it is the squeaky wheel that gets the most attention. The familiar adage says, "Can't see the forest for the trees." But I am afraid Mary was the "tree" that I missed for the "forest."

So here comes the confession:

Yesterday I handed out my first condoms to a young couple I know is having sex. He is HIV positive. I have fallen so far from the tree of my daddy's religion, and I know some of you won't approve. But this is where I am. I will continue to invite people into the Best Way, the Abundant Life—the Way of Jesus, but I will not watch another person die if it is in my power to prevent it. It's just too much.

There's more to this story, and I don't know if it makes things feel better or worse. It is embarrassing, and it is upsetting.

Two weeks after Little Mary's funeral, my older kids are in downtown Oklahoma City late one evening. As they walk to their car, they see Little Mary standing right there on the street. Jael approaches her, grabs her, and hollers, "Mary! We thought you were dead! We even had a funeral for you? What is going on?"

Mary laughs and then shrugs her shoulders. She says someone was after her. Her life was in danger, so she faked her death. Her parents even thought she had died. She says, "Yeah, my mom was pretty mad when she found out I didn't really die."

I am devastated. Destroyed. I have been through so much pain the last two weeks, only to find it wasn't even real. But then again, it was. Something has died. It just isn't Mary. It is more of my old, religious judgment. Judgment that kept me from truly loving people. It is dead, and I can't go back.

Dwayne

Dwayne has been coming to Joe's Addiction for two years. Every Friday night, he brings his laptop computer. He tells me bits and pieces about himself. He has been in the military, stationed overseas. I know he is divorced. I also know he is taking classes at the community college, and he is trying to "better himself" by getting a degree. Sometimes he asks for help with a paper he is writing. I help him with spelling, offer suggestions, and generally just try to encourage him in his pursuit of a degree.

I am surprised one night when Dwayne comes into Joe's with tears streaming down his face. I hurry over and sit down with him to ask what is going on. He ducks his head. I wait while he tries to gather his emotions.

Finally he says, "I was just at Walgreens shopping, and I passed a shelf of coffee mugs. One of the mugs said, 'GREATEST DAD EVER.'" His eyes fill with tears again, and he whispers, "I will never be the greatest dad ever." Then out tumbles Dwayne's dark and shameful story.

Dwayne molested his own daughter. As he says these words, I silently pray that my outward expression is remaining unchanged, that I can listen with no physical reaction. "God, help me!"

For ten years, I had been telling my own story of abuse. I often spoke to large gatherings of people about the relationships I had been in at fifteen years old and at nineteen. I told of my suicide attempt and the healing of shame that had happened in my soul. I even wrote a book about these things. But I had never told that the abuse did not begin in my high school years.

When I was ten years old an older teenage boy took me into the church nursery and sexually assaulted me. I had never talked openly about this experience because it seemed like too much. I feared people would think, "Why? What was it about this girl that brought her so much abuse?" Despite all the healing I had experienced, I still thought there must have been something wrong with *me*, something about *me* that caused men to do these things.

Now, this man sitting here in front of me represents the deepest pains of my life. "God, help me!"

I listen as Dwayne describes the events that led up to his heinous act. He tells me of the trouble in his marriage, the fights, how his wife had left him. He had also been laid off from his job. It was a dark time for him. He was angry. He was depressed. Dwayne then tells me of a bizarre and overwhelming temptation that came to him, and that he acted upon it. He says it was not just a one-time thing. It went on for about a month, and he knew the whole time it was wrong.

He tells me how awful he felt, and that he had to come clean, so he told his ex-wife. Of course, everything "hit the fan," and he knew it was justified. She pressed charges and he went to prison. As he is telling me his story, there is no defending, no shifting of blame. He just lays it out, simple and clear. This is what happened.

As Dwayne speaks, I continue to pray, "Oh God, oh God, oh God. Help me. How did I get myself into this? I am not this man's priest." But then I hear The Muse speak to my spirit, "Yes. You are," and I know this is how Dwayne sees me—someone he can trust, someone to whom he can confess. "Oh God, I don't think I am up for this."

Tears continue to stream down Dwayne's face. He seems unconscious of the others in the room, not even looking around to see who might be listening or watching him. I sit quietly next to him as the torrent gushes.

He goes on. "I'm lonely. I would love to find a woman to share my life again. But even if a woman would want me after what I did, I could never have a normal life. If we ever have children together, I could not live in the same house with my children. I would be required to live in a separate house until they turn eighteen and can choose for themselves." He is not angrily arguing, merely lamenting the sadness of his reality.

Suddenly, I am aware of tears on my own face.

A miracle happens in this moment. I am not angry. I am not afraid. My heart overflows with compassion for this man— maybe the vilest of sinners. I reflect on his reality and what I know of God. The Good News of Jesus is that this man's sin is forgiven—thrown into the sea of forgetfulness, never to be brought up again. But for the rest of his life on earth, he will pay the consequences for a month of horrific sin. I realize in that moment that I love him, I forgive him, and I grieve with him the loss, the pain, the loneliness. Nothing can change his reality. It just is. So I "mourn with those who mourn." Judgment falls away, and another layer of my own soul is healed.

When we first explored this part of town and we began to dream of starting a coffee shop community here, I imagined myself helping "broken" women in the clubs. This was natural. Having been abused, I had issues with men. God had brought so much healing in my life, and I dreamed of passing on to abused women the healing I had received. I even visualized the conversations and the "rescues" I would make. I had more than a bit of arrogance and some messiah complex.

But what I did not anticipate—what we could not have known—was a halfway house would open only a quarter of a mile away from Joe's Addiction and become home to over

200 sex offenders. Many of these men were fresh out of years in prison.

In the state of Oklahoma, "sex offender" has a broad definition. All sex offenses are lumped together, from indecent exposure (which includes peeing in public), to "Romeo and Juliet crimes" (i.e. a young man was 19 and his girlfriend was 15), to child molesters and rapists. The organization down the street does the best it can to screen out predators, but the potential is always there, and some of these men are not mentally stable nor predictable.

I did not know Dwayne lived at "that place," and now here he was sitting in front of me, representing my very own abuser. I tell you all of this because I want you to understand the transformation that has happened in me. It is easy to have compassion upon those who have experienced the same injuries we have. To desire to help other victims is a natural part of our healing process. In fact, it seems to be a pattern. Often The Muse inspires us to pass on the healing given to us. But it is an entirely different thing to find oneself loving and ministering to one's abuser. Maybe this is full-circle redemption. Maybe this is Love healing.

Little by little, more of these men came to Joe's Addiction. Some of them began to come to church on Sundays. Understandably, this caused concerns. Is it safe? What about the other people we want to come to church? What if they won't feel comfortable? Maybe those guys should have a church of their own. Is this who we intended this church to be for? People even threatened to leave the church if we continued to allow sex offenders to attend our services.

We did not make the decision to welcome the sex offenders lightly. John and I wrestled with these issues. It came down to this: we had been preaching the all-inclusive Love of God to our people. We had told them no one is rejected. We had told them the ones Jesus spent his time with were the outcasts, the rejects of society—even the lepers.

We realized these men are the "lepers" of our American culture. No one wants them around. In fact, in Oklahoma, their common identification card displays their "scarlet letter" in red letters. Their driver's license says "sex offender," even for those whose crime was peeing in public. Much the same as in Jesus' day, these men are required to cry out, "leper!" every time they interact with society. What would it say to our community if we now told them, "Well, we accept everyone into community except these men?" What would it say to them about everything we had told them about God's Love and acceptance of *them*?

A leper came to Jesus, begging on his knees, "If you want to, you can cleanse me." Deeply moved, Jesus put out his hand, touched him, and said, "I want to. Be clean." Then and there the leprosy was gone, his skin smooth and healthy. Jesus dismissed him with strict orders: "Say nothing to anyone. Take the offering for cleansing that Moses prescribed and present yourself to the priest. This will validate your healing to the people." But as soon as the man was out of earshot, he told everyone he met what had happened, spreading the news all over town. (Mark 1:40-44 MSG)

Some of the people who had started this experiment with us decided if we were going to allow these guys to be part of the community, they would have to leave—and they did. Even some of our early Valley Brook folks decided they could not handle the tension. We felt sad, but we tried to understand. We had to be faithful to what The Muse was saying to us, and I knew this factor was an important part of my own story.

> "Love has a hem to her garment
> That reaches the very dust.
> It sweeps the stains from the streets and lanes,
> And because it can, it must."
>
> — Mother Teresa

CHAPTER 18
JUDGMENT TO LOVE

"Our job is to love others without stopping
to inquire whether or not they are worthy."

— Thomas Merton

Jo comes into Joe's Addiction one afternoon with her two-year-old girl in tow. She orders a drink and tells me she has just been next door at Valley of the Dolls doing an interview. She says that basically means she took her clothes off and let them look at her. As she speaks, I wonder where her daughter was while she "interviewed."

She keeps talking as I make her drink, so I invite her to sit down at a table with me. She accepts and says she is not too sure she wants to work there, but she is single and needs to support her daughter. She thinks she can make decent money dancing, but again she says she isn't too sure she really wants that kind of job. As I sit listening, I hear in my spirit, "Don't you dare heap any more shame upon this girl than she already has."

Evangelism teaching in church taught me that it was our job to "get people lost" before we could "get them saved." What that meant was that we needed to show people the terribleness

JUDGMENT TO LOVE   237

of their sin and the wrath of God. We had to make sure people knew God's finger was hovering over the "smite button" and he would send them to hell, unless they realized how sinful and worthless they are. They needed to apologize to God and ask God to forgive them. Then, and only then, would God's wrath be turned into mercy.

"Don't you dare heap any more shame upon this girl than she already has."

Jo and I chat about other things for a while. She tells me she has moved to the area from Montana and she is looking for a place to rent. Someone else in the room recommends a landlord in the neighborhood and gives her a number, and this is how Jo comes into the Joe's Addiction community.

Over the next weeks and months, we get to know Jo and her daughter. I have a lot of advice to offer about things like how to help your child eat vegetables and sleep through the night. She and her baby are easy to love.

One day, I mention something about church, and Jo says, "Oh, I am not too much for the church, but I feel guilty about not taking my daughter." She starts attending our services. She seems to like the music, and everyone is nice to her, so she keeps coming back.

As relationship grows between us, Jo tells me about the man she is dating. She met him through Craigslist. He is twice her age. I ask friendly questions about him, and I notice she doesn't seem to know very much about him. I ask her what kinds of things they like to do together, and she says, "Oh, we drive around in the car until my daughter falls asleep. Then we go back to his place and have sex." Sometimes Jo has fingertip shaped bruises on her neck, and I worry about her. I ask, and she says, "Oh don't worry. It's all consensual."

Jo moves into a rental house in the neighborhood. It is pretty run down and filthy, but the rent is what she can afford. Some of us from the Joe's community go to work cleaning and fixing up the place. I spend hours cleaning grease out of the kitchen sink where apparently the previous renter repaired carburetors. We spray for bugs and create a pretty princess room for her daughter. Jo cries. She tells me she can't remember the last time she cried. She is so grateful.

Late one night, I receive a call from the Emergency Room. It is Jo. She has had a heart attack—at nineteen years old. I rush to the ER. Doctors determine Jo has a severe magnesium deficiency caused by malnutrition that has caused her heart to malfunction. They send her home with some medicine and a prescription to eat a more nutritious diet. I cannot take her back to her own house to recover while caring for a toddler, so I bring her home with me.

Jo and her baby live with us for four months, and during these months she becomes part of our family. We make sure they eat well, encourage sleep, help Jo look for a better job, and spend countless hours talking about life together. One evening, watching the movie *Runaway Bride* together, Jo cries out, "Love like that doesn't exist!"

Then Jo tells me her story: she was eleven years old and walking home from school, when a man she recognized as a cashier from the store nearby offered her a ride. He seemed like a nice man, so she got in his car. But he didn't take her home. He took her to another location where four other men were waiting. The five men raped her and then threatened her life if she told anyone.

The pain of Jo's life is almost too much to bear, for her, but for me as well, and yet the invitation to us is to allow the painful shame of others to have an empathetic claim on our lives. Not so we can fix the pain, but so we can feel it. Pema Chodron has written, "Compassion is not a relationship between the healer and the wounded. It's a relationship between equals. Only when we know our own darkness well can we be present with the darkness of others." I remember my own abuse, my own suffering, which I measure as so much less than Jo's, and I can empathize with the trauma she experienced.

This trauma did not happen to Jo once. Over the next year of her life, multiple times these men raped her. Sometimes as a group. Sometimes one or two at a time. Each time they threatened her life and the lives of her family members, her little sister, if she told. One man was a janitor at her school. Two of them attended her church. One of them was her Awana Bible teacher.

She tells me she prayed that God would make it stop, but God didn't. Then she began praying every night that God would allow her to die in her sleep, but every morning came with the promise of more pain. It is no wonder Jo doesn't think too much of church.

Her family moved to another town, many states away, and the rapes stopped. But the pain did not. At fourteen years old, Jo tried to kill herself. In the mental hospital she finally told her secret to a counselor. The counselor convinced her she must tell her mother, who, being religious, demanded an OBGYN examine her to find out whether her daughter was still a virgin. The doctor told her it was unlikely Jo would be able to have children due to the damage those men caused to her body.

For the rest of Jo's teenage years, she became promiscuous. "Why not?" she said. What did it matter? She was raped several more times, as she sometimes put herself in situations she said, "I never should have been in." She just did not care. Until. Until she discovered she was pregnant.

I am crying already as Jo tells me her story, but it is at this point her tears begin to fall. She says, "That little baby saved my life. She needed me. I was her mother. I think God gave me my baby to save me."

We do our best to love Jo and take care of her and her daughter. She gets a job, receives some supplemental help with childcare and food, and is able to move back into her own place. She is getting better. But sometimes I see those bruises on her neck. The turning point comes when Jo's boyfriend informs her he has advertised her on Craigslist, and a group of men will arrive later that night to join them in their sexual experience. Jo crawls with her baby out a bathroom window and drives away.

The next day, John and another male friend of ours stand next to Jo as she tells her boyfriend she is never coming back to see him. Their relationship is over. I start to pray for a new man, a kind and loving man, to come into Jo's life as soon as possible. I know. It is not the wisest thing to jump into another relationship. She does not understand what good relationship is like. But I know Jo. She is an addict. Hers is the kind of addiction I know from personal experience. I, too, voraciously sought for love and approval from man after man, to fix the pain in my own soul, that ever present feeling that I was damaged goods, that no one would want me. I am afraid the first unscrupulous guy that comes along will sweep Jo into another abusive relationship, and so I ask God to find her a man—a nice man.

Just a few days later, Jo needs to move. Her landlord has been violating her rights. She is sitting in her house with her daughter and, without knocking, the landlord barges right through the front door, terrifying them with his entrance. When she asks him to knock first, he tells her it is *his* house. He can do whatever he wants. He seems to enjoy the power he has and uses it to frighten her. When she is not home, the landlord comes into the house and steals her stuff. She confronts him, and he says, "You're living in *my* house. Your stuff is *my* stuff. Nothing you can do about it." I know. It's illegal. Renters rights and all that. But when you have no money and no influence, how do you fight injustice? To take him to court would cost so much more than finding a new place to live. And it would be her word against his anyway. Who would believe her over a man who owns a bunch of properties?

Some of the Joe's Addiction community shows up to help her pack and move to a new house. When we arrive, Jackson is already there. Jackson is part of our Joe's community. He attends church with us. His sister and brother-in-law help lead the music on Sundays. He has been around for a while. I notice them talking and think, "Hmmm."

At the end of the long day of packing and moving, after everything is put in its new place, we all leave to the sounds of Jo's thanks. But Jackson stays. They hang out for a while, talking. That night Jo calls me to tell me Jackson asked her out for a date. I ask her what she said, she tells me, "Yeah. We're going out Saturday night." I am excited for Jo. Jackson is a nice guy.

Sunday morning comes, and I hurry to ask Jo about her date. "How did it go?" She says it was fun. Jackson seems like a nice guy. Then she tells me he asked her if he could kiss her. My heart sinks. "What did you say?"

"I told him, 'Yeah. Whatever. I guess.'"

"Well, how was it?" I ask.

She shrugs and says, "Well, he didn't pull my hair."

Over the next months, Jo and Jackson get to know one another and practice learning to love. They have so much baggage. Jackson comes from a checkered past of his own, filled with drug running for cartels and lots of violence. Neither of them know how to love well, but they are growing. The day comes when Jackson asks Jo to marry him, and she says, "yes."

This young couple is poor. They have very little money to throw a wedding. But what a celebration it is. Members of the Joe's Addiction community contribute their talents from decorating, to cake making, to bringing a potluck dinner of all of Jo's favorites—including brussel sprouts.

It is a beautiful day for the outdoor ceremony. Family and friends gather to celebrate Love. Love unexpected. Love unhoped for. Surprising Love. Miraculous Love. There is not a dry eye in the crowd as Jackson first marries Jo by placing a ring on her finger, and then becomes Jo's daughter's daddy by placing a necklace around her neck, vowing his love to her forever.

Today, Jackson and Jo live in Montana with their *five* children. The last two were twins. Jackson has a stable job and provides well for his family. Jo is near completing a degree in Cultural Anthropology. Learning to love well has not been an easy path for either of them, but they have stuck with each other, and they have grown together. We miss them and enjoy the vacations they are able to afford to come and visit their Joe's Addiction family from time to time. I credit Jo with teaching me to love without judgment. It did not happen overnight, but she was the beginning of my understanding that I was not to be an Announcer of God's Wrath, but a Remover of Shame.

Levi

Robert brings his friend Levi to church. Levi is gay but has never been Robert's partner. They have shared a house for a few years some time back, and Robert loves him like a brother. Now Levi is living in a nursing home. He has been living with AIDS for over twenty years. He tells me once that he has seen over a hundred of his friends die from it. He used to belong to a support group, but he quit going. It was too hard watching people die. Levi sees it as a miracle he is still alive.

The third Sunday Levi is in church he walks to the front and asks John to pray for God to heal him. Prayer for physical healing has always made us nervous. You never know what will happen. Will God show up or not? But since our friend's death from pancreatic cancer, our faith- level on the whole healing thing is—well, let's just say it is much smaller than a mustard seed.

Yet, we are committed to our Jesus experiment, and this is one thing Jesus said to do, pray for the sick, so John does it. He tells Levi he knows God *can* heal him, he doesn't know if God *will*, but he is glad to pray for him.

As John launches into his prayer, Levi interrupts saying, "I think God just healed me!" John is startled and asks, "Really?" Levi says, "Yes. I think he healed my diabetes." We didn't even know Levi had diabetes. And what? Does this make any sense? Why would God heal his diabetes and not his AIDS? Weird priority list, God.

Levi's diabetes is the reason he is living in a nursing home. He is not there because of his AIDS. He is relatively healthy, not frail or weak, although he does look older than his age. He is forty- four, but I think he looks near sixty. His white hair and pale skin create a nice backdrop for his yellow-dentured, big, toothy smile that perfectly fits his ornery personality. But it is his blood sugar that is out of control. He is in the nursing home to manage his diet.

The next day, Robert brings Levi to Joe's Addiction to play cards. Levi comes to the counter and orders a smoothie. I say,

"Oh Levi. Our smoothies are not really healthy. They are full of sugar. You probably shouldn't drink that much sugar."

Levi says, "God healed me yesterday. I want a smoothie." He sees my faithless sigh and says, "I won't be stupid. I'll check my blood sugar, and I have my insulin with me. I'll be careful." I make him a strawberry smoothie.

Levi's blood sugar stays level.

He comes in the next day, and with a big smile on his face says, "Today I want to try a blueberry one."

Same thing. Blood sugar is fine.

After three days, Levi tells his nurses he needs to speak with the supervising doctor. God has healed him, and he does not need this diet anymore. He waits and waits for the doctor to examine him. Each time he asks the nurses, they tell him the doctor is busy. A week later, still no visit from the doctor, Levi walks out of the nursing home. He tells us, "I was sick to death of oatmeal!"

We baptize Levi that spring, and I will never forget his grin, as he declares God has saved and healed him, and however long he has left, he wants to follow Jesus for the rest of his life. We decide maybe God healed the diabetes, so Levi could enjoy smoothies however long that will be.

Levi moves back in with his long-time partner George and the two men hang out at Joe's Addiction a lot and come to church together on Sundays. We play cards, and we talk about life. Levi tells me more of his story. He had been married to a woman many years before. His marriage had ended in divorce. I listen, as little by little, Levi shares some of the pains of his family life growing up, even abuse he experienced as a child.

George is a tall, round black man who does not say much. When Levi tells these stories, George sits silently, cards in his hand, chewing on his bottom lip. Sometimes he shakes his head when Levi tells painful parts. George is his friend and his lover. It is obvious he loves Levi, and it is obvious he has wounds of his own hidden behind his big, quiet demeanor. We just let George be there with us, and occasionally, with no fanfare, he wins a hand of cards.

I almost always lose at cards. I become distracted with people and conversation and I forget it is my turn and where we are in the game, and then I don't know what card to play. Robert quits playing with me because he gets tired of grabbing one of my cards and laying it down for me. Robert says, "Well, let's get on over to the mayor's house," and the guys all stand up to go.

I ask them, "You're going to the mayor's house? What for?"

Robert says, "Well, that's Levi's parents. His dad is the mayor of Valley Brook. Didn't you know?"

Another evening, Levi asks if he can talk to John. He is very serious. They go over to the couch and sit down. Levi tells John he has a desire to preach. He asks John, "Do you think it would be okay if I go back into the nursing home and hold services for the people there? Talk to them about Jesus? Tell them what God has done for me?" John says, "I'm sure we can arrange it. That would be great." Levi says, "Oh good. Because I'm already doing it. I just thought I'd better run it by you."

The Gay Thing

Depending on your background, you may be wondering. Does Levi stop "sinning"? This is where I get to tell you of the evolution of my faith.

I grew up understanding homosexuality to be an "abomination," one of the worst sins one could commit. As The Muse so faithfully does, by the time I meet Levi and George, I have come to believe God's definition of sin must be motivated by God's Love. God is not random in defining which behaviors are good and which are bad. The only reason an action would be "off limits" is because it harms us when we do it, or we harm another person when we do it. God loves us and wants all of us to experience Life in its fullest. Love is the measurement.

It is easy to make judgments about groups or categories of people when you don't know them. I had never known a gay person before I met Levi. Well, I'm sure I did, just not someone open about being gay. Levi and George are my friends. They have become uncles to my children. I know there is no way God can consider them an abomination, but I am confused. I don't know what to do with the incongruity between the Love I am learning to embrace and the teachings of my religious upbringing. I know I am committed to Love, so I love Levi.

One day, sitting at a table in Joe's, Levi raises the question himself. He asks, "Should I kick George out?" John asks him, "What do you think God wants you to do?" Levi pauses for a long moment, his head bowed, eyes on his hands while he slowly rubs his right thumb over his left. John waits. Finally, Levi says, "George and I have been together a long time. He is old and sick. He can't take care of himself. He doesn't even have an income. I can't imagine Jesus kicking him out, telling him he's on his own now."

John says, "Well then, that is what God is saying. I can't imagine Jesus doing such a thing to George either."

Clare of Assisi was one of the first followers of Saint Francis. She founded the Order of Poor Ladies, a monastic religious order for women in the Franciscan tradition. I love what she said: "We become what we love and who we love shapes what we become. If we love things, we become a thing. If we love nothing, we become nothing. Imitation is not a literal mimicking of Christ, rather it means becoming the image of the beloved, an image disclosed through transformation. This means we are to become vessels of God's compassionate love for others."

Sorry and a Proud

George calls from the hospital. Levi has taken an overdose of pills. We are confused. He had been doing so well. He was happy. He was serving others. In the six months we had known him, Levi had never seemed down or despondent.

John rushes to the hospital. The doctors have saved his life, but Levi is distraught. As John tries to comfort him, the story tumbles out. Levi's ex-wife had called. They had divorced many years before. Guilt had finally overcome her, and she called to confess to him that *she* was the one who had infected him with AIDS. She had cheated on him and contracted it. All these years. Years of illness. Years of medications. Years of fear. Years of humiliation.

Levi weeps hot tears of pain and sorrow, and tears of hatred for his wife. We console Levi the best we can. We can only imagine the grief he is experiencing. Then we watch as Levi stands in church one morning to give what he calls "a sorry and a proud." He tells the whole community what his wife did and the struggle of hatred he has felt toward her. Then he says, "But today, I have decided to forgive my wife. She did not know what she was doing. Isn't that what Jesus said from the cross? Father, forgive them. They don't know what they are doing. If God can forgive me, then I can forgive her." We cry a lot of tears together in the Joe's Addiction community, and this day there is not a dry eye in the room.

Levi's Legacy

The phone rings in the middle of the night, almost a year from the day John baptized Levi. George is weeping on the other end of the phone. Levi has died in his sleep. He had not been sick. We had expected and prepared ourselves for walking with Levi through the terrible suffering of the end stage of AIDS, but it never came. He is just gone.

We visit the mayor's family and tell his parents how much we loved Levi. His dear, sweet, white-haired mother is herself breathing from an oxygen tank, and the mayor remembers us. He and John had met before when Levi was in the hospital. John had offered to take him out to lunch sometime. The mayor had said, "I don't like preachers. That Baptist preacher is always knocking on my door and telling me if I don't come to his church I am going to go to hell." He had never taken John up on his offer of lunch.

But now, in the wake of losing their son, in the tenderness of their grief, the mayor's family accepts our comfort. We offer to host a memorial service at Joe's Addiction. For the last year of Levi's life, he had been a vital part of our community, and we want to celebrate his life. They agree.

We do the service like an Irish wake (without any alcohol since Levi was a recovering alcoholic). Friends who knew Levi before he decided to follow The Way of Jesus pack the room: Alcoholics Anonymous friends are there; AIDS support groups friends, family from out of town, officials from Valley Brook city hall. All mixed together with those of us who had known him only for the last year. I have never seen so many gay and transgender people together in one place. We feel so privileged to be hosting and welcoming all.

One at a time, people share their memories of our friend, Levi. Some sweet. Some funny. Some draw tears. Some elicit laughter. His mom and dad sit on the flowered couch where Levi first announced to John he was preaching in the nursing home. John relays that story, and the room erupts. They cannot believe we knew the same Levi they had known.

After a long pause, John asks if anyone has anything left to say. Our daughter, Jewel, six years old, pulls on my skirt. I bend over while she whispers in my ear, "Mama, I want to say something, but I'm too afraid." I ask her to tell me, and I will say it for her.

"I wore this dress, because Levi told me he thought it was pretty." God is Love. Levi was Love. We saw God.

CHAPTER 19
LOVE IS THE POINT

"Love and compassion are necessities, not luxuries.
Without them, humanity cannot survive."

— Dalai Lama XIV

A young man comes to me on a Sunday at Joe's, just after the morning church service. I have never seen him before this morning, and he is one of those people you can't miss. Large, imposing stature, black hair, black clothes, colorful tattoos, and multiple piercings down the middle of his face.

He reports he went to a nearby church that morning and the pastor who met him at the door told him, "We don't accept tattoos and piercings at this church."

He was taken aback and responded to the pastor, "Well, in the Bible, Jesus was pretty much, 'Come as you are.'" The pastor said, "Yes, but we have traditional values and ways at our church."

The young man pointed to some teenagers standing nearby and said, "Well, those folks have piercings." The pastor responded, "Yes, well, they're in our youth group. You're an adult. You ought to know better."

The pastor then told him, "If you want to go to church, you should go over to Joe's Addiction. They accept prostitutes, junkies, tattoos, and piercings. They'll take anyone."

I know it's hard to believe a church would tell a person who *wants* to go to their church that they are unwelcome. Especially now, when in America church attendance is at an all-time low. You would think they would be happy *anyone* wanted to show up. But I am afraid it is an all too common story.

Teenage Mom

I am making small talk at a holiday gathering, catching up with family members and friends. One of them tells me this story of a current conflict happening in their church:

There is a sixteen-year-old, African American girl who has been attending the mostly white church. She comes with her two-year-old baby, who enjoys the nursery. Mama is grateful for both the worship service and the childcare. But now, she has gotten pregnant—again. Not married. Not even a regular guy in her life. Two different "baby daddies" (as the folks in our community say).

So here is the conflict: some women in the church want to throw a baby shower for her. She needs stuff. Baby clothes, diapers, another car seat. But the person who is telling me this story is angry, and he has authority in the church. He says "We are not going to throw a baby shower for this girl. She has to get the message this is not okay. Having sex outside of marriage is wrong. And if we give her a party and presents, she will think living this way is okay with us—and okay with God."

I try to explain. I try to appeal for mercy for the girl—for the baby. I try to help him understand poverty, cultural norms, and emotional struggles. I try. But in anger, he responds, "You are not going to convince me it is okay to condone her sin."

As Henri Nouwen said, "For Jesus, there are no countries to be conquered, no ideologies to be imposed, no people to be dominated. There are only children, women, and men to be loved." This conversation was another departure from the religion of the first half of my life. I cannot stomach it any more. Many Christians feel frustrated when people accuse them of "hating." They claim they are just standing for "the Truth." But the manner in which they do this amounts to standing against *people*, against *human beings*. There is no way this cannot feel like hate.

I hear Christians try to wrestle with the "tension between Love and condoning sin." They ask, "Where do we draw the line?" Where I am today—there is no line. There just is no line to find. No line. Perhaps where I am today is a knee-jerk reaction. Maybe so. But I think if we are going to err (and we *are* going to err), then erring on the side of Love is where I want to be. William Blake wrote, "We are put on earth for a little space that we might learn to bear the beams of love." Love is actually the point.

I had a conversation recently with a woman who is struggling with her faith. She, too, grew up in Evangelical Christianity. Some terrible tragedies in her life have left her doubting God exists. If there is a God, then why would God allow such suffering? As we mused together, trying to grapple with reality, as opposed to cliché or myth, I realized I have simplified all of my beliefs down to Love. I wonder if rather than God being the *source* of Love, what if Love is the Source? Love is God. I know the Bible says God is love, but what if the other way around is also true? Rather than God being an "entity" that exists "out there" somewhere, maybe Love is the energy force that holds everything together. Everywhere we encounter Love, we are encountering God. What if The Beatles were right? Love *is* all you need.

> "Love is our true destiny. We do not find the meaning
> of life by ourselves alone - we find it with another."
>
> — Thomas Merton

Ronnie and Dale

Ronnie is an hilarious man. He does a stand-up comedy routine in our talent show and has the whole room in stitches. His humor is not just practiced and memorized. He has that kind of on- the-spot spontaneous wit that just pops out of his mouth and lightens the mood with unexpected laughter, not just on the stage, but in everyday circumstances. Everyone likes him.

A man in our community has a heart attack and is in the hospital awaiting a pacemaker procedure. When I announce I am going to visit him, Ronnie and his boyfriend, Dale, say they want to go, too. The man is their friend, and they want to encourage him. I tell them to jump in, and they ride in the back seat.

On the way to the hospital they start arguing. It sounds like it is a continuation of an argument that has been ongoing from earlier in the day, maybe longer. Names are called. Insults hurled. It is becoming heated, and I am feeling pretty awkward chauffeuring the fighting couple. When we reach the hospital, Ronnie apologizes. He says, "Obviously, we have some communication problems. Do you think you could maybe help us with some counseling?" I tell him we can talk about some things after we have seen our friend.

On the way back to Joe's Addiction, I find myself giving communication tips and relationship advice to a gay couple. We talk about what Love is like. Love is kind. It's patient. It's not selfish. It isn't easily offended. I find myself teaching Love to people I love—people I never thought I would love. Once again, I wonder how I got here.

Climbing

Allan meets with his probation officer after an assault charge. His charge is from a fight he had with his cousin one night when they were both drunk. At his probation meeting, he fails his drug test. It is not surprising. His probation officer gives him a requirement to go to "such-and- such" place for a mental health and addiction evaluation. At first look, this seems like a merciful, and even helpful consequence. Let's provide assistance to the addict, rather than just throw him in jail.

Allan shows me the official paper from his probation officer. It includes the details of the organization where he is to report, a phone number, and an assigned case worker. The instructions read that he is to report to this place within five days.

I point out the phone number and tell Allan to call. He takes the phone, and in a few minutes comes back to me and says, "It was just a recording, something about today being the color green. Maybe I dialed the wrong number?" I take the phone and dial the number myself. A recording answers. The color of day is for addicts who are required to "check in," but the recording continues to list the names of personnel and instructions for pressing different numbers to reach them. I listen for the name of Allan's assigned caseworker. She isn't listed. I press 0 to reach an operator. A message comes on asking me to wait on hold.

I hand the phone to him and tell him to wait for someone to come on the line and then to explain that his probation officer has ordered him to come there. I tell him, "Ask how you are to do that." A few minutes later he comes back with the information they only take "walk-ins" on Thursdays from 9 a.m.-2 p.m.. Okay, so that means he has to go tomorrow. If he waits until the next Thursday, it will be more than five days.

Allan says, "I also have to show my ID." He shrugs his shoulders and flops his arms in his typical "gansta" motion. "Who Knows Who" in the homeless camp stole his wallet a few weeks ago. "Okay, that means we have to go get you a new ID today."

We then look at the address. It is in Edmond. Edmond is the suburb north of our city. There is one bus that goes to there. Allan cannot read the bus schedule. I jump online to help him figure out what time to catch the bus and where to change busses. I enter the information several times, in several ways, and discover the only bus that will get him there on Thursday arrives at 2:05 p.m.. Too late.

There is no way this young man can even understand the instructions for what his probation officer is requiring of him without help. And there is no possible way he can even meet the requirements. His P.O. knows he lives outside on the southeast side of the city, and he has no transportation.

When I start huffing and puffing and blustering my frustrations, Allan shakes his head and says, "It's my own damn fault." Yes. Yes, it is. I appreciate his honesty, and to an outsider it might even look like humility. But really, it's shame. The shame of addiction. The shame of being entirely dependent upon other people to help. The shame of failure, once again.

Codependency, enabling, "when helping hurts"—these things are all real, and figuring out the *best* way to help is complicated and messy. We cannot live other people's lives for them. I cannot prevent someone from putting the meth pipe in his or her mouth again. There is a consequence for every choice each of us makes.

But sometimes the mountain of failure and shame is just too big, too hard to climb, and the path is impossible to trek alone. In community, we climb the trail together. We hold each other's hands. And when we have the ability, we make the mountain lower. We take away some of the rocks. We move obstacles out of the way. And we cheer each other on. "Yes, the hike is hard, but you can do hard things! Don't give up!" Mother Teresa said, "Be kind to each other: It is better to commit faults with gentleness than to work miracles with unkindness." This attitude is what we must practice.

That afternoon, I help Allan get a new ID, and the next morning one of the rare folks in our Joe's community who has a car takes our young friend to his mental health and addiction evaluation. We pay for the gas with our Community Fund—dollars and pennies dropped into the bucket every Sunday to help take care of one another. Allan comes back from his meeting holding his head up high to make yet another attempt to scale the mountain that is his life. This time, he just might summit.

Or maybe he won't.

Brooks

Brooks is a transgender person who I meet at a Narcotics Anonymous meeting. Brooks starts coming to church services at Joe's Addiction. One Sunday during Prouds and Sorries, he stands and thanks everyone in the room for welcoming him. He says he has never felt welcome in any church before. He loves Jesus and is happy to be here.

From conversations with Brooks, I know Brooks was born female, but is transitioning to male. He is taking testosterone and is so excited that he has begun growing facial hair. He is sporting a scruffy beard, and his muscles are growing. Brooks shares custody of his eight-year-old daughter with his daughter's father. Brooks sometimes brings his daughter to church at Joe's. She seems to enjoy the Children's Church service. I am overwhelmed and grateful that our community has become a safe place for Brooks and his daughter.

Brooks stands one Sunday and asks for prayer. With tears brimming, he announces he is pregnant. I know. It's confusing. I look around the room, and I see the questions on people's faces. Some glance at me. Some glance at one another. There is no judgment, only confusion.

Brooks goes on. He says his daughter is the greatest thing in his life, and if God sees fit to allow him to give birth to another child, he will consider it a great joy. But he explains that because of the testosterone he is taking, it is likely that his body will reject the baby. He will miscarry. Tears pour down Brooks's cheeks at the thought of such grief.

A woman jumps to her feet, hurries to Brooks, and puts her arm around his shoulder. Another woman joins her. Then a man nearby goes to him and lays a hand on his other shoulder. A small crowd gathers around Brooks and offers prayers for him, for the baby, for peace and relief from fear. When the prayers are over, Brooks thanks everyone, and the room erupts with "We love yous" and "We're glad you're heres."

The world in which I was raised was a world in which everything was white or black, good or evil, righteous or sinful. But that is not real life. The real world is messy. It is complicated. People are messy. People are complicated. We *all* are.

Brooks miscarried the baby, and what Brooks needed was a community of people who cried *with*, people who *loved*. Love grieves with. Love holds. Love is the point.

CHAPTER 20
THEM LOVING ME

"Love is the bridge between you and everything."

— Rumi

Weary from traveling in Kansas for speaking events, I arrive at Joe's Addiction to some difficult "people stuff" going on. Conversations need to happen, frustrations need to be addressed. Not too horrible. Not too pleasant. After taking care of these things, I am sitting at the counter when in walks Sonny. He is high or drunk, maybe both, and he carefully walks to the water cooler and picks up a cup. He then looks at me and a half-toothless grin spreads across his haggard face. He flashes me a backhanded peace sign and says, "Hi Jamie." I respond with, Hi Sonny!"

He fills his water cup, drinks it all down and then fills it again. Then he asks if he can sit on the stool next to me. I invite him. As he sits down he asks, "How you doin, Jamie?" He looks down at me with half-closed eyes, and he means it. This is rare in our community. I am usually the one who asks this question. But Sonny *always* asks me, and he really wants to know. I tell him I'm tired from lots of traveling and life feels kinda hard for me these days. He says, "I know what ya mean!" And he does.

I ask him how he is doing, and he tells me he's been all right. He asks if I saw his bicycle, which I had. He has a cool, tricked out bike he has worked on all winter, and he loves it. He is so proud of it. Then I suddenly realize that just now he has ridden that bike to Joe's. I say, "Oh, Sonny, you better be careful riding your bike." He smiles his big, toothless grin, makes a peace sign with his fingers and says, "Always."

Sonny has mental illness; he hears voices. You mix in the drinking and the drugs, and it is an interesting conversation, to say the least. We talk about his fear that maybe he has ALS. He doesn't, but we look it up on the internet anyway. I read the symptoms to him and they don't fit. "Well, what about this clubfoot?!" he asks.

I had never noticed a clubfoot, so I ask him, "You got a clubfoot now?"

He says, "Yeah, didn't you see me walkin'? My foot just goes like this," and he shows me. I ask him what he thinks is causing it. He says, "My damn family. You know they're so fucked up. You know. We've talked about them before."

It is true. We have talked about them before. Lots of times. Sonny has a lot of pain in the history of his family, but I can also imagine the pain they have experienced as they have endured the tirades of a son who is mentally ill and addicted.

I ask him, "You think your family situation has caused your foot to turn like that?"

He says, "Well, you know." Then he says, "Hey, I'm still clean."

I can't help but laugh out loud. "Sonny, that's amazing." When Sonny says he's clean, he means from cocaine.

He says, "Stayin clean is hard. But it's worth it." I agree with him.

Conversations with Sonny are not straight lines. And they are interrupted by Sonny closing his eyes and muttering whispered, angry responses to the voices he hears in his head. When he feels in control again, he asks me one more time, "So how *you* doin, Jamie?" And he means it. He really wants to know.

Chris Heuertz, in *Friendship at the Margins: Discovering Mutuality in Service and Mission* writes, "A focus on friendship rearranges our assumptions. What if the resources they have also meet our needs? What if Jesus is already present in ways that will minister to us? What if in sharing life together as friends we all move closer to Jesus' heart?" Henri Nouwen writes of his experience: "The journey from teaching about love to allowing myself to be loved proved much longer than I realized." This was true for me as well.

Under the Knife

Late Christmas Eve, John and I have finished wrapping Christmas presents for our kids and filling their stockings. We can finally go to bed to catch a few hours' sleep before the early morning wake up from the kids that will come too soon. As I am putting on my pajamas, I notice a lump in my abdomen. It is about the size of a ping-pong ball, and sore to the touch. Weird. I show John, and he is concerned, but it is Christmas Eve and Friday night. We decide to wait until Monday and call a doctor-friend of ours for advice.

By Sunday evening, the lump has grown to the size of a baseball, and I am in a lot of pain. Our doctor-friend tells us to go straight to the emergency room. After a series of expensive scans, some poking and prodding and pain meds that make me vomit, they have no idea what is growing in my abdomen. They schedule me to see a surgeon the next day.

After looking through the scans, the surgeon says, "We are going to get you in for surgery tomorrow. There are two options for what this is. Either it's cancer, or it's a serious infection. We won't know what it is until we get in there. But either way, we need to take it out of there as soon as possible."

I have lived a pretty healthy life. Common colds, bronchitis here and there. When I was young, I suffered from ulcers. But nothing too extreme. Nothing out of the ordinary. I can tell you, when you hear a doctor say the word "cancer," everything stops. Surgery goes well. It does not take long, and I go home the same day. Then comes the waiting.

We wait three days for the results. Will I find out I am dying? Will I have to endure the horrible suffering of chemo? I tell John I do not think I want to do that. He will not have that conversation with me. We wait.

Finally, the doctor calls. He says, "You don't have cancer. That is the good news. What you have is an infection called Cat Scratch Fever."

What? That's a real thing? I thought it was just a 1970s pop song by Ted Nugent. It turns out Cat Scratch Fever is an infection kittens sometimes carry in their mouths. Because they lick their paws, they can transfer the bacteria to people if they scratch someone. The cat usually exhibits no symptoms, and the infection takes care of itself. When people contract it, it usually feels like a mild flu, some fever, some body aches. It usually clears up on its own as well. Most people don't even know when they contract it, but I have allowed myself to become so run down lately, so exhausted, that when I get it I get it bad.

Now I am just embarrassed. Everyone in my life has been praying for me about the possibility of cancer. People online. My family. The community at Joe's Addiction. But all I have is some dumb disease our new kitten has given me. She is fine, but I am laid out for a month, recovering from surgery and a stupid infection.

When I return to Joe's Addiction on a Sunday a couple of weeks after my surgery, I enter the building, and the band on the stage strikes up the rhythmic chords of "Cat Scratch Fever." The crowded room bursts out laughing, and one after another the people come to give me hugs. It *was* scary, and we are all glad it has turned out fine. These are my people. These are my friends, and they are glad to see me.

Shane Claiborne writes of his community, The Simple Way, "It is a beautiful thing when folks in poverty are no longer just a missions project, but become genuine friends and family with whom we laugh, cry, dream and struggle."

As I was taking on some leadership capacities in my early years of ministry, a spiritual leader in my life told me, "Don't become too close to your people. They need a pastor, not a friend." Seminary professors taught him this principle. The idea he learned is people need someone they can see as a spiritual advisor. If you become too close to them, they might not receive your counsel or follow your advice. Perhaps the reason is to maintain a professional distance from them, like a doctor does with patients.

Henri Nouwen writes, "Most Christian leadership is exercised by people who do not know how to develop healthy, intimate relationships and have opted for power and control instead. Many Christian empire-builders have been people unable to give and receive love."

Whatever the motive, I have seen this painful reality among many ministers, and the result seems sad. Pastors often have few *real* friends. If they do, the friends are far away, not part of their local community. Maybe that is just part of the sacrifice involved in having this vocation. But I don't think it has to be.

I thought we were coming to Valley Brook to help, to serve, to fix. What happened is the people welcomed us into *their* lives, into *their* family, into *their* community. We were the outsiders, and they opened the door. In their hospitality, I have found some of the dearest friends of my life. There is no longer a separation between "us" and "them." The people in our community have become the ones who share in my sadness, sit with me when I am grieving, and celebrate with me when I am rejoicing. They are the ones I want by my side when life is hard. They love me and I love them.

Pema Chödrön, a Buddhist nun, suggests compassion's truest measure lies not in our serving on behalf of the marginalized, but in our willingness to see ourselves in *kinship* with them.

Gregory Boyle believes, "Often we strike the high moral distance that separates 'us' from 'them,' and yet it is God's dream come true when we recognize that there exists no daylight between us. Serving others is good. It's a start. But it's just the hallway that leads to the Grand Ballroom. Kinship—not serving the other, but being one with the other. Jesus was not 'a man for others'; he was one with them. There is a world of difference in that."

Life expectancy is significantly lower among the poor, and John has remarked several times over the last few years to prepare me, "You know, you'll probably be the one burying all of your friends." Although I might end up outliving many of them, if I become sick, they will be the ones standing by my bed, taking care of me in my last hours, and grieving when I am gone.

A Time to Weep

"Love in action is a harsh and dreadful thing compared to love in dreams."

— Fyodor Dostoyevsky

Our resident prophet, Tisha, has a stroke. She suffers from a blood clot disorder she has battled for many years, and one of these clots breaks off and goes to her brain. Tisha's left side of her body no longer functions like it should. After months of physical therapy, Tisha regains her ability to walk, but her left arm and hand never recover.

She was a phlebotomist. That's a person who draws blood samples and processes them in a lab. She was good at her job and very proud of the fact she almost never had to "stick people twice." Because she can no longer do her job, the hospital where she worked lets her go. The Joe's Addiction community rallies around her and does our best to encourage her to find other work.

Tisha signs up with the Department of Rehabilitative Services. They help her arrange rides to and from Joe's Addiction on a small, public transportation system for the disabled. They provide her with an electric scooter and a laptop computer. She enrolls in online classes through a local community college. She decides she wants to become a counselor. We know she will be a good one.

Tisha can no longer serve as a barista, but she supports the community from her chair. She invites people to sit with her and she offers prayer. She listens to people's problems and offers encouragement. She also plays hours and hours of FarmVille and Mob Wars on the internet. John teases her that if she will grow lots of marijuana in FarmVille, she can sell it in Mob Wars and win the game. She laughs and says, "Oh, John."

Tisha is always in church on Sundays. Often she continues to play her games while the sermon is being preached. We wonder if Tisha is paying any attention at all when she motions for me to come over to her. She tells me God is speaking to her and asks for the microphone. Again and again, Tisha amazes us as she delivers the most encouraging messages of God's Love for us.

She cannot stand up for the singing, but she loves the music. Her favorite song becomes "All the Poor and Powerless" by Sons and Daughters:

All the poor and powerless
And all the lost and lonely
All the thieves will come confess
And know that You are holy
All the hearts who are content
And all who feel unworthy
All who hurt with nothing left
Will know that You are holy
And all will sing out Hallelujah
And we will cry out Hallelujah
Shout it
Go on and scream it from the mountains
Go on and tell it to the masses
That He is God

Each time we sing, "Shout it," Tisha cries out at the top of her lungs, from her broken body seated in her chair, "HE IS GOD!" The chorus repeats itself. Each time we return to "Shout it," she shouts again, "HE IS GOD!" Soon others in the room join her. "HE IS GOD! HE IS GOD!" It becomes a tradition and a favorite song for our community, eliciting more participation than any other song has before.

One Sunday morning, Tisha tells me she went to the emergency room the night before. She was in a lot of pain. They diagnosed her with a bladder infection and prescribed antibiotics and pain medication.

A month later, she ends up again in the emergency room. The infection is not gone. Tisha is on disability and could see a Primary Care Physician, but she would have to wait up to a month to fit into the overcrowded schedule. The ER physician prescribes her more antibiotics and pain medications.

More time passes, and the discomfort does not get better. In fact, it is worse. Once again she goes to the same ER where now the doctors assume she has not taken the medications as prescribed. They lecture her on the importance of hygiene and educate her on proper bathing methods. She is appalled. She knows how to keep herself clean, and she has taken the whole course of medicine as prescribed. Tisha tells the doctors off. This doesn't help her cause.

Again and again, she returns to the ER. Each time the doctors' level of annoyance and her display of anger grow more harsh, until a whole year into suffering with bladder pain, they run more tests. Scans reveal Stage 4 Bladder Cancer that has metastasized to her liver. She is furious, and so are we. Had they run these tests so many months before, perhaps they would have found the cancer and been able to treat it. Now it is too late.

The whole community at Joe's Addiction walks side by side with Tisha through the last months of her life. We take turns visiting her in the hospital. We pray with her. We hold her hand. We stand guard when estranged relatives show up demanding to see her. We weep with her as God frees her from bitterness toward these relatives and she invites them back into her life for healing and reconciliation. We learn forgiveness from Tisha, and we hand her over to some of her reconciled family when they step in to provide hospice care.

It has been four years since Tisha's death, and I am weeping as I write. I miss her so much. Tisha wove herself into my heart. She became one of the dearest friends of my entire life. I could always count on her to speak truth to me, and I could count on her to love me no matter what. I cherished her hugs and kisses. And I wanted to be like her. All the way to the end, Tisha offered prayers for me, she asked how me how *I* was doing, and she trusted God's Love would carry her into eternity.

Near the end of her life, a small group of Joe's Addiction community friends stood around her bed. One played a guitar, and we quietly sang, "All the poor and powerless, all the lost and lonely." At her funeral, we celebrated her life, and we shouted at the top of our lungs, "HE IS GOD!"

> "Life is what you celebrate. All of it.
> Even its end."
>
> — Joanne Harris, Chocolat

SECTION 5
US THEM WE

"All the darkness in the world cannot
extinguish the light of a single candle."

— Francis of Assisi

CHAPTER 21

SEX OFFENDERS, FELONS, CRAZY PEOPLE, AND TRANSIENTS

"Charity wins awards and applause, but joining the
poor gets you killed. People do not get crucified for
charity. People are crucified for living out a love that
disrupts the social order, that calls forth a new world.
People are not crucified for helping poor people.
People are crucified for joining them."

— Shane Claiborne

A woman, a regular from the neighborhood, comes in to Joe's
Addiction one afternoon and asks me, "Do you know about
the petition?"

"What petition?" I ask.

"They're going door to door asking people to sign a petition
to shut down your business."

"What?"

I don't even know how to find out what is going on. Who
do I ask? I can't call up city hall. I don't know if they might
be the ones behind the petition. Who wants us shut down?

Why? More customers make comments, confirming someone has come to their door asking them to sign.

A news report runs on the local channel. A man in the neighborhood has started the petition. His daughter was raped years before, and the man who raped her is now living at the halfway house down the street from Joe's Addiction. The father is angry. He is afraid. He knows some men from the halfway house come to Joe's Addiction for coffee and community. What if his daughter's rapist is among these men?

The news reports his concerns about the "unscrupulous people" who frequent Joe's Addiction. The reporter also points out the irony that the complaint is against the coffee shop, instead of the local strip clubs, and highlights the history of crime and violence there. The mayor, whose close friend owns two of the clubs, is quoted saying, "There's some fairly nice clientele in the clubs." A city councilman states the city doesn't have nearly as much trouble from the strip clubs as they do from "those folks hanging out at the coffee shop."

Responses flood in on the news channel website and social media. Some angry rants about sex offenders, but mostly comments about the irony that a town would target those who are helping, rather than the clubs that exacerbate addiction, sexual arousal, and crime. It is a mess, and our anxiety level rises.

I put out the call to everyone I know for legal help. We have no money. We run Joe's Addiction on a shoestring budget, and there is never extra money. In fact, most of the time we operate at a deficit. We certainly do not have enough for legal fees. No legal help is forthcoming. I understand. Who wants to get involved in defending sex offenders. Reputations are at stake. My own reputation is at stake. Will I stand with those I love, or will I cower to the pressure of the media and a few angry people in the neighborhood?

We research our situation and hope we are on good legal ground. Best we can tell, we are doing nothing illegal. In fact, targeting a group of people and banning them from coming to a place of business is discrimination. As a business, we serve any and all customers who do not pose a threat of danger. We have even brought the Department of Corrections in to train our baristas and community members what to watch for regarding potential danger. There is no legal ground for shutting us down.

However, the city council can decide they do not want a coffee shop in their town. They can choose to not renew my business license. The annual renewal date is three months away. This means we have three months to convince the city council that we are valuable to the town.

The next three months of council meetings are painful for us. After the petition is presented, we look at it. It is not a legal petition, by any means. The same names have been signed multiple times. Children have signed the petition. People who do not even live in Valley Brook signed it. It looks to be a small group of people who want Joe's Addiction gone, however, their roar is loud.

Several times, the news media runs reports about our situation. Once we are even on the front page of the Oklahoma City newspaper. Each time, the news media balances the story in our favor, highlighting the good we are doing in the neighborhood and the lives that have been changed for the better through Joe's Addiction. One city council member tells me they do not care about public opinion; they will do "what they feel is best" for their town.

At each month's council meeting, the same few town's people voice their accusations. They call our people "cho'mos" (an abbreviation for "child molesters"). They talk about the "crazy, homeless people" who hang out at Joe's Addiction, saying our people are making their town look bad. Each month, two or three of our Joe's Addiction community members stand to tell their side. They do not retaliate. Our people do not speak hateful words in return. They make no counter accusations. They simply tell their stories of how they came to Joe's, and how their lives have been changed by the Love they have receive at this little coffee shop. Every month, I weep as I watch followers of the Way of Jesus choosing to love their enemies.

John and I meet with the city council for an unofficial meeting to make an appeal and ask what we can do to change their opinion of us. The meeting is both painful and discouraging. Personal accusations against my character are most difficult for me. They say ugly things about us and to us.

The problem, as they lay it out, is I have welcomed what they call "the stray cats." They say when you feed stray cats, of course they will want to stay around. They say, "We don't want them to stay around. We don't want them in our neighborhood." I ask them to define who they are calling "stray cats," and they name four categories: sex offenders, felons, crazy people, and transients.

When I point out that these people were already here before we opened Joe's Addiction, and that many of them are residents of the town itself, they reply, "Well, we want them to feel unwelcome here. If you continue to make life easier for them they will stay, and we'd rather they move along out of our city."

I guess we had tried to anticipate the things they would say in the meeting and what our response would be. However, the most surprising element comes when a woman takes out her Bible, unzips its cover, and reads the words of Jesus from Matthew: "But whoever causes one of these little ones who believe in me to sin, it would be better for him if a millstone were hung around his neck, and he were drowned in the depth of the sea."

I ask about whom she is referring, and she says, "Those criminals." I ask if that is what she thinks I should do—put millstones around people's necks? She says, "Well, those are the words of Jesus. At least you shouldn't be helping them!"

Another man claims there is no way we are Christians because we have a smoke break in the middle of our service on Sunday.

In response to stories I tell of people receiving help from us, another man who claims to be a Christian, says, "I'm all for people getting saved, but I think you need to just give them the free stuff, and then send them on their way." The problem, they say, is we allow these people to *congregate*.

Although they state this is not an official meeting, and no one in a legal, authoritative position has made a ruling, they clearly have laid out for us that if we continue to allow "those kinds of people" to hang out in our coffee shop, they will shut us down.

The personal injuries aside, I am deeply offended for our people. The city council does not even consider "the least of these" human. The people who are making these comments are not wealthy themselves. They live in this poor part of the city. But in their own judgment, they are not like "those people."

I leave the meeting understanding that even if I try to comply with their request, there is no way to measure or monitor it. We are a coffee shop. How long is a person allowed to "hang out"? Should I go to them after they have eaten their sandwich and say, "You're done with your meal, so you need to leave now." How do I determine which ones qualify for this status? How do I determine who are the ones worthy to hang out and use the free Wi-Fi, and who are not? If a person goes outside to smoke, will that indicate I am allowing the "riff raff" to hang out, instead of sending them on their way? Their case is sealed and determined.

I, too, receive some painful personal attacks. Rumors come back through people in our community. "You know what they're calling you, right? A 'cho'mo' lover." In my defense of the rights of the men hanging out at Joe's Addiction, I have not only been taking up for them. Now, I am one of them. Warped and twisted, just as they assume all men who have committed sexual offenses are. I am no longer merely standing *for* them, I have *become* them.

Father Gregory Boyle said, "Jesus didn't seek the rights of lepers. He touched the leper even before he got around to curing him. He didn't champion the cause of the outcast. He was the outcast. He didn't fight for improved conditions for the prisoner. He simply said, 'I was in prison.' The strategy of Jesus is not centered in taking the right stand on issues, but rather in standing in the right place—with the outcast and those relegated to the margins."

I am starting to feel the sting of the reality Martin Luther King, Jr. referred to when he said, "It is hardly a moral act to encourage others patiently to accept injustice which he himself does not endure."

A police officer comes into Joe's Addiction and announces they are not required to do this, but they are giving us a "courtesy call." The officer informs us that they will arrest any people who are seen hanging around outside Joe's Addiction for loitering. (People go outside to smoke, to sit at tables and drink coffee, to socialize with each other.) The "courtesy call" is so we can let our customers know.

My emotions rage. Throughout this ordeal with the Town of Valley Brook, we have tried to respond as Jesus would respond. We have been kind; we have continued to serve and to minister. We have meditated upon the way Jesus endured persecution and death without retaliation and have tried to follow his example.

> "Count yourselves blessed every time people put you down or throw you out or speak lies about you to discredit me. What it means is that the truth is too close for comfort and they are uncomfortable. You can be glad when that happens—give a cheer, even!—for though they don't like it, *I* do! And all heaven applauds. And know that you are in good company. My prophets and witnesses have always gotten into this kind of trouble. Let me tell you why you are here. You're here to be salt-seasoning that brings out the God-flavors of this earth. If you lose your saltiness, how will people taste godliness? You've lost your usefulness and will end up in the garbage."—Jesus (Matthew 5:11-13 MSG)

However, something shifts in me. The night before this officer came into Joe's, I had seen the movie, "The Butler." I had wept in the theater as I witnessed the sacrifices made by so many in the Civil Rights Movement of the 1960s, sacrifices that were about confronting injustice through nonviolent means. I admired these heroes of not so long ago, and I wondered when is it right to receive the persecution humbly, and when is it right to take a stand and confront a wrong?

In the Gospels, we see Jesus expressing anger. His anger was never toward the poor or the outcasts, those that society called "the sinners." It was always against the religiously powerful, who were oppressing "the least of these." Once, Jesus took a whip and turned over tables, driving the money changers out of the temple. The religious establishment had set up a marketplace in the Court of the Gentiles, making it impossible for the Gentiles, the women, the sick, the lame, and the mentally ill—religiously and socially outcast people—to come and worship God. This kind of injustice seemed to get Jesus' ire up.

My anger is so often a result of *my* own feelings being hurt, or because I am not getting *my* way, or even because I feel *my* rights are being violated. Overcoming this kind of anger is a process of learning what Love looks like—learning to release selfishness, to respond in kindness, in gentleness, in laying down my rights. I have been learning to love.

Yet, it seems there is a place for "righteous indignation," and perhaps that place is when injustice impacts the "least of these." All over the nation, cities are trying to figure out what to do with their homeless populations, and some of them, rather than helping to alleviate the causes of homelessness, are shipping them out of view, or enforcing laws to limit the sight of them, or in some cases, arresting them for loitering.

I need to tell you about my friend Zach. Zach is homeless. He is a convicted felon. Zach has been given a number of mental health diagnoses. He has been told he's bipolar, schizo-phrenic, depressed. In my estimation, Zach has the mental and emotional age of maybe a five-year-old, but Zach is a grown man in mid-life.

Zach lives outside, and he doesn't bathe. His "home" is a pile of maggot-infested garbage. He smells really bad. Sometimes it's just the smell of a long-unbathed body, but sometimes he reeks of urine. I often offer a Kleenex to Zach because he walks around unaware he has white snot running out of his nose into his scruffy mustache.

Recently, Zach has lost his friend—his boyfriend actually—the one person in Zach's life who he believed cared for him. Zach's experience of loss and rejection are too much for him to bear, and every time I've seen him for the last two weeks Zach has been crying (this does not help with the level of snot production).

I understand. I truly understand. Zach is difficult to love. To the eyes of those who do not know him, I am sure he appears scary. He's big. He's strange. And frankly, fear is not unwarranted. Sometimes Zach's emotions get the best of him and his temper rages. He clenches his teeth and his fists, and then he paces, huffing and puffing obscenities. Zach carries a knife on him for practical uses living outside, but also for protection. It is not hard to imagine Zach hurting someone or hurting himself.

Zach needs help—more help than we can give him at Joe's Addiction. We give him groceries. We give him clothes. We make sure he has eaten. We listen to him cry. We pat him on the back. We encourage him to go to the mental healthcare facility in the city. He has gone. He says the drugs they give him don't work. Twice, we've even taken him to a Crisis Center. I don't know what they've done for him there, but within a day or two he shows up again at Joe's Addiction in the same condition.

Some days I cry. Some days I get mad. Zach is one of so many we know who fall through the cracks. There is no place for him. These are people, precious people with precious stories, and Zach is only one of thousands. I decide I cannot passively endure anymore. It is time to *resist*— nonviolently, of course.

I meet with the Chief of Police. It is difficult for me. I hate confrontation. I fear being hurt. I have done my research, and I discuss the law with him. I remind him it is his job to enforce the laws of the city, not just to do whatever he pleases, or even what a city council member tells him to do. I ask if he knows the loitering laws of the city. He does not. These moments of the conversation are tense, as I ask him how he can enforce the law, if he does not know what the law says. We look at the ordinance together, and it is clear that "loitering" does not include customers of my shop sitting or standing outside, smoking or drinking coffee, or even just chatting with one another.

The conversation softens as we talk about the issues the city is facing with the growing number of people who are homeless that have landed on their doorstep. Neither of us has the answer, but he finally expresses that he is not against us. He understands we are helping people. He commits that he will inform his police force to back down from this threat, and they will stick to enforcing the law. We shake hands and promise to work together if at all possible.

Following this meeting, a police car parks across the street from our coffee shop for hours at a time, just watching our people—intimidating. Our folks at Joe's Addiction wave and smile at the police officer as they drink their coffee at the tables on "the veranda."

I wrote in the beginning of this book that I was shy. I was backward. I was afraid. When we began this Grand Experiment, I would never have been able to stand up to such an intimidating force, but this is what Love has done. Love has changed me. Love has healed me. Love has given me courage. Honestly, I still quake inside in the face of so many things. I do not relish confrontation. I especially dislike having my feelings hurt. But sometimes courage rises in us when we are facing great injustice.

Day of the Vote

A few days before the city council meeting in which they will cast the final vote, John goes on a trip to India. I will spare you all the details, but you should know the day he leaves, the plumbing at our house breaks and we have no water pressure, just a trickle. "Mom, how do I take a shower in this?" Conflicts arise between folks at the coffee shop, and I have jury duty.

I said I would spare you *all* the details, so suffice it to say I am running non-stop and my stress level is off the charts. I awake the morning of the vote to a meme that passes on my newsfeed: "Never let a problem to be solved become more important than a person to be loved." This and a brief meditation on some of Mother Teresa's writings about prayer help to set my heart for the day.

In the afternoon, a woman who is a regular at Joe's Addiction becomes dangerously unstable. Of course. Of all days. She is making threats, says she has a gun and will shoot people and burn the building down. She cries. She paces. I talk and talk with her, but things are not improving. Finally, I call 911. The dispatcher listens and then says, "Are you in Valley Brook?" I tell her yes, and she says she will send the Valley Brook police. The police station is .2 miles away.

We wait, we talk, and she threatens, and she paces. Where are the police? Now we are in the street, as my *very* pregnant daughter, Jessi, and I continue to talk her down and keep her from hurting anyone at Joe's. Oh God, protect my daughter and my grand baby! I pray.

We make another 911 call, and Jessi insists that the dispatcher will stay with her on the phone until she can assure us a policeman is on the way. Jess hears the dispatcher stating this call is being recorded, and she has dispatched an officer who has now reported he is responding to the call. Accountability at least.

After twenty minutes, a police officer arrives. He puts the woman in handcuffs and takes her to the police station. Fifteen minutes later, he brings her back to Joe's Addiction and asks for her shoes, her phone, and some other items she threw around during her fit. He tells us he is taking her home, and he is restricting her from coming to Joe's Addiction for two weeks. What?! She is sitting in the back seat of the patrol car, cussing me out because we called the police on her.

Through the rest of the afternoon, she calls the coffee shop phone, texts angry profanity and threats to my phone and the phones of other Joe's regulars, informing us she will speak at the meeting that night to tell the city council every bad thing she knows about what happens at Joe's Addiction.

There is nothing we can do. It is out of our hands. Sigh. Pray. Trust.

Before the meeting, some of the Joe's Addiction community gathers in the coffee shop for prayer. We hold hands in a circle. Old Man Tom, who has been following Jesus for just a short time, asks, "Would it be okay if I say the prayer?"

"Of course," I say.

"Heavenly Father, we come before you tonight asking you to help us. Please tell them people down there at city hall that this is your place, and you are doing important things here and they should renew our license." When he finishes, he asks, "Was that okay?" and adds, "I'm sure you coulda done better."

Tears fill my eyes as I hug him. "That was perfect, Tom. Just perfect."

Another of our men who is homeless, grabs my shoulder and says, "Jamie, Valley Brook does not belong to them. It belongs to God." My tears spill over. How am I going to make it through this night?

We walk down the street for the meeting. Oh, there are just too many details to tell you. Special little things, like Biker Clint is sitting on his motorcycle smiling as we walk into the parking lot. I ask him what he's doing. He lays his hand on my shoulder and says, "Your fate is not in their hands." He turns to walk away, and I see the patch on the back of his leather jacket: "Fuck you! I don't need any friends." I cannot stop my tears.

We enter the courtroom. Seated on the front row are four men in suits. I mention to one of them that he is overdressed for this occasion. He chuckles. Our group files into an old church pew about halfway back in the room. Folks around me ask, "Who are those guys?" I don't know.

I look at our row. Drug addicts. "Crazy" people. People who are homeless. I say to one of our guys, "Oscar, you combed your hair!" His clothes are stained. His face and hands are dirty—but his hair is combed. As is typical for him when intoxicated, he becomes religious. He points up and says, "God provided the comb. God provided the motor skills, so I could raise my arm and comb my hair. All the glory goes to him." I laugh, and I cry.

The unstable woman who threatened to shoot up Joe's Addiction is there. She flits about the room from person to person, cussing, laughing, talking fast. She is high on something. I sigh and pray.

The meeting starts. The council handles other business items, budgets approved, hiring of new police officers, increasing of fees. Every time the air conditioner kicks on, we cannot hear what is being said. It is a large room, and the city manager who is directing each agenda item sits with her back to the audience. No one can hear. Several times, people in the gallery ask them to speak up. Then the air conditioner turns off.

The men in suits stand to make a presentation. They are from the corporation that owns the largest strip club on our street. They want to open another club that would be a Nude Gentleman's Club—non-alcoholic, which means state law will allow full nudity. They want to advertise all over the state.

The man assures everyone their company will also put a pizza parlor between their existing club and the new one (in the same strip mall—pun intended) that will be more "family oriented," and also a convenience store/gas station. They hand out a spiral notebook to each council member and walk through it page by page, explaining how much income they will bring into the city if the council approves this new club. Yes . . . I know. Surreal.

Because there are townsfolk gathered to hear the verdict on Joe's Addiction, there is a sizable group to witness this presentation—and they speak up. Parents express concern. Valley Brook residents say they are tired of strip clubs being the identity of their town. Emotions begin to rise, and the mayor shuts it down. She says, "We are not making a decision on this tonight. We will table it to next month's meeting, while we take it into consideration." To which the city attorney reminds her how much income this club would bring into the city.

The unstable woman who threatened to disrupt the meeting comes over and sits in the pew in front of us. She reaches her hand over the back of the pew and takes the hand of one of *our* ladies. Our group sits silent, glancing, wide-eyed at one another. The air conditioner kicks on.

Next item on the agenda, "Consideration of the renewal of the business license for Joe's Addiction." We can't hear. We all lean forward. One councilmen, the former mayor, whose son's funeral took place at Joe's Addiction, mumbles, "I make a motion . . ." What? The mayor declares, "I second." The city manager takes a vote. Ward 1: Yes. Ward 2: Yes. Ward 3: Yes. Ward 4: Yes. Ward 5: Yes. "Motion has passed."

We all look at each other. What just happened? I raise my hand and ask, "I'm sorry. Could you please clarify? We couldn't hear."

The city attorney says, "Your license has just been renewed." Stunned silence.

No more agenda items. We look at each other. We smile. What? We don't understand.

The meeting closes with a gavel strike, and the crowd stands. I notice the councilman who made the motion rushing out the door. I hurry forward with my hand outstretched to the councilman who has been most antagonistic toward us and say, "Thank you." He steps back and replies, "We will have to readdress this. That's not what we meant to do. We thought we were voting against you. We couldn't hear because of that damn air conditioner!"

He turns to the city attorney standing behind me, who says, "Nothing you can do. You just publicly voted to renew their license." The attorney reaches out and shakes my hand as I thank him. He says, "I hope next year your license will be renewed without all this trouble.

I rush out the door to the crowd milling around in the parking lot. A group stands talking with the men in suits. Another group crowds around me to rejoice. Tears, laughter, and hugs abound. Like the parting of the Red Sea, our Joe's Addiction community feels as though we are living a story of biblical proportions. We are a just a tiny little thing. Really. We love a small community of precious people, and we feel so grateful that God is allowing us to continue loving each other. We commit again do our best.

Us *for* them. Us *with* them. Until there is no us or them, only *we*.

CHAPTER 22
DESTINY

"Follow your bliss and the universe will open
doors for you where there were only walls."

— Joseph Campbell

I walk out of the kitchen and Gary is right there. He stops in his tracks and stares at me. "Gary!" I exclaim, "I haven't seen you in a long time!"

Gary lives outside and has pretty extreme mental illness. The last time I saw him, he was dirtier than I had ever seen him. His skin was brown, not from a tan, but from dirt. His layers of clothing reeked of urine. He had only come in out of the cold for just a few minutes to warm up, and then he set out again walking down the street. That's where I usually see Gary, walking down the street. I don't know where he comes from or where he's going, but he's always walking.

This day, when I greet him, Gary just stands there. Frozen. His light blue eyes always have a glassy sheen to them. He seems like he is looking right through me. No response. I ask him, "Can I help you with something, Gary?"

He says, "Yeah. I would like a tall iced tea." Then he smiles, "With lots of sugar, please?"

"I think I can handle that," I tell him.

I am surprised. In the few years I have known Gary, I have never seen him order a drink. He always drinks the free coffee or a cold cup of water from the cooler. I am surprised that Gary even has money. I've never known him to panhandle, and the uncle who was his Social Security Payee gave up helping him manage his money a long time ago.

I go to the tablet to ring up his order. "Two seventeen," I say. Gary pulls out a small fold of bills and hands me the cash.

As I am scooping ice and pouring his drink, I mention to him that he looks good. Gary has sometime recently taken a bath. His clothes do not reek, and his overgrown hair and beard seem to have been brushed, although, he still looks like the last man on earth. His hair hangs long and wild. He wears a thick scraggly beard, and his tan leathery skin is now due to the sun, not just dirt.

Gary smiles. Then he asks, "Does your iced tea have healing powers?"

I say, "I don't think I can say that it does."

"Can it cure my multiple gunshot wounds?" he asks.

"You have multiple gunshot wounds?" I ask him as I pour a steady stream of sugar into his cup.

"You can't see 'em now, but yes. I have multiple gunshot wounds."

I stir his tea with a long spoon. "Well, I'm glad you're not bleeding all over my floor," I say, as I look him in the eye. His eyes brighten, and gradually a grin spreads across Gary's face.

I hand him the tea and ask him to taste and see if it is sweet enough. He takes a sip and then says, "It presents perfectly." His head is bowed, but he smiles, looking at me through the tops of his eyes. I put a lid on the cup. Then Gary turns and walks out the door into the hot Oklahoma sunshine, sipping his tall iced tea.

I don't know how to explain to you that these types of encounters make everything else I do at Joe's Addiction pale by comparison. The Hindi word, "namaste," often said as a greeting, means: I see and acknowledge the Divine in you. I live for these moments when the real person at the core, underneath the illness, allows me to *see* them. That moment of connection feels like I have just seen *God*.

Who am I?

People often ask me, "How can I know what I am supposed to do with my life?" Some say, "I love what you do at Joe's Addiction, but I know that kind of work just isn't for me." Is there such a thing as destiny? A plan for our life that we are supposed to fulfill? A path we are to take? If we don't take that path, do bad things happen to us? Do bad things happen to the world? How do we know if we're on the right path? How can we know if what we are doing with our life is the thing we are supposed to be doing? The existential question of the meaning of life could drive one to live as a hermit somewhere in the mountains, or it might send another one of us into suicidal depression. Some just give up trying and bury themselves in the suicidal hermitage of pursuing money. It's entirely too much pressure.

All of us are not wired the same way. All of us have different backgrounds and experiences that have formed our lives. The families into which we were born contributed to our development. Some encounters were positive, some negative. Some have been wounds we have suffered. Some experiences have been eye-opening revelations. Moments of passion have ignited our soul and sent us soaring. Each of these pieces of our history has formed the person we are today.

One way we can know what it is we are to *do* in the world, is by paying attention to the things we *just can't stand*. What is it you see in the world that is just not okay with you? Personal experiences you faced in your own history may even fuel your frustration.

Maybe it is when you see or hear about bullying. Maybe it's seeing people without enough food to eat. Perhaps when you see elderly people neglected in their loneliness, it infuriates you. Maybe it is the injustices that abound in our criminal justice system. Maybe it's racial discrimination or the abuse of women. Identifying what we just can't stand helps us get in touch with a fire burning in our soul that can motivate us to step out and do things we had not considered before.

Taking action to change the world is often counterintuitive for us. When we encounter things that create discomfort, or dis-ease and frustration in our souls, we want to push them away. Feeling discomfort is, well, uncomfortable. We dislike suffering, and yet this is the very definition of compassion: *to suffer with*. If we desire to make the world a better place, we will experience the suffering of those in need. Craig Greenfield reminds us that, "We say we want to be the hands and feet of Jesus in this broken world, but we forget that Jesus' hands and feet were pierced by nails." The Dalai Lama agrees: "It is not enough to be compassionate, we must act."

Pleasure is also a good, healthy motivator. Writing those words makes me laugh. I was raised in the idea that if it feels good, it must be bad. Following the desires of our own heart could only lead us to sinful and evil outcomes, because my religion taught that by nature, our hearts are evil. But in the context of Joe's Addiction, I have experienced something different.

I have seen my personality change. Shyness gave way to confidence. Fear gave way to boldness. I have experienced joy. As Thomas Merton writes, "We discover our true selves in love." I love what I get to do, and I feel a sense of privilege on a daily basis. In fact, I feel that I found *myself* in this little coffee shop, a self that wounding and religion had obscured. What the great Sufi poet, Rumi, said is true: "When we practice loving kindness and compassion we are the first ones to profit." Inherent in the African Nguni word, "ubuntu," is the notion that a person becomes a person through other people. I am becoming me.

I no longer believe human beings are inherently evil. Inside each one of us, at the core of our being, is Love, is the Divine image of God. So it stands to reason that if there is something that brings me great pleasure, maybe it is something godly.

As I have paid attention to my soul, I have discovered that my favorite people are those who are extremely mentally ill. I mean people who hear voices and see things that the rest of us don't see. It often feels like they are living on a different plane from us. I experience great amounts of compassion for the suffering they must endure by not fitting into this world. The frustrations must be unbearable. I watch "the system" grinding many of these people under its wheels, giving them no place to live, not enough food, no sense of belonging, a constant fear for their own safety, and I *just can't stand it*.

These things cause me to suffer with them, but I also see some of the purest innocence in their eyes. When they express joy, it is often without restraint. I have encountered some of the deepest Love coming from my friends who are mentally ill, and perhaps it is that selfish motive that causes me to enjoy them so much. I *feel* loved when I am with them. They are not with me for what I can give them because they know there is little I can do for them. So the Love we experience is reciprocal. At least I hope they are experiencing the same Love from me that I am from them.

> "Don't ask yourself what the world needs. Ask yourself what makes you come alive, and go and do that, because what the world needs is people who have come alive."
>
> — Rev. Howard Thurman

What is it you love to do? What kind of people are your favorite kind of people? What settings? What circumstances, when you are in them, make you feel the most fulfilled? What kind of activities, when you are doing them, give you that feeling of "I was made for this"?

> "The place God calls you to is the place where your deep gladness and the world's deep hunger meet."
>
> — Frederick Beuchner

This has become my compass. Look for the sweet spot where these two things exist, and I believe you will find your *destiny*. I have found mine at Joe's Addiction.

Mae's Finger

Mae is a favorite character in our community. Everybody loves her. Years before we knew her, she suffered a stroke. She lost the use of her left hand, and she drags her left foot behind her. Mae rides to Joe's Addiction on her electric scooter. Her little mutt dog, Chumby, rides along beside her as Mae's guardian and companion. Although we have a "NO DOGS" policy out of concern for liability, hidden in Mae's sweater, her "baby" sneaks into Joe's Addiction on a regular basis.

Mae's speech is slurred, and understanding her takes time and patience—not only on our part, but more so on hers, as we ask her to repeat herself again and again. Usually through pantomime and guess work, we can figure out what she wants. "Coffee" and "sugar" are as clear as can be. Although because she is diabetic, I always refuse her requests for sugar. She receives Splenda instead. I tell her I am not going to knowingly contribute to her death! She always laughs, and she *always* asks for sugar.

The stroke damaged Mae's mind. She can't keep track of days or appointments. We make the laundry room available for community use, and Mae signs up. When I remind her that her name is on the schedule to wash her laundry on Thursday, she says, "Tomorrow, tomorrow, tomorrow?" It has taken me years to figure out she wants me to count the number of tomorrows to help her know how many days it will be until Thursday.

Mae scoots up to Joe's one afternoon with a rag around her good hand. The best we can understand is that Mae had been frying chicken for dinner. The oil was heating on the stove, and she didn't have a thermometer. She momentarily lost her senses and stuck the tip of her finger into the oil to test if it was ready. The tip of Mae's finger is gone—melted off. Where her fingernail used to be, now exposed bone with crispy muscles and tendons hang from it. I gasp. Mae wipes the tears from her eyes. I don't know how much Mae can feel. Years of diabetes have damaged her nerves.

I take Mae to the emergency room where the doctors fix her up. They tell me they are certain her whole finger will require amputation, but they hope that if infection can be kept at bay, maybe they can leave some of it intact. We leave the hospital with medicines, bandages, and instructions for daily care of her wound. Surgery will be scheduled later. They will call us.

Every day, Mae comes to Joe's Addiction. Every day, one of the Joe's community members washes her wound, applies medicine, and changes her dressing. There is so much that I cannot do—so many needs I cannot meet—but here is one I know how to do. I am determined to keep infection from developing. I am determined to keep Mae from losing her whole finger. Every day, she cries and asks, "They chop? They chop?" I tell her we will do our best to keep them from chopping off her finger.

A month passes, and her wound looks good. New, pink skin has closed over the wound. Her bone is still protruding, but it doesn't look infected. The day of her surgery comes, and I sit by her bedside as she cries. "They chop? They chop?" I assure her the doctor will take only as much as they need to, and I pray with her for peace before the nurses roll her away to the operating room.

An hour or so later, a nurse comes to find me in the waiting room. I sit with Mae as she slowly comes around. Her hand is wrapped in a big bandage, and I can't answer her question when she drowsily cries, "They chop? They chop?"

Finally, her doctor arrives to brief us both. Surgery went well. They removed the end of the exposed bone and sewed the skin over it. Mae has only lost up to her first knuckle. She still has her finger! She looks at me and cries, "They not chop! They not chop!" Tears of joy flow freely— hers *and* mine. The doctor says, "There was no infection. If there had been, we would have needed to take a lot more. You guys did a good job of keeping it clean."

These moments with Mae are some of my favorite in all of my years at Joe's Addiction. The practicality of changing her dressing, the swell in my heart as I comfort her fear and grief, the privilege of representing her at the hospital, the good news from the surgeon. This is my sweet spot. I can't keep Mae safe from so many other dangers in her life—drugs, abusive men, homelessness—but Mae still has her finger.

When I was a child, I considered becoming a doctor when I grew up. I decided I didn't want to be in school for that long. Like so many adults this is one of those things I wonder about what could have been. Perhaps fueled by a little of that regret and the pragmatic nature of my personality, providing basic first aid is another of my sweet spots at Joe's Addiction. I treat spider bites, lance infections, place butterfly bandages, and give out countless ibuprofen tablets. When someone comes with a cut, or a scrape, a bite, or a burn, I think to myself, "Here it is. This is my thing. I know how to do this. Bring it on."

I have thought about Mother Teresa cleaning maggots out of the wounds of the dying, and I have wondered at her compassion. I have discovered that Love takes you crazy places and gives you the ability to give empathy and dignity to the people you love. As she is so often quoted, "Not all of us can do great things. But we can do small things with great love."

Mitch's Daughter

As a perfectionist, I want to do things right. What if I don't do it well? What if there was a better way to have done it? The fear of not doing something perfectly can paralyze me from acting. But I have found this truth from the Hindu holy book, *The Bhagavad Gita*, to be true: "It is better to live your own destiny imperfectly than to live an imitation of somebody else's life with perfection."

Biker Clint brings his little brother with him to drink coffee. Mitch is quiet. He smiles and is polite, but he does not seem to want to hang out and chat. It seems like Clint is trying to tell him this is a cool place, trying to influence him to come around more, but Mitch doesn't seem interested. I sometimes see him going into the convenience store next door and I wave at him. He waves back, but I see he has bought coffee from their automated drip machine.

Over a cup of Joe's Addiction coffee, Clint tells me Mitch's story. Clint and Mitch grew up in extreme poverty. Clint remembers sometimes eating grass from the backyard of their home because they were so hungry. Both grew up hardworking and able to provide for themselves. Neither one of them has been to jail or been caught up in addiction. The flash in his eyes and the jut of his chin tell me Clint is very proud of these accomplishments.

As a young man, Mitch fell in love with a woman and married her. They had one daughter together. Her name was Jamie. I smile when Clint tells me this and say, "Hey, that's my name." He nods and says, "Yes, I know." That familiar smirk curls his lip.

Mitch's wife started using drugs, and their life together fell apart. Mitch loved her. He loved their family. But the behaviors of her drug addiction began to put their daughter in danger. He finally felt forced to make the decision to leave. He wanted to give a better life to their daughter. The courts awarded him full custody, and he moved to a city about an hour south of Oklahoma City to start a new life. Jamie was eleven years old.

What followed was the difficult life of a single-parent-family. Mitch worked hard to pay the bills. His daughter, Jamie, was a typical "latch-key kid." She most often came home to an empty house. Every day after school, she sat in their apartment waiting for dad to come home in the evening. She was bored, and she was lonely.

One day, Jamie was not there when Mitch arrived home. The search began. The police found Jamie's body cut into pieces in the freezer of another apartment in their same building. A man had initiated a relationship with Jamie over the internet, stalked her life, and then lured her into his apartment with the attraction of a cute puppy.

These are the stories of television movies, episodes of *Law and Order* or *Criminal Minds*, not the kind of thing that happens in real life, and certainly not in small town Oklahoma. Now, here sitting in my coffee shop was a family who had experienced this heinous tragedy. Unthinkable and unbelievable. And now their path has crossed mine.

The reason that Clint tells me this story is that now after the man had been captured, the long wait is over, and the trial is to begin in Oklahoma City. Clint asks if it is okay with me for Mitch to come by every evening after the day's court adjourns. He says Mitch probably won't talk much, but he just needs a place to go to be with people and not sit alone in his house meditating on his pain. I tell him, "Of course."

Over the next few weeks, Mitch comes to Joe's Addiction most evenings. He sits on the couch holding his cup of coffee and staring off into the distance. Sometimes I sit on the couch next to him and ask, "How you doin?" We never talk about the trial. We never talk about what happened to her. But after a few evenings of just sort of "hanging out," Mitch begins to talk about his daughter.

He tells me what a smart girl she was, the good grades she made in school. He tells me how much she liked animals and how he wishes he had been able to afford a pet for her. But the thing that lights his eyes is when he talks about reading to her. Mitch tells me that every evening he read out loud to his daughter. He describes their evening ritual of dinner together, one television show, and then requiring her to take a bath and brush her teeth. He tucked her into bed, and then he read. He says, "We never missed the reading. It didn't matter if we'd been really busy, or if she'd had a lot of homework that kept her up extra late. I would always read at least a little bit to her." He tells me that her favorite genre was fantasy.

Over those few weeks, I sit and listen to Mitch tell the storyline of every book he ever read to his daughter. He remembers the details of every adventure, every fantastic world they had gone to together in their imaginations. You know how it's sometimes annoying when someone tries to tell you the plot of a movie or book, because it's just not the same as you watching or reading it yourself? I never once feel that listening to Mitch. He takes me right into the details of every story in such a way that he inspires me to start reading fiction again, a pleasure I had given up for religion.

These weeks with Mitch are a privilege I cannot even describe. The notion that The Muse inspired us to open a little coffee shop in Valley Brook, OK, where the brother of a man whose daughter who was so horrifically murdered lived, that the same Muse had inspired Clint to walk through our doors wearing his "Fuck You, I don't need any friends" leather jacket, and then would inspire him to introduce me to his brother. It all feels somehow magical, a little too fantastic to be coincidence.

One evening as Mitch is talking to me about his daughter, he raises his eyes and looks directly into mine, a rare action, and says, "You know my daughter had the same name as you. Her name was Jamie."

Love, what did you do to me?
My only hope is to let life stretch out before me
And break me on this lonely road.
I'm made of many things,
but I'm not what you are made of.

Only now do I see the big picture
But I swear that these scars are fine
Only you could've hurt me in this perfect way tonight
I might be blind, but you've told me the difference
Between mistakes and what you just meant for me

— London Grammar

CHAPTER 23
FRIENEMIES

"All is like an ocean,
all is flowing and blending;
A touch in one place sets up movement
at the other end of the earth."

— Fyodor Dostoyevsky

Two years pass since the petition and the conflict with city hall. Each year, they renew my business license without a problem, so we start to dream. The convenience store next door has gone out of business. We want to create a grocery store there with affordable grocery store prices and provide mentoring to teach people how to make their food stamp budget stretch. I call the landlord.

He says, "I'm sorry I haven't told you yet. I sold the building. You'll have to take it up with the new owner." I am surprised. He had told us he wanted half a million dollars. Who would spend that much for this old, falling apart building? I ask how we can contact the new owner, and he says, "Well, I sold it to the Town of Valley Brook, so I guess just call city hall."

They have won. We know the city has purchased the building with the intention of getting us out of there. They can't legally shut us down, but they can decide they want to "go a different direction" with the kind of businesses they put in the building. When I contact the vice mayor, sure enough, he gives us a deadline. He tells me the city plans to demolish the old structure and build something new in its place, something that will attract businesses to bring income into the city.

We are sad. We are angry. We are grieving. So much life has happened in this space. It is home for many of our people. We begin the search for a new home, somewhere nearby. As most of our people do not have transportation, we want to find a place not more than a mile away. No other buildings are available in Valley Brook. Perhaps moving out of Valley Brook might relieve us from the constant tension, anyway.

We find a place just outside of Valley Brook, still within walking distance for all of our people. The space is larger than we have had in the old building. It is newer and cleaner. It even has a built-in shower that will be a great benefit to our friends who live outside. We sign a three-year lease. Our grief turns into excitement about the new space and a new chapter in the life of the Joe's Addiction community. We start painting, tearing up carpet, and reconfiguring the layout.

Once again, news channels contact us. They have heard the city is kicking us out. A reporter interviews me and some of our people, as well as the vice mayor of Valley Brook, who tells them there is no animosity on their part. The city council merely wants to improve the city by putting a more lucrative business in that location.

The Oklahoma City newspaper runs a large piece, again highlighting the way we have served the Valley Brook neighborhood. I am proud of one of our men who is a felon. He agrees to an interview and photos for the paper, telling the story of his crimes and that the Joe's community has welcomed him and brought healing in his life. The media announce our new location and encourage people to buy coffee at the new Joe's Addiction.

The day after the article runs in the newspaper, the lease manager of our new space calls me. He tells me the owner is angry he leased it to us. People from other businesses in the surrounding buildings have called him to complain. They do not want "those kinds" of people near their businesses. Business owners fear that homeless people will stand around outside panhandling, asking their customers for money, or even rob their businesses. They have threatened to pull their businesses out of the buildings this man also owns.

I assure the lease manager our people experiencing homelessness do not do such things. They are some of the best-dressed homeless people in the city, and they will not bring down the image of the other businesses. There is no convincing the owner of the building. He is adamant that Joe's Addiction will not move to his building.

I contact an attorney. Now we have a legal situation. We signed a three-year lease. The owner of the building also signed it. We have done nothing to break the lease. We have also put a few thousand dollars into deposits, paint, and labor on the new space. Surely the owner cannot legally terminate our lease. Besides, where will we go? We need to be out of our old building the next month. We don't have a back-up plan because we hadn't needed one.

The attorney examines our situation and feels we have a good case for suing the owner of the property for religious discrimination. The reason he wants to terminate the lease is because of the religious work we are doing. The lawyer wants to build a case in the media and apply pressure to the owner by creating a public outcry against him. I tell him I'll get back to him.

I call a meeting of the baristas, Free Store workers, musicians, all those who are serving the community—and I tell them the bad news. Emotions rage. It isn't fair. We have a legal lease. We have done so much work on the new space. We have ridden the roller coaster from grief to excitement. I feel terrible when I explain to them the reason. These people have been rejected by family, by churches, by society in general, and now once again they are being told they are "less than."

The personalities react in all their individual and unique ways. Some of them cry. Some cuss. Foster declares, "We will sue his ass!" I let them emote for a while. Then when the heated emotions seem to have deflated, I tell them what the attorney has said: "We can sue. The attorney feels we have a good case. We will need to go to the media and put pressure on the owner. The attorney thinks we will win without even going to trial, because the owner will probably settle outside of court to stop the media frenzy. We might win a large amount of money that could get us an even nicer place. What do you guys think we should do?

What is the right thing to do? Is all this difficulty a sign we should just be done with Joe's Addiction? Perhaps the season is over. The story is written. Maybe death is the next natural part of the cycle of life. I ask them what *they* want to do.

The room is quiet. Again someone mumbles, "It's just not fair." Then Foster speaks up. "Jesus taught us to love our enemies. We can't do it. Loving our enemy does not mean trashing this guy in the media. We can't sue him either." I look around the room. We all look at each other. Someone says, "Dammit. He's right. How do we love the owner of the building?"

We decide to ask the owner to return to us all the money we have invested and to terminate the lease without legal action. He agrees and writes me a brief note commending the humanitarian work I am doing, saying he admires us, but he cannot afford to lose the other businesses in his buildings.

I go back to the vice mayor of Valley Brook and ask for an extension of our eviction date and am surprised when he says, "There's no hurry. We'll just put you on a month-to-month basis. We'll let you know with plenty of notice when we are ready to demolish the building."

We breathe a sigh of relief and continue to serve the neighborhood. More and more people come to the Free Store, not only to receive free stuff, but to donate items they think will be helpful for other people. We continue to share food with people who are hungry and make Panera Bread donations available on the coffee table to folks in the neighborhood. One afternoon, I notice two of those people who spoke against us at city hall sneaking into Joe's Addiction to take free bagels and sandwich bread. They don't talk to anyone. They grab the bread and leave.

Frostbite

I receive a phone call from the hospital. It's Buck. When I answer, he wails in the phone, "They're gonna cut off my feet!" It is winter in Oklahoma. The temperatures have dropped far below freezing. My friend is mentally ill and addicted. The story he tells me is convoluted and confusing. The best I can gather from him is the freezing rain had soaked his socks. He fell asleep in the cold, and his socks froze to his feet.

The hospital staff is kind to him. They amputate one foot just up to the ankle, and the other one part way up his shin. They keep him in the hospital for as long as they can. He does not have insurance. When they need the bed, they put him back out on the street. The hospital generously gives him an old wheelchair, and then a nurse comes to Joe's Addiction to teach me how to change his dressings and care for his wounds that have not yet healed.

My children and I go out on the streets seeking Buck every couple of days. We usually find him "flying a sign" on a median near the entrance to a freeway not far from the coffee shop. We change his dressing right there in the median. My teenage daughter, Jewel, especially enjoys taking care of Buck.

One day, as we are peeling off his dirty bandages, cleaning and re-wrapping his wounds, a car pulls up next to us. I hear a woman call through her rolled-down window. I turn to see one of the people who was so antagonistic against us in those city hall meetings. I wave, and she says, "You just help people everywhere, don't you?" I tell her Buck's feet were amputated because of frostbite. She stares. When the light turns green, shaking her head, she says, "You are good people," and then drives through the intersection. I am embarrassed, but I also remember Jesus' words in his Sermon on the Mount, "Let your light shine before others, that they may see your good deeds and glorify your Father in heaven (Matt. 5:16). I hope the woman has seen Love in action.

Enemies Becoming Friends

One Sunday morning, as I am preaching the sermon, I see out on the front sidewalk the man who beat my friend in the head with a baseball bat. I keep my eye on him as I continue to say whatever it is I am saying. I see him hand something to one of our people who is smoking outside, and then he turns and walks away. When the service is over, the guy comes to me with a pound of hazelnut coffee beans. He says, "Rufus wanted me to give this to you. He said he wanted to contribute to the free coffee you serve to the homeless people." What?

A week later, Rufus walks through the door of Joe's Addiction. I am sitting at a table chatting with some friends. I ask him if there is anything I can do for him. "Yeah," he says, "I guess I'll have some coffee." I offer him a free donut, and he accepts. Then he sits down at the table with me. He knows the woman sitting with me. Their relationship goes way back. (I later find out he used to be her drug dealer.)

The three of us chat about life. I ask how he is doing, and he tells me his health is poor. He has a heart condition that he expects will eventually "finish him off." He tells me about his wife who died a few years before and how much he misses her. He hasn't known what to do with himself since her death. The conversation is awkward and stilted. I tell him thank you for the hazelnut coffee, and he says, "What you do here is a good thing. I just wanted to contribute in some way." He stays until his coffee cup is empty. Then he thanks me and heads for the door. I look at my friend, my eyebrows lifted as high as I can. She shakes her head, smiles, and says, "I don't know."

Scooter

One morning, Scooter comes in the front door clutching his side. Blood is oozing from underneath his tightly gripped hand. He groans, "I been stabbed."

"What happened?" I yell, as I run to him. He tells me it happened in a drug deal gone bad. This boy runs drugs for a powerful gang in the neighborhood. In exchange for his work, they pay him in drugs for his own use, and sometimes they give him a meal. He and I have talked about this before. He has told me, "This is just who I am. It's my life."

I grab the phone to call an ambulance. Through gritted teeth, he growls, "No. Don't call. The police will come with them, and I will go to jail." I ask him if he has any drugs on him. "No," he says, "but they'll ask too many questions." I don't know what to do. He needs medical attention.

As I reason with him, from the backdoor entrance, escorted by one of our community leaders, a woman comes toward me. I try to conceal my shock. It is the woman who used her Bible in the city council meeting to condemn my helping felons. She has never stepped foot into Joe's Addiction before. She says, "This boy is my adopted grandson. His mom is so strung out she doesn't watch out for him. I feed him and sometimes let him stay at my place. I can't take him to the hospital because I have to take my *real* grandchildren to school this morning." Then she hands me a small piece of paper. "Here is his social security number and his birth date. Call 911. Make him go to the hospital. Please." I take the paper from her and promise her I will do the best I can. She thanks me and hurries out the back door.

I have no time to think about this change in her. I call 911. When the ambulance and police arrive, I give them his information, and they transport him to the hospital. He survives. His adopted grandma comes once again to Joe's Addiction to thank me. The next time I see her, she is in the Free Store looking for clothing for one of her "real grandkids." Right before our eyes, we are watching enemies become our friends.

Air Conditioner

Month by month, we stay in the old building. Summer comes with its 100° temperatures, and our air conditioner quits working. I have been allowing other, small problems to go unfixed. It has now been four years since the debacle with city hall and more than a year since the city purchased our building. We have been serving and loving the neighborhood, letting our good deeds be seen, as best we can, but I do not want to bother the city about the building. It might trigger them into deciding it is time for us to leave. I can call a repairman, but the repair will cost a lot of money, and if the city is going to kick us out soon, will it even be worth repairing? But if we don't fix it, the heat will be unbearable. I pick up the phone.

Our contact person regarding the building is the man who refused to shake my hand when the city council accidentally voted to renew our license. He is now vice mayor, and the heir apparent to becoming mayor soon. When he answers the phone, I explain the situation with the broken air conditioner. I acknowledge that I know they intend to tear down the building, but I ask if he can give me some kind of time frame. I just need to know if it is worth the expense of repairing it.

He tells me they have no time frame in mind. They have ideas, but they don't have a solid plan, nor do they have the money to do anything soon. Then he says, "Um, Jamie, you know this is what I do, right?" I don't know what he means. He says, "I have an air conditioner and heating repair business." No, I do not know this. He says, "I will send one of my guys over there this afternoon to take a look at it."

"Wow. That's great," I say, "but can you let me know what it will cost before fixing it. If it's too expensive, we might need to figure out some other way."

"No," he answers, "I'm saying *I* will take care of the air conditioner. Whatever it needs. You won't need to pay anything."

My throat tightens. "Are you serious?" I ask.

He says, "What you are doing is a good thing, and I would like to contribute by fixing the air conditioner."

When I tell about this conversation during the next Sunday's Prouds and Sorries, the room is silent. We look at each other, and then the room erupts in applause.

Love Gang

The call to love our enemies is, without a doubt, the most difficult thing Jesus invited us to do. It makes no sense. The most natural thing is to hate back. To take an eye for an eye. To seek revenge upon the one who harms us. For gang members, the decision to not retaliate can be a life and death decision. It is a ridiculous call, and yet, as the cycle of violence is broken and Love spreads, the ripples of Love change the world.

Some gang members in our community have a teardrop tattoo under their eye. For some, it represents the loss of someone they loved. It can also mean a person was raped in prison and then branded as a victim forever after. But for most, the teardrop is a symbol of having killed someone. For my gang friends, loving a member of a rival gang or a person of a different race, or resisting the urge for revenge are places where the rubber meets the road in this "Love thing." So many have lived on the broad road of violence that leads to destruction, and this Way of Love is an invitation to walk a narrow path that leads to life, and life abundant.

As pastor at Joe's Addiction, I am often the one who teaches the words of Jesus to these who are steeped in violence. I am the one who issues the oft' repeated call to love, to forgive, to believe the best, to give a second (or third, or fourth, or seventieth chance). I am often the one reminding people in our community that this is how we live. And I am the one who most often is modeling for them how to do it.

One day I give two dollars for bus fare to a man in our community who is harming others and causing a lot of fear in our homeless camp. I don't want to. I am mad at him for being mean to my other friends. But it is hot . . . he has to make it to a probation meeting seven miles away . . . and, because love is kind, I give him two dollars. Several people in our community notice and wonder why. We have yet *another* talk about loving people who don't deserve it. And we agree together that I did the right thing.

Loving ex-cons who have murdered and raped is not so hard for me. Loving people who steal from me is not hard either. But loving people whose ideology differs from mine, especially those who have "ghosted" me for not believing the way they do, is incredibly difficult. And honestly, much of the time, I don't do it well.

But we are committed to the Better Way. The Jesus Way of life. The Way of Love.

Martin Luther King preached a sermon on the topic of Loving Your Enemies. He said: "Now there is a final reason I think that Jesus says, 'Love your enemies.' It is this: that love has within it a redemptive power. And there is a power there that eventually transforms individuals. Just keep being friendly to that person. Just keep loving them, and they can't stand it too long. Oh, they react in many ways in the beginning. They react with guilt feelings, and sometimes they'll hate you a little more at that transition period, but just keep loving them. And by the power of your love they will break down under the load. That's love, you see. It is redemptive, and this is why Jesus says love. There's something about love that builds up and is creative. There is something about hate that tears down and is destructive. So love your enemies."

I decide to try out an idea. I put a black stamp of a heart under my left eye where gang members place their teardrop tattoo. I wonder what the folks at Joe's Addiction will think. The first day I wear it, Scooter notices and asks, "What's that heart on your face about?"

"What do you think it means?" I ask.

He says, "Well, usually people put a teardrop there, and that means you've killed someone." He tilts his head and rubs his chin. "But yours is a heart. A heart means love, so yours means love not killing?" I raise my eyebrows to let him know he's close. "Loving people instead of killing them? Like loving your enemy?"

"Exactly," I say.

He slaps his thigh and laughs, "You're crazy, Miss Jamie."

Brian Zahnd says, "Quite simply, we are disciples of the one who would rather die than kill his enemies."

I have the same conversation numerous times in the month I wear the heart stamp, so one afternoon, standing in the coffee shop, I announce I have decided to have it permanently tattooed. One of the guys says, "Really?"

I tell him, "Yep. I'm ready to make a permanent statement that I am going to love my enemies."

He smiles and says, "Then I'm gonna do it too."

Another one stands up and chimes in, "You're our O.G., if you do it, I'll do it."

Another stands. You can feel the excitement, the energy rising in the room. He says, "I want one too."

The first one then says, "We're gonna make a new gang: the Love Gang!"

A tattoo on my face pretty much seals the deal on my departure from my fundamentalist religious upbringing. The heart also symbolizes my standing in solidarity with my community at Joe's Addiction. For eleven years, these precious people have welcomed me into their world, into their neighborhood, into their homes, into their lives. They have become my family. My best, most loyal and supportive friends. I have experienced more love, more forgiveness and more tolerance for my character flaws in this community than anywhere else in my life. I am humbled and so grateful. So this tattoo on my face is my way of saying I am all in, no reservations, no turning back. What started as "me" for "them," has become "we."

Nine of us go together to receive a tattoo of a heart on our face. We create a hand sign that combines the sign language of "I love you" and "Fuck you." Our gang mantra is "I fucking love you." Word has spread in the neighborhood that a new gang has come on the scene. The message is out that instead of fighting, instead of violence and hatred, we are here to spread Love. And the Love Gang continues to grow.

I had no idea when we decided to do this thing what a deep commitment it means for those who take the tattoo. I hear them, daily, reminding one another of their commitment to Love. "You can't do that. You're part of the Love Gang." "Hey, remember Love, man." Many times, when I become angry, one of them points to their heart tattoo and reminds me of *my* commitment to Love. We are learning to love together.

One of the Love Gang guys introduces me to another young man sitting in the coffee shop. He says, "This is our O.G."

The kid asks, "What does O.G. mean?"

From another part of the room, someone says, "Original Gangster."

Another one pipes up, "It can mean Old Gangster too."

The kid looks surprised. Mike jumps in, "In her case, I think it just means Old Grandma!" The room explodes with "Awws" and "Ohhhs," as they howl their love for their gang and for me.

I walk up upon Forklift telling a new guy—a big man covered in tattoos from his chin down—all about his history and how he left the gang and violence to follow the Way of Love. I stand there and listen as he talks about the things he gave up and about the Love he has received in their place. He explains our heart tattoos and talks to the new guy about loving our enemies and how it makes the world better for everyone if we love instead of hate.

The new guy hangs his head and says, "I want to leave the violence, Dude. I keep tryin' ta change myself, but I can't seem to do it." Then he looks at me and asks, "Will you pray for me?" I hardly ever do that kind of thing anymore. I told you my uneasiness with prayer these days, but I lay my hand on his shoulder. Forklift looks at me seriously and then puts his hand on the guy's other shoulder and bows his head. We pray together. Tears roll down the new guy's face, as I ask God to help him.

When I finish, I tell him we'd love to have him come around more often, and we will support him, as he begins to walk a different way. I tell him "We like you a lot."

Forklift says, "Not just like. I *love* you, Homie."

Forklift then says, "He'll be getting the heart tattoo soon."

The new guy nods and says, "I'll get it put on my neck. I don't want to mess up this pretty face."

A few weeks after we got our tattoos, I am standing in the coffee shop showing our gang sign to someone. I'm explaining what the tattoo stands for and how we tell one another, "I fucking love you." After I say these words, I hear a woman's laughter behind me. I turn to see a husband and wife standing at the coffee table where the weekly Panera Bread donation is piled. I recognize them as folks who attended those city hall meetings and sided with those condemning Joe's Addiction. "Oh! Sorry," I say to them. She runs to me and hugs me. "I love it!" she says, "Thank you so much for all you do here in the community. We get bread from you every week. We are just so grateful for you." I stand amazed.

Christmas Eve

It's a busy afternoon at Joe's, and the phone rings. One of the baristas answers and hands it to me. She says, "They want to talk to the owner." I sigh. Companies contact me all the time, offering a better deal on this or that. I take the phone and say, "This is Jamie." The voice on the other end of the phone says, "Hello. This is Jacob from Whispers (the new club next door). You guys do things to help the homeless there, don't you?"

I hold my breath. What had our people done to upset them? I had seen someone digging in their dumpster a couple of days ago. Maybe they had left a mess. Had someone been panhandling their customers? I answer, "Yes, we do."

He goes on, "Well, we would like to cater a Christmas Eve meal for the homeless of Valley Brook and any other needy families in the neighborhood. Would you like to sponsor it together with us? We will provide the meal. All you need to do is provide some hot chocolate." He keeps going. He says, "I talked to the mayor, and I asked if we could host the meal at city hall. He said, as far as he was concerned, it's okay with him. He'll have to check with the city council, but if they don't let us have it at city hall, we'll just rent a tent and set it up between our club and your coffee shop. Hopefully the city will let us do it at city hall. Are you in?"

I feel like I have been punched in the gut. I have difficulty finding breath to respond. I ask him, "Are you serious?" I am crying.

He laughs and says, "Of course. We think what you are doing is wonderful, and we want to do something nice for the homeless people you guys help every day."

I find my voice and tell him I am so grateful. Yes, we would love to do it together with them.

Later that week, I go to the strip club to nail down the details. Love Gang members whoop and holler, teasing me from our front sidewalk as they watch me walk into the club. I come out with the news that Whispers, Joe's Addiction, and the Town of Valley Brook will cosponsor a Christmas Eve meal held at city hall on Christmas Eve.

Some of our people are thrilled. They celebrate the change in attitude toward us. But some say, "I'm not goin' to city hall to eat some dinner they wanna give us!" Hatred for police and city officials who have done them wrong rises from deep places of wounding. One guy recalls the times police officers have shoved him to the ground, twisting his arm and grinding his face into the concrete, only to let him go after they look at his ID. Fines they couldn't pay. Jail time they have served. All the injustices suffered cannot be erased by a free meal. A Love Gang member called, Cajun, declares, "That mayor is one of the reasons the State took my daughters from me. I'm not goin' in there an' eat dinner with that man!" His hatred fuels every bit of spittle flying from his mouth as he barks the words.

Most often, love for our enemies takes the form of action on our part, or at least the choice to resist our natural responses of revenge. But this time, the call is to *receive* Love from the very ones who have harmed us. We talk together about it multiple times that week. What does Love look like? Christmas Eve arrives and a group of about fifty of us from the Joe's Addiction community head to city hall.

As I'm driving a few of us in my car, I see Cajun walking on the side of the road. I roll down my window and ask, "You comin' to the dinner?"

He says, "Yeah. I'll be there."

The others in my car say, "He won't be there."

I watch him walk right on past city hall and down the street.

The strip club caters a fancy meal. There are pork chops *and* fried chicken. Roasted potatoes, dirty rice, and green beans. And they serve chocolate cake. Huge pieces of cake. Everyone eats until they are stuffed. We laugh and joke about the hollow legs some of our men must have. Joe's Addiction hot chocolate adds a homey dose of warmth to the scene.

I move around the room greeting people and filling drinks. Several ask if I am going to eat, and so I take a plate. When I turn to find a seat, the only empty space is right next to the mayor and his wife. I sit down next to the man who refused to shake my hand four years earlier, the man who told me he would do everything in his power to shut down our coffee shop, but who recently fixed our air conditioning. We eat Christmas Eve dinner together. His family and my family. He and I. I thank him, and he says, "It's nothing. Thank *you* for all you do for our community." I wonder if I have entered an alternate universe. Perhaps I have—The Kingdom of God. Beloved Chaos.

When some of our men are on their second or third plates, the door opens and Cajun saunters in. I go to him and say, "I'm so glad you came."

With head bowed, he says, "I made a decision when I took this damn tattoo on my face. What else could I do?" Cajun eats his fill of pork chops and chicken and then asks for a "to go" plate to take to his brother who kicked him out of his house a short time before. He says, "I'm sure he's hungry, and he'd love some good hot food on Christmas Eve."

Gregory Boyle writes in Tattoos on the Heart, "If we choose to stand in the right place, God, through us, creates a community of resistance without our even realizing it. To embrace the strategy of Jesus is to be engaged in what Dean Brackley calls 'downward mobility.' Our locating ourselves with those who have been endlessly excluded becomes an act of visible protest. For no amount of our screaming at the people in charge to change things can change them. The margins don't get erased by simply insisting that the powers-that-be erase them. The trickle- down theory doesn't really work here. The powers bent on waging war against the poor and the young and the 'other' will only be moved to kinship when they observe it. Only when we can see a community where the outcast is valued and appreciated will we abandon the values that seek to exclude."

Belonging

In *Chocolat*, the town authorities reject Vianne, the owner of the chocolate shop. They do not appreciate that she has welcomed the nomadic people who the town calls "river rats." In a painful crisis of rejection and wounding, Vianne decides to leave. She doesn't have to stay. She can just as easily move on to another place, a more welcoming town perhaps. As she is packing her belongings and announcing her plan to leave, Josephine, an abused woman who Vianne has loved into freedom and new life, says to her, "If you leave, everything will go back to the way it always was." Vianne snorts, "It *is* the way it always was."

When I look around our little part of Oklahoma City, I agree with Vianne. Nothing has changed in the grand scheme of things. The powers-that-be still rule. Not only our little town, but the world at large. Greed still reigns. Injustice still wreaks havoc. Poverty still steals life from those who struggle to survive each day. Many of our people in the Joe's Addiction community still suffer from drug addiction. We have not been able to provide housing for those who are living outside. Despair still drives many of our people to give up on life for good. Vianne was merely pointing out the truth, the reality of things as they are. "It *is* the way it always was."

Josephine responds: "Not for me."

Each year, Christmas Caroling has become our measurement of the growth of the Community of Hope in this town. Some of those drug houses now have families with children living there instead. We send out a newsletter letting the neighborhood know what night we will be coming and we invite them to join us. Strangers now gather at Joe's Addiction to join us in caroling their own neighborhood. We laugh, we sing together, and we enjoy the warmth of cookies and hot chocolate at Joe's Addiction. This year, as our group of carolers approaches a front porch the door opens to a woman holding a plate of cookies. She knew we were coming, and she has baked them to share with us.

The atmosphere is changing. Hope is replacing despair.

He rules the world with truth and grace
And makes the nations prove
The glories of His righteousness
And wonders of His Love
And wonders of HIs Love
And wonders and wonders of His Love.

Civil rights activist, John Perkins, has said, "We live out our call most fully when we are a community of faith with arms wrapped about a community of pain." I don't know if starting a coffee shop community is the best way to spend a life. We honestly stumbled into it. I cannot say whether there is a more strategic place to plant oneself, or a more important kind of work one can do. Certainly, the physical needs of a poor town in Oklahoma City are not even near the extremity of the needs in the slums of Mumbai, India.

What I do know is, as I drive around the neighborhood, people recognize me. They wave from their front yards. They smile. I wave back, and a rush of emotion floods my soul. I have found a place of belonging in the Beloved Chaos.

AUTHOR'S NOTE

I have used various Bible translations and paraphrases through-out this book. Sometimes my choice was for what I felt was the most familiar translation. Other times I chose a version or paraphrase that made the verses more current and unfamiliar, in hopes that the reader would potentially be more awakened to the things that Jesus said. I enjoy *The Message* paraphrase for this reason.

It is an amazing privilege to write my story and the stories of my friends. I did change the names of the people in our Joe's Addiction community to protect their privacy. I had to create a "cheat sheet" for myself, so that when readers tell me, "I loved the story of Tisha," I can remember who that is in real life. I hope that you experience some of the love that I have for these people who are not characters in a story, but real humans, many of them still living their lives in the day to day struggle to survive.

If You Loved This Book . . .

Connect with Jamie on facebook.com/jamie.w.zumwalt, Twitter @jamiezumwalt, Instagram jamie zumwalt

Visit www.jamiewestzumwalt.com for regular updates about the Community of Hope at Joe's Addiction

To schedule Jamie to speak for workshops or events contact Jamie here: www.jamiewestzumwalt.com/contact

ACKNOWLEDGEMENTS

To my editor, Sandra Moore: I am so grateful for your kindness and for your willingness to ask me the really tough questions.

To my friends who read early manuscripts and gave me feedback: Buddy, Sarah, Josh, Patrick, Chris, Paulette and Scott. Thank you so much for your time and your honesty.

To my husband, who has ridden the waves of this adventure with me: Thank you for your support and your help and for giving me freedom to discover my own destiny in this Grand Experiment.

To my children, Jessi, Josiah, Jael, Jewel, and James and my son-in-law, David Scott, who had no choice but to go through the adventure with us. I am forever grateful for your support and your affirmation, not only for the work I do, but in writing this book. You helped me to have the courage to write these stories down and to be my true self in the process. I admire each of you, and I want to live as authentically as you do.

And to the Community of Hope at Joe's Addiction: Thank you for loving me, for letting me be your pastor, and for encouraging me to tell your stories and my own. You have made my life an amazing adventure.

FURTHER READING

I love Further Reading pages! If you feel inspired to explore some of the theological, philosophical, and community development topics raised in this book, here are some books that have been helpful to me:

On the Kingdom of God:
>Brian Zahnd's *Beauty Will Save the World*
>Brian McLaren's *Everything Must Change*

On Faith Shifting:
>Kathy Escobar's *Faith Shift: Finding Your Way Forward When Everything You Believe is Coming Apart*
>Rachel Held Evans' *Faith Unraveled: How a Girl Who Knew All the Answers Learned to Ask Questions*
>Rachel Held Evans' *Searching for Sunday: Loving, Leaving, and Finding the Church*
>Sarah Bessey's *Out of Sorts: Making Peace with an Evolving Faith*
>Richard Rohr's *Falling Upward: A Spirituality for the Two Halves of Life*

Reba Riley's *Post Traumatic Church Syndrome*
Lisa Gungor's *The Most Beautiful Thing I've Seen*

On Violence and the God of the Bible:
Brian Zahnd's *A Farewell to Mars: An Evangelical Pastor's Journey Toward the Biblical Gospel of Peace*
Gregory Boyd's *The Crucifixion of the Warrior God*

On a theology of Love:
Jimmy Spencer's *Love Without Agenda*
Tom Oord's *The Uncontrolling Love of God*
Brian Zahnd's *Sinners in the Hands of a Loving God*
Mother Teresa's *No Greater Love*
Gregory Boyd's *Repenting of Religion*

On a psychology of Love: M. Scott Peck's *The Road Less Traveled*

On Compassion: Henri Nouwen's *Compassion*

On Jesus and the Gospel:
Shane Claiborne's *The Irresistible Revolution*
Jesus for President
Red Letter Revolution
Brian McLaren's *The Secret Message of Jesus: Uncovering the Truth that Could Change Everything*
Craig Greenfield's *Subversive Jesus*
NT Wright's *Simply Christian* and *Simply Jesus*
Kent Annan's *Following Jesus Through the Eye of the Needle*

On Love and Community:

    Chris Heuertz's *Unexpected Gifts* and *Friendship at the Margins*

    Jonathan Wilson Hartgrove's *Strangers At My Door*

    Father Gregory Boyle's *Tattoos on the Heart* and *Barking to the Choir*

On Hospitality: Christine Pohl's *Making Room*

On Missional Community: Hugh Halter's *The Tangible Kingdom*

On Heaven and Hell:

    Rob Bell's *Love Wins*

    NT Wright's *Surprised by Hope*

On Christianity, the Bible and Homosexuality:

    Justin Lee's *Torn: Rescuing the Gospel from the Gays vs. Christian Debate*

    David P. Gushee's *Changing Our Mind*

    Matthew Vines' *God and the Gay Christian: The Biblical Case in Support of Same Sex Relationships*

On Community Development:

    John Perkins' *Beyond Charity: The Call to Christian Community Development*

    Bryant L. Myers' *Walking With The Poor*

    Any of the books sold by Christian Community Development Association at www.ccda.org